RHETORIC AND HISTORY
IN REVOLUTIONARY NEW ENGLAND

Philemon Robbins, ms sermon July 12, 1741, Robbins Family Papers, Yale University Library. (Discussed in pp. 23–26)

Rhetoric and History
in
Revolutionary New England

DONALD WEBER

New York • *Oxford*
OXFORD UNIVERSITY PRESS
1988

Oxford University Press

Oxford   New York   Toronto
Delhi   Bombay   Calcutta   Madras   Karachi
Petaling Jaya   Singapore   Hong Kong   Tokyo
Nairobi   Dar es Salaam   Cape Town
Melbourne   Auckland

and associated companies in
Beirut   Berlin   Ibadan   Nicosia

Library of Congress Cataloging-in-Publication Data

Weber, Donald, 1951–
Rhetoric and history in Revolutionary New England.
Bibliography: p.
Includes index.
1. Preaching—New England—History—18th century.
2. Rhetoric—Political aspects—New England—History—
18th century.   3. New England—History—Revolution, 1775–
1783—Religious aspects.   4. United States—History—
Revolution, 1775–1783—Religious aspects.   5. United
States—Politics and government—Revolution, 1775–1783.
I. Title.
BV4208.U6W4   1988   251'.00974   87–12248
ISBN 0-19-505104-1

2 4 6 8 10 9 7 5 3 1

Printed in the United States of America
on acid-free paper

*To my mother
And to the memory
of my father*

Preface

I did not set out originally to write the book that appears below. I had intended, during the summer of 1982, to expand my dissertation on Jonathan Edwards and American culture, which still needed a section about the Edwardsean legacy to his eighteenth-century guardians to fill out my earlier narrative. Of course I had already encountered this generation of evangelical ministers—which included figures like Joseph Bellamy, Samuel Hopkins and their many faithful disciples—in my previous researches. In virtually all accounts of New England religious culture these New Divinity men (as they came to be called) were cast as unwitting agents in a saga of decline; the group, according to critical observers like Ezra Stiles, Harriet Beecher Stowe, Joseph Haroutunian, and Edmund S. Morgan, that helped atrophy, fossilize, or betray (one could usually choose among these verbal indictments) Edwards's social, religious, and intellectual vision.[1]

So I began to reconsider the case against the New Divinity ministers, hoping to continue the story of Edwards's influence by examining the career of his son Jonathan, whose absolutely *huge* corpus of extant manuscript sermons had frightened me away a few years before, when I was rummaging through the archives at the Hartford Seminary Library. Now I decided to confront all those sermon folders in order to test what had emerged in my reading on religion and the American Revolution as a key issue in the debate over the influence of the New Divinity (and the Great Awakening in general) on the Revolution: namely, that the ministerial generation after Edwards remained for the most part aloof, otherworldly, above all apolitical during the revolutionary crisis. Further, I noticed that while other Congregational pulpits sounded with the high strains of Whig ideology—inflected, to be sure, with familiar Puritan idioms voiced earlier by seventeenth-century Jeremiahs—Edwards's guardians preached away their congregations with the abstractions of high-level theology, a scene that engaged them more than the political whirlwinds swirling around them.

In light of this debate I began reading through the Edwards, Jr. Collection, especially those sermons composed and delivered between 1770 and 1790. To my amazement I discovered that Edwards had preached throughout that critical interval on virtually every important event or battle of the war in a homely language that (so I imagined) would have been readily grasped by most of his audience. In fact, Edwards's sermons incorporated every trope characteristic of whig political discourse. Thus the logic of one important line of interpretation, perhaps best represented by Nathan O. Hatch's *The Sacred Cause of Liberty* (1977), was refuted by the manuscript evidence itself, which clearly proved the so-called otherworldly New Divinity preacher to have been *immersed* in revolutionary history. Before, during, and after the Revolution Edwards performed his oracular, explanatory office for his people. Rather than standing as an emblem of apolitical aloofness, then, the testament of the manuscript sermons revealed him to be firmly embedded in his own time.

After a while, however, I was no longer amazed by the manuscript evidence or perplexed by the apparent disjunction between scholarly claim and historical fact; after all, shouldn't we expect *all* colonial pastors, whatever their doctrinal stance, to have been attentive to the meaning of revolutionary events unfolding in their midst? I was excited by the materials (and the overturning power of their implications) and began to read the sermon series, which preserves Edwards's performances often in week to week (and sometimes in mid-week) sequences. Soon, however, I became puzzled by the formal character of this daunting cache: only a portion of the sermons were written out in full; most survived in a kind of private shorthand penned in a severely circumscribed prose. This syntactic foreshortening even had a spatial coordinate, for the preacher would usually divide his page in half, in effect delimiting the room available for inscribing full, sweeping sentences. Was this mode of composition unique to Edwards, I wondered. Where did he learn this habit of fragmentary composition? Were there connections between New Divinity affiliation and this vision—and method—of preaching? And what, if anything, could his literary remains tell us about his understanding and above all, his experience of the American Revolution?

These questions intrigued me, and steered me away from my original project. But they also returned me to the archives, where I reaped a rich harvest of primary materials practically unnoticed by students of early New England religious and intellectual culture.[2] I decided, therefore, to linger in the rhetorical world represented by hundreds of fragile sermon pamphlets. I have now surfaced in the following study to chart that world's mental terrain and gauge the psychological affects issuing from the sermons themselves. "Sometimes," observes historian Gary B. Nash, "the documentary evidence takes command of the investigator and demands that one set forth in unexpected directions."[3] *Rhetoric and History* is the result of the compelling, indeed commanding weight of the documentary record revealed in eighteenth-century sermons. It is an attempt to answer a series of curious questions that, unexpectedly, took hold of my imagination.

What follows, I hope, is an interdisciplinary study in the best sense: a fruitful, mutually enriching incorporation of work being done in a host of areas (including American Studies, symbolic anthropology, religious studies, and narratology), as well as a reconsideration of the debate over political ideology and religious discourse during the American Revolution. I hope, too, that my methodological assumptions (about the ritual aspect of ministerial language, multivocality, how sermons refract the mental world of the ministers) together with my general claims about the fragmentary form of religious rhetoric and the ministerial loss of social and political authority by the end of the century will spur debate and generate further archival study.[4] Above all, I hope that the mental world of the five patriot preachers recovered here will be recognizable to contemporary readers, for ultimately they struggled to make sense out of history spiralling out of control, and in response they tried to forge a seamless narrative out of the fragments of a shattered world view.

"History at its best is vicarious experience,"[5] Edmund S. Morgan notes in a recent interview. I would suggest that the manuscript sermons unearthed and reread in this study bring us as close as we are likely to get to the hearts and minds of the evangelical clergy, those profoundly human actors who, by their collective example, helped a generation through a critical passage in our cultural history.

Acknowledgments

In researching, thinking through, and writing any book, one learns to rely on the advice, support, criticism, and generosity of friends and colleagues. In my own case I have been lucky to have received all of the above from three scholars of American culture who followed the progress of this study from its beginning and read and criticized the entire manuscript. I wish to thank Sacvan Bercovitch, who has been an important friend and mentor over the years and from whom I first learned about the intellectual excitement of doing early American studies. I also want to thank my colleague Paul J. Staiti, who from his vantage in American art history proved to be an ideal reader, reminding me about audience and forcing me to make my ideas clear. Finally I wish to thank Jay Fliegelman, from whom I have learned more than I can possibly acknowledge. He first explained the implications of my project and later offered a continuous stream of insights into the religious, political, and psychological dimensions of the American Revolution—a dialogue which provided constant inspiration and encouragement.

I would also like to thank a host of friends, colleagues, and fellow Americanists who in one capacity or another—as willing listener, engaged critic, colloquium director—gave me opportunities to try out my ideas and, in the process, helped improve this book in numerous ways: Ruth H. Bloch, John L. Brooke, Andrew Delbanco, Emory Elliott, Joseph J. Ellis, John M. Faragher, Robert A. Gross, David D. Hall, James A. Henretta, Daniel Walker Howe, Wilson H. Kimnach, Michael P. Kramer, Mason I. Lowance, William S. McFeely, Paul McNeil, Susan Meyer, Gary B. Nash, Jeffrey Rubin-Dorsky, Peter Shaw, Harry S. Stout, and Rafia Zafar.

I wish to thank Mount Holyoke College for a Mellon Faculty Fellowship in 1982 that helped me begin this study, and for a Faculty Grant in 1986 that helped me complete it. During the academic year 1984–1985 I was fortunate to receive a NEH Fellowship which I spent as a Fellow at the Charles Warren Center for Studies in American History. To Professor Bernard Bailyn, its Director, to Pat Denault and Susan Hunt, its administrators, and to my colleagues at the Center I owe thanks for creating an ideal environment for scholarship and a wonderful forum of exchange. I owe thanks as well to Alan Heimert, who sustained me through the year with occasional meals at Eliot House. That same year I was designated a Five College Scholar through the auspices of Five Colleges, Inc. and its lively director, E. Jefferson Murphy, who provided a spacious office while I was on leave from Mount Holyoke. Above all else, however, I wish to thank Janet Nelson, my colleague and neighbor, for lending me a room with a view to work in; without her kindness and generosity this book literally could not have been written.

I owe special thanks to the various research libraries and manuscript librarians who greatly facilitated my research efforts: Diana Yount and the Trask Library, Andover Newton Theological School; Baker Library, Dartmouth College; Ruth Blair and the Connecticut Historical Society; the Connecticut State Library; the Historical Society of Pennsylvania; Houghton Library, Harvard University; the Huntington Library; the Massachusetts Historical Society; the New York Historical Society; the New York Public Library; Polly Pierce and the Stockbridge Library Association; the Beinecke Rare Book and Manuscript Library, Yale University; and Yale University Library.

At Oxford University Press I am grateful to Cynthia A. Read for seeing the manuscript through publication, and to Carole Schwager, Joan Bossert, and Paul E. Schlotthauer for their numerous editorial suggestions and improvements. For typing the manuscript, which meant learning to decipher my notorious scrawl, I am indebted to the heroic labors of Nimfa Gehman and Susan Hunt. And to Tamara Ankarstran I owe thanks for collating the array of manuscript materials used in this study.

Finally, I reserve my deepest thanks to my wife Barbara, who listened, edited, and somehow lived through the completion of this work; she alone knows the challenges, struggles, and triumphs that this book has come to symbolize. And to Jennie and Daniel Weber, thank you for letting me be away for more hours than I care to remember.

Cortlandt Colony   D.W.
Mohegan Lake, N.Y.
June 1987

Contents

RHETORIC AND HISTORY
IN REVOLUTIONARY NEW ENGLAND

Our sermons should be well studied.

—LEVI HART, July 1781

Introduction

The Religion—Politics Debate Reassessed

By all accounts the American Revolution was an overturning event for the Protestant clergy, those attentive watchmen who, from the beginning of New England's settlement, were obliged to explain the course of history to their congregations. What was the meaning of the political and military drama unfolding before the colonists' eyes? How did the often strange, perplexing scenes of contemporary history fit along the predetermined grid of Providence? And what were the proper, legitimate responses to collective threat, or perceived divine judgment? The patriot preachers of late eighteenth-century New England were absorbed by these ultimate questions, among others, and from their pulpits they were called upon to pronounce on the ambiguities of revolutionary history and discern, like the biblical prophets with whom they identified, the signs of the times.

It was not an easy task, to judge from surviving testimony. "If fail now, lose all," Jonathan Edwards, Jr. nervously uttered on the eve of Independence, partly in despair, yet partly in an effort to alarm his people to the dangers of complacency. To mobilize a fearful populace toward political action was, of course, the foremost office of the patriot preachers; from their pulpits they translated revolutionary ideas into ideology—a social–rhetorical process that helped the colonists act in history and, in time, forge a new identity.[1]

But what of the patriot ministers themselves? How did they respond to the religious, political, and social overturnings in their midst? Can we recover some version of their subjective world view? The following study addresses these questions by describing the connections among religious rhetoric, political discourse, and narrative form in the revolutionary pulpit. In most general terms I am concerned with how the clerical mind actively constructed a rhetorical world in the effort to impose narrative order onto the experience of historical contingency. That mode of cultural work, we should note, is often a strenuous, frightening business, especially if (as was the case for the evangelical ministers) one's entire world view is rent by the emergent ideologies of a new age. In response to crisis the mind tends to seek a shred of coherence from tattered history by spinning out both personal and collective myths, cohesive stories the mind tells about itself in an act of psychic restoration, in the desire to extract a seamless thread of narrative out of historical fragments.

In this respect my subject also concerns the tension or dialectic between myth and ideology during historical and political crisis. Myths, we know, are the stories a culture invents to confer identity; they give shape to collective history in the smooth flow of the myth's narrative, which, Richard Slotkin notes, transforms "temporal contingency into divine law." Slotkin observes that "the logic of myth" literally flows from "the logic of . . . [its] narrative," and the weight of the myth's narrative agency enables a culture to achieve and maintain consensus—in religious, social, and political spheres—through the ordering powers of narrative itself.[2]

Ideology, by contrast, often challenges the self-evident aspects of the mythic vision. Oppositional in intent, adversarial in stance, ideology halts the historical fluidity that myth seeks to generate by exposing the social and ideational disjunction between myth and history. In this respect it is important to observe the contrasting literary modes of myth and ideology: historical narrative is the vehicle of myth, whereas sermons, polemical pamphlets, and propositional literature in general are the literary expressions of discontented ideology. Still, as Slotkin reminds us, the end of ideology, so to speak, is the generation of a *new* narrative, a new myth of cultural consensus.[3]

The creative dialectic between myth and ideology provides a rich, suggestive context for the following analysis of the transformations of religious rhetoric in the revolutionary pulpit. In trying to recreate the mental world of a series of historical actors, I seek to describe, from the evidence of surviving manuscript sermons and letters, diaries, as well as printed works, how the evangelical clergy experienced the American Revolution; and how political events shaped their rhetorical response to revolutionary experience.

Of course, by posing a connection between sermonic expression and the social world of revolutionary New England I assume that such a cultural-linguistic dialogue exists, and that ministerial inscriptions preserved for over 200 years register, however indirectly, a portion of social reality. More important, I assume that the *forms* these jottings took are reflective as well; that is, form can be as socially expressive as intellectual content. And, finally, I assume that we can recover *some* sense of the psychosocial inflections of colonial America from manuscript sermons. In this respect, Nathan Hatch's constraining assertion, that "the printed sermons of Revolutionary New England are probably more representative of what was understood and believed in the pew than sermons that failed to arouse anyone's interest and thus were buried quietly in a minister's dusty file of manuscripts," is too narrow and ungenerous. On the contrary, manuscript sermons highlight the dynamics of individual minister–congregation interaction; indeed, they echo, at times in poignant and more powerful ways, the popular ideals and anxieties of the moment.[4]

But *Rhetoric and History in Revolutionary New England* is not, let me emphasize, a study of lay or popular piety on the eve of the American Revolution. I have not sought to recover the affective world of the pastors' audience. Instead, I have entered a long and often acrimonious debate in American cultural history over the way religious and political idioms interact in the revolutionary pulpit. I seek to raise the debate to a less polemical and more textually attuned level by asking different questions of its scholarly factions and about the literary remains of the historical actors themselves. In the process, I build on the exciting work in symbolic anthropology, contextual analysis of political discourse, and recent studies of eighteenth-century religious and intellectual history. Before posing those questions or explaining a methodology, I will briefly sketch the history and current state of ferment in the religion–politics debate.

As with so many important questions in American cultural history we must begin with Perry Miller. Writing in 1961, in his now classic essay "From the Covenant to the Revival," Miller argued that the colonial jeremiad offered the key to political mobilization in the Revolution. What had eluded the secular historian, Miller claimed, was "the wonderful fusion of political doctrine with the traditional rite of self-abasement"—a merger that fueled "a dynamo for generating action." Thus political language alone, in and by itself, "would never have supplied the drive to victory"; only what Miller termed the energizing effect of religious rhetoric could have propelled a generation, steeped in Puritan habits of imagination, to revolt.[5]

For Bernard Bailyn, on the other hand, the foundations of the revolutionary impulse were cast from the intellectual inheritance of English Whig republican principles which enabled the populace to embrace the "logic of rebellion" as the cause of liberty. And more recently, Bailyn presents a trio of case studies to highlight "the difficulty of explaining by any simple formula the role of religion in the origins of the American Revolution."[6] Viewed together, Bailyn's examples reveal a kind of ideological leveling among the Protestant clergy. Both Old Lights and New Lights preached the rhetoric of English tyranny and conspiracy; both shared a political, if not theological stance that explicitly challenges the constricting categories (so the charge usually goes) imposed by Alan Heimert: New Light = zealous patriot, Old Light = lukewarm (at best) participant.[7]

The debate over religion and politics thus centers on their mode of interaction. How did the revolutionary clergy came to espouse and preach across denominational lines a political rhetoric of Whig liberty? The question, however, contains a hidden, instrumentalist assumption. As posed by Hatch, and others, the question often reads, "How were political concerns instrumental in renewing sacred rhetoric?" Hatch's own reply, that there was an "unconscious sanctifying of political values" in the revolutionary pulpit, posits a virtually moribund evangelical clergy who simply retreated into a vision of an apolitical millennium after the fires of the Great Awakening had died away, after the long-awaited prophecies of the kingdom of God, believed imminently to descend in America, were not fulfilled. In response to Heimert, Hatch contends that the "New Light millennial vision could never have provided the intellectual foundation for the historical optimism prevalent among ministers of the revolutionary era." Instead, subsequent events and crises in American history inflamed the ministerial imagination: France replaced the Whore of Babylon in the book of Revelation as the object of wrath and rebuke, to be replaced (shortly) by the British Tyrant in the wake of the Stamp Act and other plots of enslavement. To Hatch, it was not (as it was for Heimert) the Awakening but rather the French and Indian wars that ushered in a rebirth of residual Puritan idioms, grafting religious formulas onto emergent political rhetoric.[8]

Of course most scholars would agree that political issues, however shrouded in religious language, lie at the core of eighteenth-century American discourse. But viewing religious idioms as merely the *vehicle* for political sentiment drains the discourse itself of its complex dynamic.

As J. G. A. Pocock reminds us, "any text or simpler utterance in a so-phisticated political discourse is by its nature polyvalent; it consists in the employment of a texture of languages capable of saying different things and of favoring different ways of saying things." And in an inter-pretive directive crucial for those latter-day exegetes who would estab-lish the "authentic" meanings of texts, Pocock advises: "It is a large part of our historian's practice to learn to read and recognize the diverse idi-oms of political discourse as they were available in the culture and at the time he is studying."[9] It seems to me that students of religion and the American Revolution have missed the key contextual overtones sounded in the revolutionary pulpit; they have missed, as a result, what Pocock calls the "polyvalent" or, as the symbolic anthropologist would say, "multivocal" aspects of religious rhetoric. This audible failure can be illustrated by the example of Joseph Bellamy, a guardian of the Ed-wardsean tradition, whom Hatch and others have viewed as a model of the aloof, otherworldly New England Divinity man who preferred lofty metaphysics to engineering for the Revolution.[10]

Bellamy himself, it appears, chose to preach to the patriot troops. In 1775 a soldier by the name of Simeon Lyman recorded his experience of listening to the famous minister embolden the encamped army. "We had a sermon preached to us by Mr. Bellowmy," he recalled, "which I think I never heard outdone in my life for liberty."[11] To what meaning, to which contexts should we ascribe this characterization of Bellamy's af-fective impact? Is this the "liberty" of Country ideology, as explained by Bailyn? Had Bellamy been preaching in the Whig mode? As Rhys Isaac notes, "The phrases that recur again and again in the preachers' writings concerning their striving were pregnant in this time of political revolu-tion—'had liberty,' 'had not as much liberty as at some other times.' "[12] "Pregnant," of course, is the key word. Is Bellamy *delivering*—as oracu-lar midwife—emergent Whig rhetoric to the patriot soldiers? Isaac's gloss, we should note, ignores the normative meaning of "liberty" as a pastoral ideal of preaching. To preach "under" liberty, as Private Ly-man's rendering seems to refer, is to speak with the agency of the holy Word, with the enabling freedom of the prophet's oracular power. My point is that the rhetoric of liberty yields multivalent religious and po-litical meanings.[13]

Indeed the multivalent aspect of revolutionary rhetoric is more clearly and suggestively understood if that discourse is situated, or reenvisioned, as the cultural product of colonial rituals, the appointed Fast and Thanksgiving ceremonies revived everywhere during the Revolution. By ritual I mean those public, formally structured gatherings when ministers, spurred by the momentous occasion and sense of temporal urgency, spoke to their auditors of the hopes, fears, and promises of the infant nation. Following Victor Turner, I understand these public gatherings as incorporations of the ritual process, whereby a culture in historical transition refashions the mythic stories it tells about itself. Ritual language, Turner argues, often contains the key words of a culture; during the passage from an old identity to a new one, its symbols become charged with ideological and affective valences, and in their dynamic interchange these symbolic "linguistic formations . . . stand *ambiguously* for a multiplicity of meanings, evoke emotions, and impel men to action."[14] Thus ritual language often acquires a social agency empowered by the liminal, "betwixt and between" aspect of the collective passage under way. In this respect, the multivalent quality of ministerial discourse bespeaks the processual nature of the Revolution itself: the religious and political valences which inhere in liberty announce the rhetorical office of liberty as ritual symbol.

Of course the ritual dimension of the American Revolution (and of early American culture in general) is a fertile subject of late. Scholars from various fields have summoned a "hermeneutic anthropology" or a "processual symbology" to map the mental terrain of colonial America.[15] David D. Hall, for example, recently urged that a "ritual process" framework may yield the most compelling descriptions of religious culture; and he observes (in light of the perspective I have been sketching) that "fast days were moments for restoring boundaries." That is, on those occasions of collective assembly, the people *actively* restored their sense of communal purpose by collectively purifying the kingdom. On these days of public ritual, clearly separated from the community's weekly routine of hearing regular preaching, the people ceased their work and listened to their expounding minister foretell sometimes an arc of spiritual descent, sometimes a prophecy of imminent glory. Above all, the message reflected both the historical consciousness of the minister and his attentive, assembled audience.[16]

This study seeks to inhabit the consciousness of those Fast Day and Thanksgiving Day orators. What were the anxieties, the hopes, and the sense of history voiced by the evangelical ministry, and perhaps revoiced among the people? What stories did ministers invoke to help effect the collective passage from political dependence to Independence? *Rhetoric and History* shows that the patriot clergy were often uncertain about the course of history and about the outcome of events. Indeed, rather than restoring boundaries, their fast day orations often reveal ministers at the anxious edge of contingency (akin, perhaps, to Emily

Dickinson's psychic straddling of "circumference"), where the designs of Providence no longer seem apparent or self-evident. Instead of collective affirmation, Fast Day rhetoric refracts a world caught in liminal midpassage; the future lay "open," a blank page of history to be inscribed orally by the comforting words of the communal spokesman. Only *after* the Revolution could a new narrative grow out of upheaval. The revolutionary historians created a new myth after ideology (reflected in both the form and content of sermons) had voiced its discontent; we might say that the historians' creative efforts restored boundaries through the cultural work of mythic narrative.[17]

But the evangelical ministers whose manuscript sermons this study unearths and recontextualizes often could not sustain or even summon a fluid narrative to mediate revolutionary history. In their private (as opposed to published) writings, at least, they moved from full-scale narrative to a kind of sermonic shorthand, characterized by fragmentary syntax, vertical catalogues, and incantatory phrases—what I call the fragmentary style of the Awakening pulpit. Perhaps the clearest example of this striking formal shift is that of Philemon Robbins (who preached for over fifty years in his Branford, Connecticut pulpit); by the summer of 1741, on the threshold of the Great Awakening, he radically altered his habits of sermon-writing. He was not alone. Other New Light preachers, including Eleazar Wheelock and even Jonathan Edwards, changed from linear narrative to fragmentary, disfluent modes—and all at virtually the same historical juncture.[18] Of course the itinerating presence of the incendiary George Whitefield and the impact of his affective (and affecting) preaching style may have spurred imitation. My point, however—and it is perhaps one of the more controversial issues raised by this study—is that modes of communication are linked to religious stance. In effect, I am describing evangelical pulpit modes *as a cultural style.*[19] The format and formulas of these sermons reveal the shared religious, social, and political identity of the New Light ministry.

Thus the following case studies of religion and revolution offer variations within the evangelical mentality. Viewed together, they portray the narrative struggle to accommodate the bewildering experience of revolution at the historical moment when the language of Providence, in Lester Cohen's words, "could no longer provide categories adequate for explaining the Revolution."[20] In the example of Philemon Robbins, the blend of narrative and fragment in his prerevolutionary and revolutionary discourses demonstrates how Awakening styles inhere in the patriot rhetoric of the 1770s. The shape of Robbins's career thus presents an alternative way of conceiving the links between Revival and Revolution:

their affinities may finally be rhetorical rather than doctrinal or political.[21] I restore Jonathan Edwards, Jr. to the revolutionary pantheon (this study also joins in the current rehabilitation of the New Divinity men) and show how he, faithful guardian that he was, imbibed the historical imagination of his more renowned father. The son, we might say, labored to continue the work of redemption (both vision and text) through and beyond the Revolution. Chapter 3, on Levi Hart, examines the dialectic between public utterance and private discourse in a reading of his manuscript sermons and recently found manuscript diary. At the end, Hart provides a moving testament to the way private anxieties issued in public celebration—the impulse to translate fear into affirmation. With Stephen West I show how Whig ideology came to western Massachusetts and blended with West's apocalyptic timetable for all those huddled nervously in the hills of Stockbridge, awaiting the outcome of events.

Chapter 5, on Samuel Cooper of Boston, addresses the question of sermonic form and religious imagination in a more theologically moderate, less doctrinally rigid minister preaching to an elite, urban congregation. In light of the shared sermonic style among the Edwardsean adherents, Cooper's continuous narrative and his habit of repreaching earlier sermons suggest a cyclical view of history against the progressivist vision bequeathed by Edwards to his New Light heirs. Yet when Cooper preached directly about revolutionary events, he also discovered the power of evangelical modes.

"How do historical actors comprehend the flux of daily existence? How can the observer reconstruct their subjective world view?" asks historian James Henretta. The project of historical reconstruction must, at some level, remain impressionistic and necessarily partial; after all, we can no longer recover fully the mental world of revolutionary ministers composing in their studies or declaiming from their pulpits. Still, the recovery effort "move[s] us onto new terrain."[22] *Rhetoric and History* maps the psychic landscape inhabited by the generation of patriot preachers who were at times witnesses to and at times agents of the country's rite of passage.

I invoke again the language of ritual process, for if we imagine the American Revolution as a liminal episode, if we listen carefully to both the religious and political overtones that filled the revolutionary pulpit, then the following portrait of eighteenth-century ministers struggling to construct public narratives that might restore—or at least give some meaning to—their besieged world view strengthens as it enlarges the emerging scholarly consensus about the multivocal dimensions of revolutionary discourse itself.

It is during the passage from an old identity to a new one, during moments of cultural upheaval, that symbols take on their ritual office. And it is during these often dangerous but culturally creative and obligatory junctures that language itself acquires what anthropologists call a subjunctive mood or tense; meanings become unmoored from fixed referents, discourse is multivalent; imaginatively, and socially, everything is possible.[23] From this perspective, the rhetoric of the Revolution may be styled subjunctive. Ministers, to varying degrees, recognized the politically subversive in the ideology of republicanism, but through what the famous patriot orator Samuel Sherwood termed the "dark, emblematical, figurative language"[24] that filled their performances, the Protestant clergy eased the country through the historical passage being enacted.

In the end, the alternating valences of revolutionary discourse register the dynamics of interaction itself, for during the charged rhetorical atmosphere enveloping the America Revolution the religious and political poles of the rhetoric of liberty, in a moment of creative potential, were connected.

1

From Awakening to Revolution:
The Example of
Philemon Robbins of Bradford

On September 19, 1730, his twenty-first birthday, young Philemon Robbins began a diary on the self-effacing note characteristic of Puritan mentality: "O! The wonderful patience and forbearance of God to such a sinner! how many years have I lost and how little time have I spent for God." Eager to begin a ministerial career, the recent Harvard graduate (1729) taught school for a while in Andover, kept up his theological reading in Poole's *Annotations* and Samuel Willard, attended the Thursday Lecture in Boston for 1731, and then, as if to mark the crossing of a personal threshold, announced in his Diary for November 20, 1731, "I preached my first sermon." Preaching the gospel Word was of course the most important office in the intellectual and pastoral life of a minister in colonial New England, and Robbins's subsequent diary entries, which record when he had "finished a sermon" or question whether he should accept an "invitation to preach," suggest that the fledgling minister's initial preaching before the Branford, Connecticut congregation (to which he was called in the fall of 1732) were something of a rite of passage, a public performance enabling "such a sinner" to improve the time, and thus gain a social identity.[1]

Little is known of Robbins's early life, either at home on his parents' farm outside of Cambridge or while at Harvard, but the circumstances of his college and later pastoral career place him among that generation of rural, lower middle-class farming families who struggled to prepare their sons for the ministry in early eighteenth-century New England. Robbins's father, Nathaniel, "paid his son's college bills partly in bricks and by carting ashes, dung, hay, and sand." While at college, his Harvard biographer tells us, Robbins "waited on table" and, perhaps as a response to his financial and social standing, was "a quiet and frugal student." Still, despite the hazy portrait, when perceived as a whole Robbins's career neatly conforms to the pattern of New Light ministry as described by recent social historians of colonial New England.[2] After preaching in the Branford pulpit throughout the late fall and early winter of 1732, Robbins accepted that congregation's call on December 30 and received the right hand of fellowship—the clerical ritual of fraternity performed by local ministers—from Isaac Stiles at the ordination ceremony on February 7, 1733. Recording the fact of this public sanctioning, Robbins penned a line that, given the urgency and self-consciousness attendant with the notion of career among the ministry, privately registers the relief accompanying professional arrival, the resolution of his identity as one of God's messengers. "And now," Robbins confided, "I am by Divine Providence set over a flock and engaged in this work." Fittingly, by late February the twenty-three-year-old pastor was already preaching on the duties of ministers and congregations.[3]

I do not wish, however, to rehabilitate the figure of Philemon Robbins merely to place him within prevailing notions of the evangelical ministry, although his New Light sympathies, embroilments in pastoral and institutional controversies during the Great Awakening of the 1740s, and longevity in the pulpit (he preached to his Branford flock for almost fifty years, until his death in 1781) collectively summarize the current historical portrait.[4] Robbins is important because he lived through the event we label the Great Awakening—*our* term for what seems to be an upheaval in colonial society may be a scholarly fabrication, as a recent polemic argues, but surely for those who observed, experienced, and later remembered events between 1741 and 1745 *something* happened to alter the psychic and social landscape of their world[5]—and the problematic, bewildering (to the historical actors themselves) era that begins with the Stamp Act crisis and "concludes" with the creation of the American republic. Moreover, Robbins is important because, as spiritual and, later, oracular guide to his congregation, he explained and eased his people through the often terrifying journey leading to Independence. Finally, Robbins is important because his rich legacy of sermonic performances, from his very first orations to his Awakening sermons, Stamp Act sermons, and Revolutionary efforts, enables us to follow the shifts and turns of his imagination over time—the shifts in narrative form, the turns of biblical and secular metaphor—as he tried to make sense of and give shape to his experience of history.

The example of Robbins, in short, tells us much about how at least one eighteenth-century Connecticut minister understood the course of events and perhaps, as Emerson remarked of his own clerical ancestors, *"experienced* life for his flock" (italics in original). If Robbins is indeed "a fair representative" (in Emerson's phrase),[6] then this first case study may illuminate a variety of issues in the continuing scholarly debates over rhetoric and history in colonial New England: the linguistic agency of oral versus print culture and mobilization on the eve of revolution; the blurring of Whig and Puritan idioms in the revolutionary pulpit; and the legacy of the Great Awakening to the Revolution.[7] By examining the extant remains from his pulpit—in effect, reconstructing the mental world of Philemon Robbins—we may enter these continuing debates in American intellectual and cultural history.

The weeks after the New Haven Commencement of 1732 must have been exhilarating for Robbins; he met fellow New Light evangelicals whose doctrinal beliefs and temperamental style were perhaps more compatible than those of his college friends at Cambridge. His last pulpit performance before he accepted the Branford call on December 30—the neophyte preacher's "25th discourse"—was finished December 16, 1732 and delivered on December 24.[8] The sermon, written out in full narrative, builds on the famous and, a generation later, much-invoked text from Galatians—the example of spiritual liberty that girds the Christian saint in resistance to "the yoke of bondage" of the law. Of course, the rhetoric of liberty would be empowered with a political valence in the revolutionary pulpit; "liberty," in Rhys Isaac's phrase, would become "pregnant" with radical meaning.[9] What is intriguing about Robbins's 1732 thoughts on liberty is how the sermon turns from a conventional meditation on the dangers of social and doctrinal deference to an implicit attack on the authority of all fathers, Biblical and historical. In Robbins's reading, Christ's gospel liberty "does not only consist in deliverance from the burdensome ceremonies under the law but . . . from the curse of the moral law [.] and this is a glorious liberty indeed." This "liberty," in effect, sanctions the sons' denial of the fathers: "It implies that we beware of the irrational or unscriptural traditions of the Elders"; indeed, "it is foolishness for any man to pin his faith upon another man's sleeve, or take any man for a perfect pattern of faith and *manners"* (emphasis added).[10]

I highlight "manners," for it prophetically registers the social fractiousness that would cleave the Connecticut clergy during the Awakening, when discord over preaching style, modes of worship, and ministerial behavior reflected a larger cultural strain.[11] Moving quickly from "Elders" to "forefathers," warning his eventual congregation of "the folly of those that adhere to such traditions" (as did those Galatians, who "conformed" and "regulated" themselves to "Judaising teachers"), Robbins identified the adherence to tradition as the source of "the unhappiness of many at this day."[12]

On what grounds did Robbins argue for the Fathers' "unauthorized" pattern for the self? In effect, his rhetoric seeks to overturn the historical continuity between "our forefathers" and what he styled "the equal authority of scripture." The fathers, in his view, were not prophets, not a "perfect pattern for us to copy"; rather, "they had the same Natures that we have and were prone to the same evils as we. They were doubtless erroneous in many particulars."[13] Here Robbins *reverses* the logic of Old Light Charles Chauncy's famous attack on the enthusiasts in *his* midst. In 1742 Chauncy challenged the revivalists' appropriation of a prophetic stance, arguing that only Paul (and those similarly authorized Biblical figures) could arrogate that special office unto themselves; he summoned the fathers' "pattern" to chastise the upstart, dangerous, latter-day antinomians in the land.[14] Robbins, however, asserted that the fathers were merely "natural" (that is, not under spiritually bequeathed grace), and therefore not binding as either moral or spiritual exempla; his challenge denied, in this respect, their oppressive biblical and political weight.

Still, as if recognizing the risky dimension of his message, Robbins sought to temper its impact at the close: "I would by no means," he retracted, "be understood *to speak* anything against the worship and discipline of the churches in New England . . . our land has been wonderfully favored with an able[,] pious and faithful ministry" (emphasis added).[15] This oblique apology registers Robbins's (perhaps inchoate) sense of the connection between oral discourse and the social/linguistic agency of the spoken word—of the link between public utterance and political challenge to traditional authority. Of course Robbins was only twenty-three when he spoke his "25th Discourse" before the Branford church, at *the congregation's* behest. At some level, however, Branford was prepared to embrace the new pastor's antipatriarchal perspective. For as Richard Bushman argues, prerevolutionary Connecticut was in transition from anxious Puritans "in struggle with the social order" to autonomous Yankees who "inwardly revolted against the old and authority."[16] From this perspective, Robbins's 1732 sermon embryonically foreshadows the oppositional stance of the Awakening in both its ideological and social vision. "We should not," he warned at the end, "take the best saints that have ever lived, the Apostles, our forefathers, or any creature for our pattern and example in all things."[17]

As we shall see, Robbins's preaching career from the Great Awakening through the Revolution amounts to a struggle to mediate the claims of private conscience with the need for communal harmony: the anti-authoritarian stance latent in the doctrine of Christian liberty with the social ideal of political order. One of the great ironies of Robbins's "prelude" sermon before his institutional passage is that the linguistic vehicle which carried its implicit challenge—the unimpeded, fluid narrative line—would soon be replaced by a new style that spatially (as it survives in manuscript) and rhetorically (as the words were uttered before audiences) subverted the traditional forms of the sermon itself. The new message of the revivalists, we might say, needed new modes of expression. As we follow Robbins in this phase of his pulpit career we can observe how doctrinal content and narrative form interact and sustain each other; how, during the Great Awakening, rhetoric itself met the demands of history.

By his own admission, Robbins's pastoral efforts in the early years of his ministry were uninspiring. "There have been but small additions to my church in the year past," he privately confessed on his twenty-eighth birthday. He persevered, however, reading and rereading the Scriptures: "Oct. 15, 1737 I began to read the Bible in course the 7th time." (By the early 1740s, in what becomes his only diary entries for that period, Robbins records the onset of each new biblical cycle. It may be that the distractions [or judgment] of religious controversy silenced his personal accounting.) But it was his office as preacher which, above all, conferred social and spiritual identity. "I am weekly preaching at private meetings," he noted in April 1738, "and where God's people meet in his name." Yet with each public display came a private, Dimmesdalean anxiety, as Robbins prayed in consecutive birthday meditations (1738 and 1739): "While I preach to others," he worried, "let me not be cast away" into Hell.[18]

Throughout the late 1730s, then, Robbins's pastorate appears utterly conventional: he delivered sermons on various domestic and moral themes (the conduct of wives, adultery, on bearing false witness); moreover his relations with the Branford congregation were free from discord. Like many early eighteenth-century pastors, Robbins engaged the affections of his flock. He took pleasure (for example) in noting the various signs of their unprompted love: "I have received great kindness from my people this last fall [1738] and they are cheerfully handing in some tokens of their respect"—a "good parcel of wood," or the surprise threshing and binding of his wheat upon his return from Boston. But if pulpit performances are an index to pastoral success, then Robbins might have replayed his earlier lament over "but small additions to my church" through the early 1740s.[19] A sermon of 1740 summons the figure of Jesus, at whose sermon on the mount "many were captivated and charmed";[20] in general, though, Robbins's sermonic art expounds standard biblical themes, explores conventional biblical tropes.

For example, a fast sermon of March 1741, at the threshold of revival, speaks in the key of Jeremiah:

> God expects that we take notice of his frowns and his corrections. We have agreed to separate this day to be solemnized as a day of humilia- tion, fasting and prayer . . . the earth groans and the beasts of the field languish. we have reason to be humbled for the severe frowning season that has occasioned so much evil abroad and been so distressing with us at home. how many souls are lost shipwrecked and cast away in the seas. how many have doubtless frozen to death and perished with the cold on this continent . . . and God is still frowning upon us O Israel thou hast destroyed theyself.[21]

Of course the Revolution (and the political events leading up to it) would transform this formulaic ritual, temporalizing Robbins's other- worldly stance and quickening the static urgency of the preacher's ad- monition. He concludes on a note he would return to a generation later: "Sometimes the judgment of war is brought on a people for their sins. Tis a distressing time to a people when visited with this calamity."[22] An earlier performance resounds with the martial rhetoric of Christian soldiers exhorted "to fight the good fight of faith," to fight through the darkness of this world "to the light" of the next. Our enemies, Robbins warned, may be "subtle and crafty . . . powerful and yet treacherous"; still, those "quick-sighted in arts and sciences, civil politics or the affairs of the world," they are blind to "spiritual things"—an "Enemy to be overcome."[23] The enemy, of course, would later be objectified in the subtle and crafty designers of the Stamp Act, and ministers, in turn, would become alert, if not quick-sighted, to political affairs, but the smooth linear narrative of these pre-Awakening exercises did not (or so it appears in church records) quicken the spiritual springs of Branford.

The dullness changed, however, in the summer of 1741, when Rob- bins dramatically altered his sermonic style. Against the advice of some members of his own congregation, against the appeals of the settled (that is, institutionally confirmed) ministers of the New Haven Consociation, Robbins preached on January 6, 1742 to a group of Separate Baptists upriver at Willingford at *their* invitation. Both his decision to speak and his sermon sparked a "storm of controversy" issuing in professional banishment, a drawn-out intraministerial battle (accompanied, as always, with charges and defense, feigned apologies and power moves), and a protracted season of discord between pastor and church.[24] The Wallingford Controversy (as this incident is usually called) is a chapter in the chronicle of Baptist revolt against the instituted churches, an episode in the saga of religious dissent and freedom. For the Standing Order Robbins's willful itinerancy was characteristic of the civil and doctrinal threat posed by New Lights to the autonomy of settled ministers and their congregations. For my purposes, Robbins's single moment of public celebrity (or ignominy) lets us examine how the Great Awakening led to a new style in preaching *and* temperament, both of which were labeled by that all-purpose epithet of scorn and fear in eighteenth-century New England, "antinomian."

The ecclesiastical uproar that sounded in the wake of Robbins's pulpit transgression was the response to his mode of preaching. Robbins, so the charges went, stood before the Baptists of Wallingford under a "strange heat of spirit"; he was continually "craving to be preaching," day and night, in church and, more dangerously, in "frequent public preaching." Moreover, he was a religious agitator, always "consorting with, and improving [exhorting] those to preach and carry on in public."[25] Finally, he countenanced the miscreant James Davenport's "singing along the streets," and judged "carnel and unconverted" any "that did not approve of the late religious stir that has been in the land."[26] The case against Robbins thus reads like a roll call of charges brought before the pro-revival enthusiasts. In his defense, Robbins appealed (as did all New Lights) to the authority of the extraordinary religious moment. "The people," he observed later in his own published defense, "seemed to be seriously attentive . . . some considerably affected." (Robbins also cited the precedent of fellow New Light Joseph Bellamy, who had earlier accepted the Separatists' invitation to preach.) He also offered a series of printed confessions designed to appease the Consociation, but each of his conciliatory efforts was refused.[27]

The people of Branford, however, were less adamant. Meeting in January 1747, the church voted Robbins its support: "We are generally steady attendants on his ministry, and don't remember that ever he has expressed himself as charged. . . . We think Mr. Robbins preaches the

Doctrines of Grace more clearly and pungently than in some of the first years of his ministry among us."[28] Publicly, Robbins dismissed the charges as unscriptural: "I am not sensible that my preaching was contrary to Divine Law"; privately, he channeled his church's support into the language of Christian defiance. "My people," he wrote to the Controversy's moderator, Nathaniel Chauncey, "have in form cast off the yoke which my Rev'd Predecessor and the church in his day could not bear, to submit their necks voluntarily to it. And as for myself I find an increasing Disinclination to Ecclesiastical Bondage." The language recalls, of course, the antiauthoritarian rhetoric of 1732 as it reveals the conflation of religious and political categories in a time of (perceived) cultural crisis; how religious idioms (drawn from Galatians) could authorize a rejection of consociational "bondage" and "oppression."[29]

But what was so dangerous about Robbins's preaching? What was so objectionable in the eyes (and ears) of his ministerial peers? The answers are complex, but one way to explain the Wallingford Controversy is to read it as a response to cultural strain, as a reaction to the weakening of an old order and the arrival of a new—in short, as a reflection of ideology in crisis. Robbins's Awakening sermons, fragmentary in literary form and radical in doctrinal content, are the rhetorical correlative to what might be described as the breakdown in narrative in the Awakening pulpit. Of course Jonathan Edwards and Charles Chauncy published traditional narratives defending or attacking the Revival. I refer to the wholesale transformation of the narrative mode by evangelical preachers during the Awakening—indeed, sermon fragments betray the anxiety and sense of cultural dislocation of the overturning moment itself. By the summer of 1741, Robbins had discovered a new form in which to embody his spiritual and social message.[30]

Most descriptions of this new rhetoric remain vague, often relying on the "spiritual travels" of Nathan Cole, whose vivid account of dropping his farming tools in mid-plow, running behind his wife "as if we were fleeing for our lives," and "trembling" in reaction to the spectacle of George Whitefield's open-air preaching exhibition offers an unmediated view of what it was like to experience, as a recent study of New London in the Awakening puts it, a "frighteningly new cultural landscape."[31] It was Whitefield's voice, of course, which imbued the scene with the sense of apocalyptic anticipation and anxiety. "My hearing him preach," Cole relates, "gave me a heart wound." Indeed, the "almost angelical," "young, slim, slender youth['s]" charismatic presence translated Cole from the dusty field of this world to a conviction of sin leading to a stance of "a sweet submission to His will."[32] Cole's "deliverance" was thus effected by the agency of the spoken word. Faith comes through hearing, Paul reminded the deaf Romans; and Whitefield, self-authorized, latter-day prophet that he was, seems to have understood the Apostle's precept with a vengeance. Whitefield also understood the social power at the root of the Latin "fides"—the "conviction which," in Walter Ong's neat aside, the public speaker of ancient oral cultures "was supposed to arouse in his audience."[33]

From this perspective, the pamphlet wars, doctrinal squabbling, and notorious spectacles of the Awakening (like James Davenport's book-burning antics) may be viewed as reflections of a cultural crisis centered on the meaning, nature, and spiritual efficacy of the spoken word. Davenport's "crime," a recent study declares, "was in his speech"; if so, then we can gauge the psychosocial threat of the revivalists' message, along with the medium in which its message was conveyed, to that arch-defender of the faith, Charles Chauncy. The New Lights, he railed in 1743, deviously sought to "make the Relation, between Pastor and people, a meer nothing; a sound without meaning." The source for this anarchic state of communications was the "prophetic" utterance of itinerant preachers—self-styled oracles who confused the "meer" sounds of their enthusiastic speech with social and doctrinal meanings sanctioned only by Holy Writ. If Davenport's audience was "prepared" to receive the "new style," it was because he appeared to speak under the mantle of a biblical prophet whose utterance, as both sacred "Word" and "Event," proffered a new identity, a selfhood for which people (like farmer Cole) would immediately cease their worldly labors to embrace.[34]

Philemon Robbins, we know, imbibed the New Light style virtually created by Whitefield. The Wallingford Controversy, wherein Robbins was expelled from his professional union as a stiff-necked itinerant, is a minor, yet emblematic episode of the Great Awakening in general. The case against him—that he was hankering after preaching—turns (as noted earlier) on his oral style, the novel manner of his sermonic delivery. In short, the Robbins affair involves what anthropologist Richard Bauman describes (in another context) as "the legitimacy of religious *speaking* and the source of legitimate religious words."[35] We will perhaps never recover the authenticity of the spoken word that stirred people in earlier times (Who can imagine or reconstruct what Whitefield or Patrick Henry might actually have sounded like?), but we may gain some measure of its effect by listening to verbal discourse with our contemporary ears attuned to inflections, reverberating, incantorial phrasings, and vertical catalogues—all characteristics of Robbins's revival preaching. Robbins *was* perhaps "subversive" in his pastoral nonconformity during the winter of 1742, for his preaching *had* changed radically by the previous summer, at the height of the Great Awakening. A sermon dated July 12, 1741, preached at least a dozen times (in pulpits throughout southeastern Connecticut), illustrates the message and method of Robbins as itinerant. That he considered this particular sermon of special import is not surprising, for among the many audiences who heard this most frequently delivered of all Robbins's orations was the lay congregation of Separatist Baptists of Wallingford.[36]

What distinguishes the sermon is not so much its text, from Genesis 6:3, "And the Lord said, my spirit shall not always strive with man," but its spatial arrangement. The four spare pages (in contrast to the usual twelve or sixteen of earlier efforts) are not filled with fluid lines of linear narrative but rather with sentence fragments, kernels that root the speaker at the essence of his thought yet allow for a tremendous freedom of rhetorical invention. The sermon's "context," which follows immediately below the text, quickly sets forth the biblical world at the threshold of destruction: "old world destroyed by flood." Then, after citing God's particular threats in later verses of the chapter, Robbins continues with the sermon's "Doctrine," which amounts to a slight but telling inversion of the original text: "That tho God's Spirit strives with man a while it will not strive always." In effect, Robbins transfers the authority of God's voice, the oracular "And the Lord said" of the Biblical text, unto himself, thus appropriating the power of the word to create temporal anxiety in the hedging, tension-filled tag of "will not strive *always*."[37] The reversal sounds the theme of the generic awakening sermon—the need for a true sight of sin, of true conviction, of true repentance, *now,* for the day of judgment is at hand. Again, it is important to emphasize how Robbins's fragmentary, compartmentalized sections simply announce his shifting arguments, or various sermonic "reasons," which collectively "improve" the Doctrine. Significant, too, the mode of persuasion is dialogic, providing Robbins with, in Richard Bauman's words, a "high degree of control over the dynamic and direction of the interaction" and at the same time nurturing a "collaborative dimension" with his audience:[38]

```
4. God sends his sp[irit] to strive a while
How [?] Ans. by word/read—sometimes
                  preached—sometimes
```

word not effect without—we see some are others not
When strive conscience is judge
            made look inward   what I am
                                where going   O Darkness
                                what doing   Hell
                                                 before[39]

In this example Robbins combines the "catechetical" style with a "cata-loguing" technique, a vertical cascade of words, or, more usually, paral-lel phrases that, viewed cumulatively (or, better, heard), add rhetorical weight to the sermon's urgent message.

Moreover the catalogue is at times "incantorial" in effect, eliciting an active participation between speaker and audience. Repetition leads to anticipation, or, in Kenneth Burke's apt phrase, a "collaborative ex-pectancy," which "invites participation." Catechetical dialogue and in-cantorial fragments set off in vertical catalogues are thus the stylistic innovations that appear to have frightened the established clergy, not so much in their inert existence as markings on a page, but in their affective agency in public performance, when the power of the spoken word as event—as collective ritual—aroused some dozen rural audiences in 1741–42.[40]

Of course a new preaching style alone cannot transform a psychic landscape. The Great Awakening, we know, had its greatest appeal among the rising generation; some languished under a protracted adolescence characteristic of fourth-generation status in colonial New England; others felt guilty over the material gains easily won in Yankee America. In both cases, the new birth functioned as an ideology offering a new identity to those sons and more often daughters anxious about the future.[41] The Awakening, that is, eased the psychic and social transition attendant with upheaval.

Demographically there was dislocation as well. The age of most Con-necticut New Lights, social historians calculate, hovered around twenty-five, while the average age of their Congregationalist opponents veered above forty.[42] Robbins's July 1741 "Wallingford" sermon strikingly registers this generational chasm. Returning to the opening Doctrine (about the transience of God's spirit) he underscores the urgent argu-ment of this theme, warning that man should never stop striving for conviction of sin:

every mans limited time   life fixed Job 14.5
must be a [last?]   Day grave—text
most [to?] age   if done dreadful—live monument

when after 40 rare [emphasis added]   Damnation sure
not always, Sabbath calls offers only in season of 'em
Some flatter are convt. [convicted]—Spt. [Spirit] strive—in vain . . .

then farewell *profit*—means— hope never come . . .
Make haste Sinners to accept of X for Lord & Savior
O make haste   life uncertain
                    time——   now calls offers
                    strive Spirit——   waiting

And then, toward the end of the Improvement, embedded within a corner of the manuscript, Robbins directly exhorts specific auditors, first addressing "Christians," then "sinners," and finally, in the dialogic mode, answering objections with a catalogue of imploration:

            work to do
O realize   pow[er] [of] God to do
            Damn[ation] if not
            text
& that, except you repent, the Hour is at hand wh[en] Judgment & wrath, Sin & anguish [will be your] portion[43]

This plea for repentance was Robbins's special revival message for southeastern Connecticut during the "frenzied" summer of 1741. Like other New Lights, Robbins assumed that the time of judgment was indeed at hand; sinners who stopped striving for conviction (according to the morphology of conversion) were doomed—especially those adamant souls hardened to the heart-softening power of the Spirit, those lost souls beyond the age of forty.

The most effective—and affective—dimension of Robbins's pulpit rhetoric is his use of direct address, his verbal gambit to speak "individually," by blurring private and public voices; I refer to the strategic use of ejaculatory phrases (which often appear at the culmination of a diary passage) at key moments of a sermon. Both diary entry and sermon build toward a verbal crescendo, as in this passage from his diary, February 1738: "I have dayly experiences of God's care and goodness but have a hard heart and am backward to acknowledge it. O that God would form me for himself." Robbins's awakening sermons appropriate this technique, usually closing with a passionate, "O let us turn to God with our whole Hearts and vow and pay our vows that wherein we have done iniquity we will do no more."[44] The rhetorical transfer highlights Robbins's desire to extend his own voice from private hope to public entreaty—to insert himself simultaneously within the oracular "And the Lord Said" of the textual opening, the "Noah preached" of the contextual gloss, and his own Doctrine-inversion ("yet it will not strive always").[45] This layering of voices implicitly creates a kind of oral continuum, with Robbins's exhortation serving as the galvanizing "word" of a latter-day prophet. By the end of the sermon, the voices of Genesis and that of Branford's pastor blur—sacred and secular, public and private—and therein lies the agency of Awakening rhetoric and power of oral discourse in general.

That discourse is empowered through the ritual process. "The very essence of the symbol," writes Michael Walzer, is that it "simultaneously provokes thought and evokes feeling"; it is "perhaps our most important means of bringing things together, both intellectually and emotionally." Although he does not name this complex dynamic, Walzer indirectly describes the distinctive social agency of ritual language, its ability to generate intellectual and affective responses that enable people to believe and *act* in social dramas. If the Puritan sermon (especially the fast day variety) functioned as collective ritual, "integrating" all segments of New England society, then the integrative power of oral discourse issues from its ritual aspect: to invest abstract ideas with an emotional valence and transform, in their interaction, ideas into ideology.[46]

Of course a fuller analysis of Robbins's pulpit rhetoric—especially during the Revolution—is required to establish the ritual dimension of his sermonic language. For now, let me highlight a curious change in his sermons after the fires of the Awakening died away, a change that reveals Robbins's self-consciousness about matters of pulpit delivery and audience.

"Sermons when read are not delivered with Authority and in an affecting way," Solomon Stoddard admonished in *The Defects of Preachers Reproved* (1723); in contrast, "when Sermons are delivered without notes, the looks and gesture of the Minister, is a great means to command Attention and stir up Affection."[47] Perhaps in response to spiritual ebb or congregational dullness, Robbins began to lace his sermon fragments with the inscription "amplify." "In a revival Christians may rejoyce in coming [to] God *amplify*"; "to rejoyce in him implies a love to his Dispensations. Heart all open. *amplify*."; "Enq. Who should weep and mourn? a.[nswer] All God's people—*amplify*." What did Robbins mean by this private notation? On one level, to "amplify" means to enlarge, to extend in power, although a more obscure meaning, "to make additional remarks, expatiate," is perhaps what Robbins reminds himself to orally perform in the pulpit.[48] But the term's most suggestive implication, in my view, is its source in Ciceronian rhetoric, which theorists of Puritan preaching (most importantly William Perkins) adapted in their formulations of sermonic theory—above all in the Application, whose purpose is "to recapitulate and to amplify." "To Cicero," Eugene White explains, "amplification meant 'to win Credence' by arousing the emotions . . . through the use of 'powerfully illuminating' language."[49] In this respect, Robbins's textual notation to amplify signals more than just persuasion; it was the key moment in the sermon event when he compelled himself *beyond* the fragment of written directive, beyond the prescribed text, into the realm of pure, extemporaneous preaching. "Amplify": the verbal sign to extend orally the theological argument; to *affect* the hearer; to *effect* an interchange between idea and emotion.

As mentioned earlier, we may never be able to recover fully the mental world of the Great Awakening as experienced by historical actors; through the example of Robbins's rhetorical response, however, we can gain some sense of the dislocations of 1741–1742, for the Revival wrought a profound shift in *his* sense of how the world could be represented. Language, we have been told often enough, gives linguistic shape to the chaos of experience. By the summer of 1741, fragments replaced narrative as Robbins's literary mode of representation; they were, we might say, the grammatical reification of the spiritual and social upheaval that historians assume the Awakening engendered. Fragments, then, were perhaps the only form Robbins could trust in a time when traditional narrative could no longer mediate experience. In this respect, the shift from narrative to fragment limns what Clifford Geertz describes as a loss of orientation when received traditions reel under the strain of emergent ideology.[50] The Awakening, that is, demanded a new rhetorical mode to render a new experience, and fragments met the requirements of the ideology of the new birth.

Robbins continued to translate experience into disjointed fragments and sweeping catalogues through the 1750s while preaching on standard pulpit themes. A Thanksgiving sermon of November 1757, for example, sings out the "praise [that] is due God for Englands preservation in many dangerous seasons:

> a protestant Prince
> a nursing Father
> a defender of the faith"

as it employs the commonplace of paralleling Israel and England: "God saved Israel of old from Enemies. So England also from Enemies—Enemies more numerous and powerful."[51] By the 1760s, with the fractious history of the Awakening a memory and thirty years of pastoral labors behind him, Robbins arrived as oracular authority to his Branford congregation—an "awesome" figure who had a "virtual monopoly over the public forum."[52] As patriarch, Robbins served as both spiritual and secular guide—an intermediary whose public utterances helped explain the course of history, sacred and political, to a community on the threshold of upheaval. There is, again, another telling shift in the shape of Robbins's preaching career in the 1760s; one might call it a "return to narrative," and it occurs at yet another key historical juncture, when Robbins was obliged to pronounce upon the meaning of the Stamp Act, which he did before the people of Branford on December 18, 1765.

The colonists' violent response to Parliament's passage of the Stamp Act on November 1, 1765 puzzled the parent country and bewildered her outraged children. Whatever issues one chooses to highlight—the political and economic dimensions of the crisis, the clash of ambitious personalities, and so on—the fact remains that the Stamp Act was felt as an event of unique emotional and psychological significance that exposed an "uneasiness over implications of freedom" in colonial America.[53] And from this perspective Robbins's Stamp Act sermon registers the collective trauma the act is said to have inflicted.

The sermon opens with a troubled text, from Isaiah 59: "We wait for light but behold obscurity; for brightness, but we walk in darkness." Immediately setting the occasion ("The Stamp Act so called whereby a tax is imposed on the north American colonies by the British Parliament"), Robbins moves reflexively to the "consideration of [the] mournful state of the Israelites when in the Babylonish Captivity." The strong narrative line continues, as Robbins works backward from New England's sacred origins in the Bible to the remarkable providences of God "in conducting our Fathers hither," delivering them from early Indian scourges ("time after time") to the "late general war" which "appeared the most universal gloomy and threatening that has been known upon this continent—a treacherous Enemy with Barbarous Salvages had almost edged around us designing to come upon us unawares."[54] Confronted in 1765 with perhaps a more insidious design edging its way toward Branford, Robbins's narrative suddenly breaks down; it is as if his rhetorical effort to summon a historical explanation cannot sustain itself in the face of the "gloomy" challenge of current events. And as if in reaction, the sermon moves from narrative to catalogue, incantatory phrases, and the continuous invocation of "amplify"—in effect, the literary modes characteristic of his Awakening rhetoric.

For example, after listing *vertically* a series of recent military victories ("Cape Breton reduced/St. Johnsbury taken/Niagara subdued") the preacher offers a litany of parallel phrases which, heard in sequence, spatially reduces "little" Branford to the physical and spiritual battlefield where, at the very moment, the fate of all devout Christians was being played out:

> & now North America—now New England—now Connecticut—what will you render to the Lord for all his benefits now wont join selves to Lord in everlasting covenant
>
>   watch   strive
> now wont you pray   war   against every sin
> wont you lead holy lives & train up children for God
> wont you tell ages to come of Gods wonderful works
> wont you sanctify Gods sabbath—love odinances walk in ways
> wont you make religion your business & know that your chief end is to glorify God
> wont you improve . . .
> & wont you consecrate.[55]

The rhetoric moves from the unstated but implicit narrowing toward "now Branford" in the first litany to the second "wont you" refrain of the catalogue (with the twice-repeated "now wont you" as mediating phrase). The cascade of imperative verbs is striking in its blend of passivity and agency (watch, pray, sanctify versus strive, war, tell). How can a people fulfill their office as prophetic witness to unfolding history and yet "create" history? The verbal ambiguity of the catalogue captures that very dilemma. Still, the rhythmic strains of Robbins's Stamp Act sermon convey powerfully Burke's notion of "collaborative expectancy" as it rivets the struggle for the continent within the soul of each prospective saint.

In the afternoon portion of the sermon (many of Robbins's performances were composed for morning and afternoon delivery) Robbins returns to the theme of historical origins, rehearsing New England's beginnings with the example of John Robinson and his band of Pilgrims who chose to settle in England (as opposed to Holland, France, or Spain), "to subject themselves to its laws and [thus] are entitled to the same priviledges of British subjects." At this point Robbins introduces the pulpit convention of "English liberty" as argument against the Stamp Act, but his ultimate defense of the colonies is made by a curious logic appropriated (as he tells us) from theological discourse:

the colonies all seem universally to be agreed against it [the Stamp Act]—universal consent is an argument that divines use to prove the Being of a God—& in this case that all the colonies should so universally agree & be of one mind—we may think the hand of God is in it———if you say tis an act of the King & parliament, and we ought to submit to every ordinance of man for the lords sake—ans. things are right or wrong in their own nature—if wrong authority cant make them right— Such as plead for King[']s prerogative in acts unconstitutional and wrong are going apace to the Doctrine of passive obedience and non-resistance[,] a Doctrine held only by highflying churchmen & Torys.

He might have inserted "amplify" in the margin to ensure the appropriate response.[56]

Yet for all its similarities to the contemporaneous rhetoric of the Stamp Act discourses, Robbins's performance ultimately leaves its speaker (and perhaps its auditors) neither with the mobilizing logic of Whig ideology nor with the reflexive typological formulas of (say) Charles Chauncy, but rather with the apocalyptic anxiety that is the touchstone of awakening sermons. For unlike Chauncy's ministerial assurances about the course of providential history in his Stamp Act repeal sermon, Robbins's attempt to impose narrative order opens out on the ambiguities of interpretive contingency. Returning to the terrifying "day of darkness" announced in the textual opening, Robbins intones, "We send our prayers & humble remonstrances to our rightful Sovereign but the event is uncertain & we know not what is before us—thus God has tryed us with mercies and our fruit has been sin and now he is trying us with a new & before unheard of strange tryal which leads to _____ [.]"[57]

Thus abruptly does the passage "end." Indeed, Robbins refrains from completing the unsettling thought for, like the narrative itself, the once-assured course of history now seems uncertain, *unparalleled,* without apparent biblical or historical antecedent. Retreating from the metaphysical abyss into which the logic of his words forces him to stare, he "safely" concludes with a traditional jeremiadlike warning, perhaps a reflection of the "disburdening" of self accompanying the "anguished ordeal of choice between patriotism and loyalty" that marked the crisis of conscience in 1765. "Let none be mobishly or riotously inclining at every trouble or uneasiness. ampl." Robbins cautioned. And, as if to swerve his congregation from the terrors of contingency and social anarchy in the direction of selfless Christian devotion, Robbins appended a peroration of passive verbal directives: "be thankful"; "Eye the hand of God"; "pray for the King"; "Remember that"; "pray ear-

nestly"; "Take heed." But perhaps the most resonant phrase of the sermon's Improvement, *inserted* within the catalogue, is a line that summarizes, in its multivocality, the range of pre-revolutionary feelings in
the wake of seeming judgment: apocalyptic fear; millennial hope; and
the ultimate image of human passivity in the face of God's miracles:

> The flood is coming—get into the ark.[58]

The flood seemed to be even more imminent by 1766 when Robbins,
in a sermon preached on the repeal of the Stamp Act, again offered his
pulpit as a haven from the ambiguities of history. Detailing the story of
Mordecai, Haman, and the plight of the Jews (Robbins would, in 1774,
return to the Book of Esther, but with different rhetorical result), Robbins portrays the mood of the colonies as filled with "apprehensions,
distempers, and fears" attendant with the "vicious . . . tendency and
consequences" of the heinous act itself. The discourse tries to establish
narrative flow, but two curious asides betray Robbins's own self-
consciousness as communal spokesman who, on this occasion at least,
could not sanctify the integrative, sustaining myth of the culture. "The
Repeal of the *Stamp Act* whereby we are instated in our ancient Rights &
priviledges is (I suppose) the occasion of our being called together this
day to worship god in his House." The parenthetical aside is intriguing.
Is it a private notation tinged with weary irony or the public acknowledgment of an exhausted, strained ritual? In any event, the juxtaposition of "ancient rights and priviledges" (the line rings more provocatively if "rights" is read as "rites") with "(I suppose)"—a personal
aside which deconstructs the collective myth—is striking. Of course Robbins believed deeply in the cohesive nature of the moment, but his next
line, "I have made a choice of words now read *for your entertainment*
on this occasion" (emphasis added)[59] bespeaks a rare moment of self-
judgment, perhaps even a shock of recognition over the disparity between the "distempers and fears" following recent events and the "mere"
Biblical analogues designed to contain intractable history by absorbing
it into the redemptive continuum of the sacred.

Significantly, the typological formulas of the Repeal sermon cannot
seem to accommodate the social realities of urban unrest. To be sure,
as providential artist, Robbins paints the "joyfull scenes [which] open
to the Jews" in Mordecai's time, but his portrait shifts quickly to contemporaneous issues in describing Haman's fate. "The former prime
minister is turned out and Hanged," Robbins reminds his audience, "not
in Effigie but in Person." The allusion to the restive Stamp Act crowds

is not perhaps immediately telling, except that Robbins's sermon goes on to pronounce on the looming anarchy envisioned in mobs and effigies. Indeed, the Lord's remembrancer would even have the "immemorial first of November" (the date inaugurating the enforcement of the Stamp Act in the colonies) struck from the calendar of providence: "let it not be numbered with the days of the year—but left out of the Christian calendar that its Era may not have a return to renew our sorrows." (The passage suggests that the Stamp Act had no coordinates on Robbins's linear axis of providential history; if it were plotted, it would disrupt the sequential patterns of the Christian calendar.) The memory of wicked oppression may be banished by an act of selective historical amnesia but not so the discordant scenes of recent experience, when "some in despondency, some in outrage and tumult[,] acting as sons of violence, under the spurious name of sons of liberty" have "in an unlawful way" been swept up by "a spirit of licentiousness and outrage" rather than "a wonderful spirit of liberty."[60]

Robbins's language, which echoes that of Chauncy's printed Repeal sermon (including Chauncy's own epithet for the Liberty men, "sons of wickedness"), registers an uneasiness with the political forms of human agency unleashed by the response to perceived oppression; it also registers how the palpable reflections of politics can in some ways immobilize (rather than inspire) the religious imagination. Although Robbins's rhetoric would never reduce to the almost casual typology of Chauncy (*"It may be said* of these colonies," he remarked in his Repeal sermon, "as of the Jewish people upon the repeal of the decree of Ahaseurus" [emphasis added]—Robbins's invocation of Esther, Mordecai, and Haman never becomes "mere" analogy), the Branford minister, like his Old Light counterpart, was anxious over the disjunction between events and the course of providence, a historical divergence to which "some have been perplexed with the thot [*sic*] of fatal consequences."[61]

That perplexity accounts, I believe, for the uncharacteristic, self-conscious glossing of the Repeal sermon's occasion and import. The parenthetical "I suppose" is the lament of the doubting patriarch chagrined over children *"acting* as sons of violence"—outside of accustomed social roles, playing at incendiary games. Haman was *really* hanged, the Bible tells us; do not mock Scriptural exempla with your mere "effigies." Still, in the end, Robbins deferred to the authority of contemporaneous voices, specifically the voice of William Pitt ("the Darling of the Nation"),[62] whose Parliamentary orations were more affecting (and effective) than any Old Testament discourse, and the voice of

Mayhew, in his famous sermon on the Stamp Act Repeal, *The Snare Broken*. "I am beholden," Robbins confessed, to "sundry texts in the present performance."[63] Other texts, that is, replace the authority of the Bible; as a result, the weight of recent political history achieves a kind of interpretive, indeed, "intertextual" sway to which Robbins himself acknowledges rhetorical deference and dependence.

Thus frightened by the anarchic "sons of violence" in his midst, threatened by the "spirit of licentiousness" abroad in the land, Robbins oratorically responds to crisis with the famous image from *The Snare Broken;*[64] with Mayhew, Robbins tries to mediate the socially disruptive claims of political liberty with the purely spiritual, a stance that is not adversarial but rather adheres to the belief that "the King and Parliament have the interests of the colonies so much at Heart."[65] If in retrospect we view Robbins's confidence as naive or innocent, we ignore the psychic bonds of allegiance that determined colonial attitudes toward England. What alienated the hearts and minds of the colonists so suddenly still remains unresolved. However, we can describe the reaction of at least one Connecticut minister to the social dislocation and metaphysical trauma that occurred between 1765 and 1776; we can follow his attempt to explain the course of history to himself and to his Branford congregation; and we can gauge in the process how, in Bernard Bailyn's formulation, "the incandescent theme of liberty . . . blazed forth" from his pulpit.[66] Though Robbins's rhetoric never leaped with high incendiary flames, he did join with other patriot ministers to keep the fires burning. More enlightening is the shifting of pulpit identities (or stances) during the Revolution: the transition from his pastoral role as comforting witness to his revolutionary office as historical agent, engineering for America.

That transition was not, of course, tantamount to a conversion experience; the "fusion of piety and politics" characteristic of the revolutionary pulpit was not immediate. Yet "for those who continued to confront the world in religious terms"[67] the emergent scene of politics, war, and death was perplexing and intractable—in Robbins's case he often confessed to a personal ignorance and impotence before the complexities of civic affairs. Nevertheless, his pulpit rhetoric from 1774 through 1779 reveals him neither retreating from the political world of revolutionary America into some otherworldly realm of millennial wish-fulfillment, nor preaching away his congregation with the abstractions of high theology. On the contrary, the Revolution fired Robbins's imagination; his patriotic sermons represent the flowering of his pulpit rhetoric as the Revolution revived the pastoral demands of his office.

Although the revolution "would in time destroy [the clergy's] special role as authoritative intermediaries"—perhaps the greatest irony of eighteenth-century American religious culture—it recalled ministers to their "task to awaken the people to the dangers confronting their liberties" and returned them to their original role as faithful shepherds, leading a frightened flock through the bewildering psychic landscape known as the American Revolution.[68]

Much has been written about how the Black Regiment, as Tory historian Peter Oliver styled the patriot ministry, lent their physical and spiritual energies to the sacred cause. From early studies of Whig propaganda to more recent scholarship that treats "the great outpourings of the spoken word" as the spur to passionate involvement and political enthusiasm among the populace, the question of language and religious rhetoric, political ideology and mobilization continues to engage students of the Revolution.[69] Over and again we hear and read of revolutionary *"schemers* [who] set out to *inflame* the public temper"; of the *"dynamic* interactions" between "rhetors and audience"; of preachers' words *"pregnant* in this time of political revolution"; of religious minds which *"took fire* in the *explosive* atmosphere" of revolutionary America (emphasis added).[70] The very language is revealing: "infused," "spread," "energized," "agitate," "triggered," 'took fire," and so on. Incendiary rhetoric summoned tautologically to describe incendiary rhetoric may not explain much of anything. Still, the language does raise the question of ideology and its mode of transmission: that is, how ideas become the source of belief and the basis for action. According to Stout and Isaac, the transforming agency of the spoken word enabled patriot preachers to challenge the elitist world of print—and the ordered, hierarchic, deferential world it symbolizes—with the leveling power of oral discourse.[71]

The example of Philemon Robbins allows us to enter the debate over the "blurring" of Whig rhetoric and Puritan idioms,[72] along with current investigations into the social power of oral discourse during the Revolution. On August 31, 1774 Robbins joined Samuel Sherwood, Benjamin Trumbull, Jonathan Edwards, Jr., and other Connecticut ministers in preaching "the day before the Congress in Philadelphia at a public fast"—a collective ritual designed as "a summons to renewed obedience and vigorous action" to a people on the threshold of political unity and identity.[73] How can rhetoric both "summon obedience" *and* empower "vigorous action"? Robbins's fast day sermon exemplifies how the Black Regiment could at once inspire resistance and contain the radical potential of the rhetoric of "liberty."

Robbins returned in 1774 to the biblical source of his Stamp Act Repeal oration, the Book of Esther, drawing his Doctrine from the political plight of the Jews under a wicked king: "When kings or earthly powers frame decrees against their subjects 'tis matter of lamentation and calls for repentance fasting and prayer." The Doctrine follows after a long narrative summarizing the saga of Mordecai, who would not, "out of conscience," defer to Haman. Mordecai, as Robbins tells it, "did not deny reverance to Haman out of pride, nor any personal grudge against him—much less out of contempt of the king[']s authority and command—but meerly out of conscience, because he was a Jew who was obliged to give divine honour to none but God only."[74] The political application of the story of Esther was a typological commonplace of revolutionary literature, but Robbins's Mordecai is not quite a "conscience patriot," despite his proto-revolutionary stance toward the King's "designing" minister. If anything, the sermon, which weaves Old Testament antecedents and contemporaneous contexts in an infinitely flexible and continuous style,[75] retreats from the political implications of its own rhetoric. Though Robbins invests his discourse with virtually every theme derived from Whig ideology—"bad advisors and malicious and corrupt ministry"; the "liberty we received from our ancestors"—he simultaneously warns against what he calls the "imprudent discourse" of would-be patriots who have made themselves "obnoxious" by their speech. "Why need any thing be *said*," Robbins asks, "to justify those measures that are taken to bring unconstitutional burdens upon us[?]" (emphasis added). "Imprudent" speech is politically impotent; it is "talk [that] will do no good." Indeed, the ultimate admonition of this sermon concerns the dangers of orality itself: "let not your speech be provoking."[76]

Of course the ironies of Robbins's warning against provocative speech resound in a sermon that is itself a model of orally imbued political resistance. At key moments, Robbins inserts the tonic phrase of the textual opening, thus forging an incantatorial effect that is the hallmark of suasive preaching:

> This is matter of lamentation and calls for repentance fasting and prayer
> tis matter of Lamentation
> When king Ahaseurus's Decree came out against the Jews, the Text says, there was great mourning and fasting and weeping and wailing and many lay in sackcloth and ashes—

and have we not reason at this Day for weeping and mourning. tis a day of darkness, a dark day—perhaps the darkest that ever our eyes or our fathers have seen.[77]

The authority of biblical history blurs with current; in turn, the leveling power of Robbins's typological imagination enacts a ritual response to oppression across the historical continuum, from biblical Persia to Branford.

The sermon is laced with further rhetorical ironies. Despite his nervous nod to "provoking speech," the speaker himself intones a litany of rhetorical questions, the answers to which a latter-day chosen people already knew:

> Shall a whole province—nay a whole country have their dearest priviledges be taken from them and burdens laid upon them, which they are unable to bear—Shall they all be enslaved and have no right to their labors . . . Shall all be sufferers[,] the innocent with guilty . . . What shall we do for relief, What course can we take?
> To pretend to resist King and parliament and oppose all the force of fleets and armies would be madness and folly—and to submit to internal legislation and taxation and have statutes made to bind us in all cases whatsoever—we cannot we may not never never never, Duty to God our Country, ourselves, and posterity forbids it, let the case be whatever it may.[78]

Resistance leads to madness (only "feigned" action, as the pretender selves of 1765 who acted as "sons of violence"); yet to submit would be a denial of conscience, both to God and history. *"Let the case be whatever it may."* The line signals Robbins's entrance into the world of contingency. "Surely we ought to exert ourselves to the utmost," the patriot preacher urges, but how can we "detest and abhor all things of a mobish riotous aspect" and yet forge a new nation? "Which way is best," Robbins confessed, "I can't determine."[79] The sermon, we might add, rhetorically objectifies the same dilemma. The *figura* of Mordecai disappears before the indeterminacy of future events, the biblical trope which might have guaranteed the future gives way to the secular world of factional debate and political dealing—the *real* world of the Congress preparing to meet in Philadelphia the next day.

Still, despite Robbins's self-confessed immobility, his deference to and dependence on a God who "would undertake for us," the fast day rhetoric spurs as it warns, mobilizes as it retreats from authorizing political resistance. As ritual discourse, it invests abstract ideals with an affective valence, dismissing the logic of submission with the moving, summoning injunction, "never, never, never." The psychosocial implications of Robbins's impassioned nay-saying were indeed terrifying to the Protestant ministry—Robbins, we recall, had in 1765 peered into the abyss of rebellion; in 1774, he looked further into the dark, indecipherable world of contingency. After Independence, his pulpit would bravely assert the cause of America and give comfort to those who, with their minister, ventured forth into the ambiguities of revolutionary experience.

Throughout 1777 Robbins mounted his pulpit to explain the course of history to his Branford brethren, struggling to place the judgment of war—"our unnatural civil war,"[80] he called it—within the scheme of sacred history. These 1777 sermons represent the flowering of Robbins's sermonic art and offer an index to the mental world of their speaker, and perhaps their auditors as well. Viewed together, they reveal how Robbins enlisted the services of "providential language . . . to blur the distinction between sacred and profane history by wedding events of the Revolution to the history of redemption." The example of Robbins, however, complicates that observation: rather than reflexively calling on providence as "a principle of historical explanation,"[81] Robbins's revolutionary rhetoric exposes the tensions within that imaginative convention itself. In general, his 1777 sermons cannot sustain the narrative mode inherent in the historical parallels of typological exegesis. Perceiving the time as yet another moment in the ongoing battle between God's people in America and the enslaving forces of darkness, Robbins revived many of the rhetorical strategies of his awakening sermons—the ejaculatory phrase, vertical catalogue, litany, and incantation—in his effort to create metaphysical order out of historical chaos. In the process, Robbins assumed the mantle of Jeremiah to remind and exhort his congregation, but the prophetic voice could not so easily envision an approaching millennium; the future was never assured—at least as of January 1777. To read (and listen to) Robbins's sermonic efforts over 1777 is to follow the ministerial mind in process, from excoriation to hope. Through the ritual language of his series of "war fast" sermons Robbins helped his people act in history by charting the country's devious-cruising course set by the Revolution.

I allude to the famous closing lines of *Moby-Dick* for, like Melville's great epic about the American ship of state, Robbins's major trope for the country's wartime passage through the Revolution is that of a ship forever tossed on perilous seas; like Melville, Robbins probes the ulti-

mate question of design, providence, chance, and futurity: Are the cir-
cling movements of the white whale patterned or contingent? Where
does the current upheaval of revolution fit onto the grid of God's plan
for America?

In partial reply, Robbins's War Fast sermon of late January 1777 answers with the familiar jeremiadic anxiety and lamentation for an apostate people. The text itself, from Jeremiah 18:7, 8, establishes that tone,
reminding the audience of God's whimsy "to pluck up and pull down" a
kingdom. "If that nation . . . turns from their evil," God's voice announced in the words of the biblical prophet, "I will repent of the evil
that I thot to do unto them." The notion of divine premeditation may be
unsettling, but a chosen people knows that "by repentance and reformation men escape the evil[.] So that one design of the threatening may be
to reclaim and rescue"—only, of course, in recognition of "unfeigned repentance." Still, providential reclamation did not seem apparent in a
land afflicted with "violence and cruelty, inhumanity and barbarity, what
horrors and devastation have they spread in this land."[82]

The litany inaugurates a series of portraits of the physical ravages of
war: "the pestilance has walked in darkness," visiting a contagion among
the Northern armies, whose soldiers are "rotting in their blankets before
their souls set loose from their bodies." Branford may not as yet be
scourged by the disease but the contagion of revolution has imprisoned
its people. "We can't tell," Robbins bemoans, "which way to go or step
out doors but at the hazzard of our lives." Against this image of a town
barricaded and quarantined by sin and disease (both physical and spiritual) the preacher opposes the spirit of the forefathers, from whom
"how sadly we have apostasized . . . How pure were their intentions,
how fervent their prayers, how delighted in ordinance making." The
contrast in religious affections explains the "perilous and dark aspect in
the country," in a "land [which] seems to be full of self."[83]

The times in January 1777 were indeed bleak, and human agency was
helpless in a season of "agitation" and "convulsion." "We must reform
and alter our course," Robbins urged toward the end, but the collective
action implied by the ministerial imperative is immediately qualified:
"We cant sit at helm and steer the ship in this boisterous [sea]/we cant
hold the reins of providence nor know what to do." Robbins's trope recalls the image of Noah's ark from the Stamp Act discourse (but note
the mixed metaphor, which anthropormorphically invests providence
with a bucking as well as a rocking movement). By 1777 the ark is
reeling through tumultuous waters, "plucked up" and "pulled down"
without the steady winds of providence to guide it safely along its pre-

destined course. Thus Robbins leaves his audience metaphorically at sea, contemplating the horrors of divine judgment, listening to their helmsman confess an inability to steer into the future. The sermon leaves us, in effect, at the edge of contingency reflected, in Robbins's long catalogue of fragments which limn the requirements of "unfeigned" piety. "This is a people that God has adopted for himself," the preacher scrawls along the vertical edge of the catalogue[84]—perhaps an afterthought that tries somehow to *insert* a "marginal" people into a familiar narrative of the self's prophetic journey along the morphology of conversion.

Robbins returned to the foundering ship metaphor in subsequent sermons of 1777. "America is undone," he warned on the fast day of April 29, "if they dont take a new course," for it appeared a "stormy[,] floody time." This public effort reveals Robbins struggling to establish narrative before the challenge of *intractable* experience as he both chastises and emboldens his audience. In the morning portion of the oration the ominous forecast of "clouds and thick darkness" (a variation on the textual opening from Joel 12:2, "A day of darkness and of gloominess, a day of clouds and thick darkness," which becomes a tonic phrase chanted over and again in the afternoon) is brightened by the dispersing agency of the "faithful body of men engaged for the welfare of the country"; their "skill and wisdom" will scatter the "clouds that now hang over us" and reveal "a mountain of [holiness] and a dwelling place of righteousness." Furthermore, "our children . . . will rise up and call us blessed," Robbins prophesies at the close, extending the theme of generations introduced a few moments before; "as Elijahs go off Elishas may come on the stage."[85]

The generational metaphor is, of course, tinged with irony: by 1777, at sixty-eight, Robbins was himself an Elijah bequeathing his mantle to a rising band of Elishas assembled in Philadelphia. (Of that important shift in American cultural history, from theology to law, he was not unaware.)[86] Fittingly, then, the afternoon portion opens with a portrait of new beginnings, detailing, in a vigorous, sustained narrative, the story of Exodus, implicitly linking the morning's concluding vision with the continuing saga of God's "covenanted people of old." The current historical context reinforces temporal continuities; Branford, Robbins implies, remained within the covenant. The afternoon's opening in effect *translates* the audience back into biblical history, placing the community within the teleological vision of the redemptive spiral. And that telos is stylistically objectified through a sequence of "yet" phrases ("yet at length"; "yet he remembered"; "yet he raised up Joshua") which propels the narrative inexorably along, moving from the story of deliverance through the secular example of "our forefathers in Europe" whom God "transplanted . . . hither[.] The winds and sea obeyed his voice to waft them into America—then a howling wilderness."[87] Thus does God's *voice* impose design on Nature's contingent elements. But when Robbins's ritual chronicle arrives at his own time the narrative sputters; current history cannot be gleaned for *figurae*. "We have long set under our vine and fig tree enjoying the sweets and comforts of life and how happy might we yet have been if we had cleaved to God with all our Hearts." Instead of its conjunctive office, the "yet" of this sentence almost arrests the sequential flow. The shift in rhetorical valence compels Robbins to repeat the ominous tonic phrase ("Tis now a dark day"; "Tis a day of darkness"), along with litanies and catalogues, as if only the revivalist mode could accommodate the unnarratable (but not unutterable) times.[88]

Perhaps the clearest reflection of Robbins's narrative dilemma occurs after he describes the strange, unnatural reversals that have accompanied the country's siege by "an implacable and relentless enemy":

> The temple of God turned into horse stables, colleges into barracks, towns and cities pilledged burnt and destroyed. They have marched in person when the Land like the garden of Eden was before them but behind them left a desolate wilderness.[89]

These spatial inversions are not the worst of it, however. There follows a catalogue of woes (each prefaced with the refrain "how many"), culminating in the most unsettling of inversions to Robbins's imagination—the unnatural generation of Tories, whose collective portrait he brushes in these fragmentary, poetic strokes:

> O tis a Day of Darkness . . .
> ad to this the *tories* that rise up against us
> from amongst ourselves
> born with us,
> fed at our tables
> lodged in our beds
> priviledged & protected by our country
> tied to us by Relation[90]

Here was the ultimate familial horror: rebellious Elishas who spurned the nurturing, sheltering family and turned against country. No narrative could ever mediate the illogical reversal of a generation cut loose from its own history—a discontinuous progeny, denying its hereditary connection to family and to American history in general.

If the afternoon performance opens with a recalling of God's promise to Abraham's children (to construct a legendary past), it closes with an attempt to scatter the clouds of contingency and return the ark on course. "The war continues," Robbins sadly acknowledged, "and tho we have exerted ourselves so much and suffered so much—the event is uncertain[.] let it be so[.] events are Gods." Nevertheless, the authority of God's commandments justifies political exertions ("the 6th Commandment requires all lawful endeavors to preserve our own life," he reminded). Robbins concludes with the by now familiar pattern of conditional sentences that move in tone from anxiety to hope, despair to encouragement. "If that spirit prevailed thro the states as appeared in the beginning of the war the prospect of danger would not much deter us; . . . if we have a permanent trust in God we shall be safe and easie"—preserved in the biblical ark, buoyed up on boisterous waters, *safe and easy within narrative.* "But if our hopes and fears rise and fall at the [event] of every skirmish we are unsteady"—afloat on the turbulent waters of historical (and narrative) contingency.

What did the people of Branford hear in 1777 as the solution to their political and spiritual plight? Robbins urged them "not to be at all discouraged but freely, cheerfully, and voluntarily exert [them]selves to [the] utmost—Tho clouds and thick darkness are roundabout . . . yet justice and judgment are the habitation of his throne forever. Tho weeping endure for a night/Joy will come in the morning." On this hopeful vision Robbins stops speaking; the conjunctive "yet" performs a prophetic linguistic office, guaranteeing that from the eyes of redemptive history there is no contradiction between patriotic exertion and the saint's "inclination" toward God. The "yet," we might say, looks forward to the millennial morning after the night-weeping of uncertainty.[91] Above all else, however, Robbins's rhetoric converts uncertainty into faith, thus enabling his people to endure the historical passage into collective selfhood.

In many respects, then, Robbins's 1777 performances represent the flowering of his pulpit art. It is as if the Revolution became a consuming subject, the matter for his imagination to transform and render as public discourse. Donald Scott writes of how the commanding office of the ministry in prerevolutionary America gave way later in the century to the self-enclosed coterie of professionals lamenting their weakened status.[92] Robbins's example suggests, though, that the evangelical ministry reached the height of pastoral efficacy and oracular power at the very threshold of decline.The significant shift in Robbins's pulpit stance through 1777, from angry prophet denouncing the sins of the nation to seer forecasting a glorious future, offers testimony to the Black Regiment's mobilizing and comforting role in a time of crisis. In the dialectic between interpretive ambiguity and the seamless narrative of providential theory, Robbins found his preaching voice. He also discovered, in the process, the usable past and ideology of Whig rhetoric.

The sermons preached during the summer of 1777 were delivered, as Robbins attests in his running title, "to give courage in war": specifically, to encourage those afflicted with a "backwardness to enlist" to come to the aid of God's army. Invoking the well-known "curse of Meroz," Robbins berates all those "timorous and slouthful [who] refuse to come to the help of the Lord." To combat fear and lethargy Robbins calls for a revival of that "enlisting Spirit." Note the preacher's ambiguous play on the agency (in joining the army) and passivity (in joining for Jesus) of "enlisting" a quickening spirit which God sends "to wake up his people and engage all the courageous in the country." In contrast to the devious Tories ("Enemies . . . among ourselves, that keep in the dark") who "may *act* the traitor," we need the "unfeigned" religion of true patriots who "fight with [their] hands and pray with [their] Hearts."[93]

But the war sermon is not simply an early version of recruitment propaganda; its larger purpose, as Robbins himself declared (perhaps in the afterthought of titling the manuscript), is to give psychological and historical comfort: to *enable*—in the sense of the enabling power of ideology to help people in history. Rhetorically, the incantatorial tonic phrase ritually confers identity as well. Resounding throughout the oration, the tonic phrase "Yet we are God's people" prefaces a quick lesson in Whig history, with Robbins reminding the audience how "England was once eminent for Religion," a "people after God's own heart—but how is it with most of them now?" The contrast with the Stamp Act sermon is telling; now the unnamed agent of horror stands revealed: "are they not," he asks, speaking of the mother country, "murderous, tyrannical and cruel?" The segment concludes with a spatial and geographic move from the old world to the new. "I dont know where we shall find God's people," Robbins asks (in a version of the dialogic mode, whose question already voices an expected answer), "if not *here* in America" (emphasis added). As if to highlight this temporalizing of the sacred, Robbins intones the optimistic strains of the jeremiad: "Tho our land is defiled with sin and we have many abominations—yet we are God's people. He has built his Church upon a rock and the gates of Hell shall not prevail against it." The assurances of prophecy and promise impel those of an "enlisting" spirit; "at such a time," the preacher exhorts, "our all is at stake."[94]

At such a time. The apocalyptic urgency of the times demanded patriotic exertion, but Robbins, faithful providential historian that he was, knew that only God determined events. If earlier in the year his preaching acknowledged man's limited agency, by the summer of 1777 he could speak of the Spirit bequeathing "a pattern and example for action" to a generation of soldier-Elishas. Significantly, Robbins's later sermons are *filled* with allusions to contemporary events and local geography, weaving his rehearsal of Old Testament providences with "scenes" of latter-day victories and "God's Mercies." The Lord "does not make a people his to destroy them—no—He may allure them and bring them into the wilderness but then he will speak comfortably to them." So too with Branford's faithful shepherd. Robbins's revolutionary sermons voiced the secular sounds of assurance as they conflated secular and redemptive history. In a stunning phrase (again, toward the close) Robbins summarized both his Sunday theme and his oracular office: "O tis comfortable to anticipate the time" when "this land may be Emmanuel's Land & this people & _____." We may imagine that the preacher's private notation to "fill in the blank," to fulfill the rhythmic cadence of the sentence, was completed in public utterance, or else in hopeful, silent unison with the congregation. To find comfort in anticipation of future events is to rest easy in the ark of the collective covenant, safe within a narrative that envisions America as the dwelling place of her "Christians of Canaan." Rather than highlight the disjunctions of contingency, by the summer of 1777 Robbins chose to anticipate the future. "Let us be hearty to God in the present struggles," he advised, "hearty to improve for him all the success he intends to grant us."[95]

By that summer, too, Robbins's language became fully immersed in Whig rhetoric, the "everyday inheritance" of intellectuals in eighteenth-century America.[96] Robbins, however, did not exploit religious idioms on behalf of an ascendant ideology, nor was his immersion a calculated grafting of Whig idioms onto obsolescent Puritan formulas.[97] Rather, he imbibed the currents of Whig rhetoric to fashion an explanatory system that could mediate the doctrine of providence with the ambiguities of revolutionary history. A telling example of this process is the synecdochical revision in a Thanksgiving sermon of December 1777. "Praise God," Robbins enjoined, "for his smiling upon us in the prosecution of a just and necessary war for the Defense and Establishment of our ~~necessary~~ inalienable rights and liberties."[98] Of course this remarkable substitution could be read as the author's wary avoidance of redundancy, but the revision (in my view) bespeaks the blurring of entire world views. "Necessary" suggests a world of providential design, of liberties sanctioned by the testament of God's plan. The shift to "inalienable" signals a rhetorical crossing into the discourse of English political thought and ideology (which of course had its own version of "providential" history invariably summoned by Whig pamphletists), a transition that reverberates a new tone, and with it, a new vocabulary.

Right after the revisionary invocation of "inalienable" there follows a recapitulation of recent history that, in its already retrospective stance, conforms to the familiar logic of Whig hermeneutics:

> The states as such are united. They have felt the oppression of the British nation—they have tried petitions, prayers and remonstrances, which have all been rejected—they know their cruelty and unrighteous Demands, declaring their right to give law[,] to bind us in all cases whatsoever & that nothing will satisfy but entire submission & so our liberty and property must be all at their command . . . the good hand of the God upon us we are united to oppose them & determined to be free—[99]

The passage rings with the high strains of Country Party rhetoric. Of course Robbins would not have recognized (or much less have acknowledged) the incorporation; he continued to see the times as ripe for another of God's remarkable seasons of renewal; "We are . . . to pray for a blessing on the United States," he announced, and hope "that religion may revive in them." He repeated the call in November 1778, following the most overtly Whig-infused sermon of his career. That he continued to long for a revival does not bar him from the secular world he helped, if not usher in, at least ease into being. Like Gordon Wood's collection of Whig spokesmen, Robbins embraced his "task to awaken the people to the dangers confronting their liberties."[100] From this perspective, the Thanksgiving sermon of November 1778 stands as the culmination of his patriot vision.

Let us listen to a portion of Robbins's oration at an "incendiary" moment where he expounds the recent woes to beset the country and offers the logic of Christian dissent as a mode of deliverance:

> We are particularly to praise God this Day for the preservation of our Rights, liberties & priviledges. We live amidst the calamities of a grievous & unnatural war[.] our enemies have sought our destruction, the effusion of our blood, our wounds captivity imprisonment & Death with merciless rage endeavouring to devour burn & destroy all before them but . . . God has made his power and grace known in saving the United States of America from the cruel hand of Tyranny that has been out against us, and memorable is that day wherein we were declared

Independent of those who by cruelties and horrors of war have sought
our ruin, while we were dependent in our former connection with
Great Britain we were obnoxious to tyranny and the cruel hand of it
bore more and more heavy upon us. But God has wrought our deliverance therefore stand fast in the liberty wherewith Christ has made
you free and be not entangled with the yoke of bondage.[101]

Here is an evocative example of the conflation of biblical and secular
worlds, the political uses of Christian "liberty," and the biblical reso-
nances that fill Whig accounts of American enslavement. Throughout,
Robbins's language is "multivalent"; it registers both the high-level ideas
of Whig discourse and the affective dimension of the speech to the Galatians; it recalls, in turn, Robbins's early sermon challenging the authority
of fathers (as well as the 1747 letter decrying the "yoke of bondage" in
the wake of the Wallingford affair); and it reveals, above all, the rhetorical blurring of "liberty" in its office as ritual symbol.[102]

The blurring is evident as well in the subtle change in the by now familiar sermonic tropes. "God's works of providence are glorious," he
states conventionally; "he preserves upholds and governs all things, or-
ders the affairs of nations & kings, peace & war life & death & all the rev-
olutions and *changes of time.*" But those revolutionary "changes, from
a King to a Congress"—the cultural passage that has been his subject
since 1765—are fraught with uncertainty, as we have seen; only Providence could steady the ark through the stormy, floody voyage to its millennial haven. By 1778, Robbins's incorporation of the secular world of
statesmen and politics is complete, as he implicitly links the once atemporal ship with the guidance of "such wise and faithful men . . . who
decree rule & govern" from *their* "pulpits"—the "assemblies and public
councils of the state." "Tis a very difficult thing," Robbins admits, "to
set at helm and steer in such a tempestuous and boisterous season."[103]
His ark now floating on the rough waters of politics, Robbins indirectly
names the pilots of the revolutionary cause as the new helmsmen of the
republic.

Fittingly, too, by 1778 Robbins's ship of state sails on a millennial
course despite the buffetings, the ebb and flow, of the winds and seas of
revolution. Changing metaphors, Robbins closes the oration with a vision
of Ezekiel's wheel spiraling toward the fulfillment of redemptive history:

all the wheels of Religion are set agoing when God pours out his spirit
in a pleasurable manner. but if he withold [sic] or withdraw his spirit
they stand still. let us be ardent that god would pour out his spirit bring
us to general repentance and reformation—dwell in our Land & make it
a Mountain of holiness and dwelling place of righteousness.[104]

"Let us be ardent"—the phrase registers the affective springs of social and spiritual mobilization. ("O then let us be hearty," he chants at the end, glossing the textual opening from Psalms 9:1, "I will praise thee O Lord with all my heart.")[105] To be ardent is to strive for the kingdom that is imminent, to engineer for its descent upon *our* land." Before, Robbins's "mountains of holiness" represented the otherworldly type of spiritual desire; now, after the Revolution, in the wake of Robbins's temporalizing rhetoric, they have a secular (geographic) and sacred locale.

A great emblem for this transformation occurs at the end of one of Robbins's last sermons, where the aged minister, in a sequence of revisions, lets us observe the ministerial mind in a rare moment of selfconscious process: "May God grant . . . our Independence" to "all people in ~~America~~ Branford[,] in ~~New England~~ Connecticut[,] in America & thro the world."[106] Clearly, Robbins perceived the wheels of Independence as an engine of redemption moving from his pulpit in little Branford and extending out in ever-widening geographic circles to encompass state, region, country, and the world. (Note the remarkable reversal from the Stamp Act sermon, which narrowed the geographic focus, *from* the universe *to* Branford.) For a moment in 1779, the patriarch attained his oracular office: his vision of millennial fulfillment expands, propelled by geographic litany, from temporal to sacred, in a continuous act of spatial extension and spiritual translation.

In this respect, Robbins's revising impulse may be viewed as the rhetorical correlative to the movement of revolutionary discourse itself: the ritual leveling of autonomous, self-interested colonies through the power of the spoken word; the attempt to fit revolutionary experience within the comfortable narrative of redemptive history. For over fifty years, through seasons of upheaval and bewilderment, celebration and despair, judgment and hope Robbins's words sought to explain, soothe, chastise, defend, mobilize, and confirm both the obscure village and emergent nation in their shared pilgrimage. "I will hear your prayers," the minister assured, emulating the voice of God, "and [will] make America my special case."[107] The career of Philemon Robbins is an extraordinary testament to the sustaining power of religious rhetoric to meet, listen, and answer to the political and spiritual needs of people in times of cultural crisis.

2

The Edwardsean Legacy:
The Example of Jonathan Edwards, Jr.
of White Haven

Of course the role of oracular spokesman and communal authority was not the only office to which the New Divinity men aspired; besides charting the spiritual progress of their flocks, easing the passage through revolution, these latter-day prophets charged themselves with the education of a rising generation of Elishas, a progeny who would continue the sacred calling of the faithful shepherd. Perhaps the most famous and influential figure in the process of New Divinity socialization was Joseph Bellamy, who, from his "school of the prophets" in Litchfield County, personally directed the training of a majority of patriot preachers, later styled (by Loyalist Peter Oliver) the Black Regiment. Bellamy's parsonage, the fathers assumed, offered the proper religious and pedagogic environment to form those sons who felt the ministerial call. Philemon Robbins, for example, sent both his sons off to Bellamy. "My son that now comes to you," he wrote Bellamy in 1757, "has a great desire to be with you . . . his eagerness, engagedness & strong desire . . . is such that if I should deny, it seems as though his mind would be perplexed." For his own part Robbins confessed that "the chief good I can do in the world is to bring up two sons for public service."[1] Indeed, the meager legacy of Robbins's printed works (which include ordination sermons for his sons, Ammi and Chandler, both of whom served as Revolutionary chaplains) suggests that Robbins viewed himself not as a "leading" intellectual figure (as did Jonathan Edwards and Bellamy) but rather as a literal progenitor of the true faith.

The image of Robbins as father connects the figures who comprise the subject of the next two chapters: Jonathan Edwards, Jr. and Levi Hart. Like Robbins's sons, both Edwards the Younger and Hart studied under Bellamy; viewed together, they offer a portrait of how the rising generation of New Divinity experienced the American Revolution. What, for example, was their sermonic response to political events? How did they attempt to order and explain the course of history to their congregations? Were they, like their mentors (I include Robbins in this category along with Bellamy), able to attain the status of the prophetic pastor? According to their more theologically and temperamentally moderate colleague, Ezra Stiles, this "younger class" wished "to become oracles themselves" ("they all want to be Luthers," Stiles once remarked, with a tinge of irony) but instead preached away their congregations by invoking the so-called arid, high-level discourse of New Divinity metaphysics. Following Stiles, Edmund Morgan describes Edwards, Jr.'s generation as "fearlessly consistent," inveighing against helpless congregations with "complex, abstruse, metaphysical" sermons "devoted to the details of theology that the layman found incomprehensible."[2]

Significantly, Morgan's account simply rehearses the contemporaneous debate among the New Divinity men themselves about the nature and art of preaching. Edwards, Jr., for one, already knew the case against those preachers styled "Edwardsean"; they "are too apt," he confessed, "to run into an argumentative & what is commonly called a metaphysical way of preaching." Indeed, Edwards remarked that they "almost all fail thro' want of zeal & devotion." Edwards, Jr.'s self-conscious pronouncements anticipate as well the nineteenth-century caricature of the aloof, abstracted evangelical theologian. One midcentury memoirist recalled the heavy shadow cast by the younger Edwards himself: "In the pulpit he was too profound to be interesting, or always intelligible to ordinary minds."[3]

The question of otherworldliness is important, for according to Morgan's logic, even if these ministers were aware of the political events leading up to and beyond the Revolution, they were not inclined intellectually, socially, or temperamentally to descend from their lofty pulpits into the mire of history itself—thus Morgan's assertion of a dramatic and virtually clean break in the transition within eighteenth-century American life, from religion to politics.[4] Thanks to the efforts of religious and cultural historians since Morgan, however, we have come to view the dialectic of religion and politics in more complicated ways.

The following chapter continues the rehabilitation of the New Divinity by describing how one of its younger adherents translated the collective upheaval of revolution into private and public modes of discourse.

In the case of Edwards, Jr. I am concerned with both his office as preacher and his self-appointed role as guardian of his father's literary and theological legacy. "He often said he had spent his life in his father's writings," a nineteenth-century custodian of the Edwardsean tradition noted;[5] study of the son's response to the Revolution lets us observe how the father's historical vision, especially as drawn from *The History of the Work of Redemption,* helped shape that of the son.

What little we know of Jonathan Edwards, Jr.'s youth reveals a harrowing and tragic childhood. He was six when his father removed the family to the wilderness of Stockbridge, and its native environment shaped the son's earliest sensibility. "All my thoughts ran in Indian," he informs us; "It became more familiar to me than my mother tongue." At the age of ten (1755) Jonathan was sent by his father to the wilds of New York state with the Indian missionary Gideon Hawley, but when fighting broke out they fled amidst continuous danger, eventually finding their way back to Stockbridge. (In a letter to Edwards, Jr.'s son, Hawley's gripping account of his adventures with "my Jonathan" describes how the pair escaped: we "disguised ourselves . . . we had one alarm upon another—till we finally got hardened.")[6] By the age of thirteen the younger Edwards had lost both parents. After attending school in Princeton, he went to the College of New Jersey and eventually, keeping the faith, he studied under Bellamy, from whose Bethlehem pulpit Edwards's initial sermonic efforts issued. His brief diary, kept while an undergraduate, is thoroughly conventional in its ejaculatory phrases of self-doubt and formulaic confessions: "I find my life has been no means answerable to my profession [of faith]." "Several days have now passed," he recorded in May 1764 (age 19), "without anything scarcely beside hurry & confusion with much ambitious jangling in the class. But O! that my God would make me ambitious of nothing so much as of his favour."[7] After being stirred by the preaching of President Finley, Edwards made a confession of faith, and by the winter of 1768–1769 he received and accepted a call to minister to the White Haven Church in New Haven. The church vote was not unanimous, however, for as a strict follower of New Light church discipline Edwards demanded that White Haven rescind its earlier advocacy of the Half-Way covenant (the softer, liberal doctrine that allowed for a wider church membership); in its stead Edwards restored the mandatory practice of public rather than private confessions as requisite for visible standing in the church.[8]

Fittingly, Philemon Robbins preached the sermon marking the occasion of Edwards's installation in White Haven, thus claiming "the dear young orphan" as one of his own ministerial sons and, in turn, bequeathing to Edwards—at least for the ritual scene of professional sanctioning—a palpable paternity. Fittingly, too, Robbins's discourse concerned itself with the art and aims of preaching: the issues of ministerial language, sermonic tone, stance toward audience, and so forth. His 1769 thoughts on preaching provide an index to the ministerial ideal (in the wake of the Revival) and let us measure the example of Edwards, Jr. against what he heard on that cold January morning in New Haven.[9]

We should note first that Robbins's remarks on preaching recall directly the ministerial wranglings that he himself was embroiled in a generation earlier. Ministers should "preach carefully, plainly and intelligibly," he advised before Edwards and the assembled coterie; "they are not to indulge themselves. . . . and as to stile, it ought not to be mean, contemptible & dirty but yet easie, plain, & familiar. I repeat the word familiar because I am persuaded it has a tendency by the grace of God to rivet the truth in the memory & so in the H[eart]." Perhaps in response to—and in an effort to rebuke—the "metaphysical" aspect of the younger generation, perhaps as a nod to the memory of heated disputes among ministers over "familiar" preaching styles (the charge against the eccentric James Davenport in New London over twenty-five years earlier was, among other things, that his style was *too* familiar, too potent, unsanctioned both textually and rhetorically) Robbins now asserted that only an "easie, plain" discourse can enable the preacher to perform his affective (and affecting) office. "Ministers may not prevaricate," he warned, or "be double-tongued or use double-dealing. They may not use ambiguous phrases." And to rivet the truth into the believer's heart they "are to make use of the threats & promises for the designed ends. The threatenings, to awaken sinners to fly from the wrath to come—& the promises to allure them to draw & engage them after God."[10]

Given this formulation, we might say that Robbins's own preaching career is a moving testament to the fulfillment of his theories of sermonic art; the figure of Jonathan Edwards, Jr. offers less an example of oracular accomplishment than a portrait of a self-styled Edwardsean struggling to reach out, to communicate, to *rivet* his own fears and hopes in the hearts and minds of his congregation. To be sure, Edwards the New Divinity preacher is far from Stiles's and Morgan's negative portrait; rather than propelling him into some otherworldly vision of heavenly solace, the cultural trauma of the American Revolution shook Edwards loose from the atemporal sequence of "regular preaching"—Harry Stout's phrase for the weekly pronouncements on religious, moral, and spiritual matters[11]—into a world of political danger and economic threat, a world where the minister as communal authority was obliged to fashion an explanation of current events and reinscribe secular history as a function of providential design. Rather than preaching away his congregation with an inaccessible metaphysical style, Edwards's language, both in the sermon fragments (which constitute the bulk of his extant performances) and a few fully penned discourses, emerges as plain and familiar. Indeed, the example of Edwards challenges a number of prevailing assumptions about the Edwardsean (lack of) response to revolution; instead of dismissing him as apolitical, or relegating him to New Divinity oblivion, he should be reinstated as a vocal member of the Black Regiment in his own right. After two hundred years of obscurity, it is time for Edwards the Younger to join the consensus.

Edwards, Jr.'s nineteenth-century memoirist, aware of the manuscript evidence, had already added Edwards to the revolutionary pantheon. Tryon Edwards, the midcentury guardian, described "the intelligent and warm interest" which his ancestor, "in common with the great body of the New England ministers, felt in the welfare of his country"; a later custodian of the literary remains advised, in bequeathing the collection of sermons to Hartford Seminary, that "a careful study of these Patriotic discourses will reveal some of the reasons why the clergy were zealous for the war & will reveal the causes of their great influence therein."[12] Careful study, however, reveals that Edwards was not overly zealous; incendiary rhetoric (à la Tom Paine) was not his style. His sermons before August 31, 1774—the date of the colony-wide observance on the eve of the Continental Congress (and the date of one of Edwards's many statements about the imperial crisis)[13]—convey the hesitant, fearful, anxious mood that characterized prerevolutionary America.

Exactly five years before the Continental fast Edwards spoke at White Haven from Exodus 3:7, 8: "And the Lord said surely I have seen afflictions." Except for the earliest surviving sermons, which are written out in full and delivered from pulpits in Bellamy's Bethlehem, Samuel Hopkins's Great Barrington, and at Princeton—one senses that the young Edwards was showcasing his fledgling talents before the living shades of his father's Connecticut Valley world—the bulk of Edwards, Jr.'s huge sermonic corpus remains in note form, with each page divided in half so that only the fragment of a point or thought could be expressed on paper. Whether he arrived at this method of composition from quickly acquired pastoral confidence is not self-evident (the sermon notes begin too early in his preaching career; they are not the pulpit shortcut one might associate with the easy confidence of a long-settled pastor). More likely, Edwards's sermon form links him with the extemporaneous mode of his New Light forebears who took their identity from the evangelical method of brief, shorthand notes and exhortative delivery. In any case, we should not be too quick to discern in every surviving fragment a representation of a world in chaos. It may be that Edwards felt he could work best from suggestive, inferential notes to public narrative. Still, this early oration of 1769 (Edwards was twenty-four when it was delivered) allows us to enter a world where the White Haven congregation was asked to consider the far from rhetorical question, "Are not our national affairs in the utmost perplexity?"[14]

Perplexing they were, and Edwards's rhetoric voices in revealing ways the psychic and political perplexity of prerevolutionary New England. After invoking the biblical doctrine from Exodus, assuming, in turn, his audience's familiarity with the portion under exposition—"you well know," he notes, "how the childen of Israel came to Egypt"—Edwards moves quickly from sketching the Israelites' physical plight (and by typological extension his congregation's as well),

> Here we find/em—
> & under a yoke/of bondage—

to his proposed Doctrine: "It is the duty of a people under affliction & public calamities to cry to G[od] for deliverance." As Edwards works through the "logic" of his discourse he opposes the implicit antinomian stance of "not crying"—that is, the stiff-necked refusal of confessed dependence, of spiritual deference that God's children are obliged to acknowledge—"not to cry to him is to deny" our dependent status, "to set up to be independent, to act . . . as our own Lords"—with the proper (and necessary) habit of crying out in times of affliction. "To cry," Edwards explains, "is to act in our proper place." Note, in this respect, how the passivity of crying is verbally expressed as action, as agency, reaffirming the hierarchies that order the world—"placing God in his place & ours in ours," as Edwards confirms. The theological and social point, of course, is the equation between ritual supplication and promised deliverance: the portion of the covenant that prescribes passive cryings out as the proper response to "public calamities."[15]

What is important in Edwards's application of this standard theme is his (almost) shifting conflation of the typological example of biblical deference with the currents of antiauthoritarian posturing abroad in the land. To be sure, he provides a requisite litany of "Ancient examples" to authorize the necessity of supplication, but his more pressing concern

erratum

For
Rhetoric and History in Revolutionary New England
by Donald Weber

Page 53, line 16 should read:

to petition ~~the~~ a king & chief magistrate*S* of any nation for deliverance

is the textual sanctioning of contemporary dissent. "Tyranny is no ordinance of God," Edwards declaims; yet

> Some would insinuate—
> divine rights
> But why so angry in this instance?
> not agreeable to him
> This was civil tyranny
> Yet
> Ought to seek deliverance from civil tyranny in proper ways

On the threshold of the Revolution patriot preachers continuously asked,
What *are* the "proper ways to seek deliverance"? In effect, the 1769
oration bespeaks the strains attendant with filial breaking away, the
psychic costs of independence. The sermon registers that anxiety in its
blurring of religious and political language, in Edwards's investment of
"crying" with a political valence, as the following key passage reveals:

> To petition ~~the~~ king & chief magistrates of any nation for deliverance
> from oppression is not contrary to any divine command.
> Did not G[od] command Moses & others?
> Therefore not rebellion
> How can it be ———?[16]

Chosen people must cry to God for deliverance during times of oppression; so too must a saving remnant petition *a* king—the revision of the
article swerves the preacher from directly affronting King George himself, and thus amounts to a psychologically less threatening confrontation. Still, Edwards's reflexive summary of Old Testament examples of
supplication (to sanction the colonists' current actions) barely obscures
the self-conscious denial implicit in "therefore not rebellion." Worried
over the charges of blasphemous rebellion, the ultimate primal taboo,
the revolutionary preachers labored to deny its potential insurgency by
reinserting the "apostate" sons into an alternate genealogy, from British
patriarchy to the true patrimony of liberty proffered by the Founding
Fathers.

Yet Edwards's rhetoric is far from the incendiary style of, for instance, Thomas Allen of Berkshire County; rather, this early performance conveys the New Divinity man trying to accommodate religious
and social doctrine in the face of intractable history. "Are not our
national affairs in the utmost perplexity?" (emphasis added), he asks,
assigning a temporal dimension to (earlier) sacred analogues. In frag-

mentary, hurried prose Edwards sketches the following portrait of the times as he works toward the closing exhortation:

> Are not our national affairs in the utmost perplexity?
> great darkness?
> ~~war already begun~~
> on the very verge of a ~~civil~~ war?
> yea already begun as the constitutions being untimely overthrown—?
> But if either should happen, what evils will ensue†!
> in one case expect slaughter & devastation
> father against son
> such times we never saw

Such was the extreme perplexity—apocalyptic and generational—imagined by the young minister in 1769. Even the shift in grammatical inflection, from the doubting, incredulous question mark canceled in favor of the assertive exclamation of expected judgment, registers the preacher's mood. In a few years he would be able to utter, instead of crossing out its woeful implications, the phrase "civil war." But for now the unthinkable needed to be repressed/erased with a call to prayer, supplication, and biblically authorized petition. "Unless we cry," he intoned at the end, "may deprive us entirely" of our "greatly favored/great religious liberty."[17] The unspecified, unnamed agent of deprivation is telling, in this respect, for the resulting ambiguity highlights the political and psychological dilemma of the revolutionary clergy. In a short time, Great Britain would become the devious agent of deprivation, perceived as designing the overthrow of providentially planted religious liberty in America. Yet Edwards, Jr. and his fellow patriots were always wary of the charge of filial rebellion, always nervous that although temporal affliction demanded passive, "proper means" of response, events were tending toward the abyss of *unutterable* civil war. Thus the arc of Edwards's preaching career begins in anxiety; it ends, however, with a brave yet troubled effort at reading what he eventually called "the fate of America."[18]

"The events of providence," Edwards observed in a Thanksgiving day oration of 1774, "are the language of G[od] to men."[19] From 1770 on he translated that language for a people well-versed in the biblical grammar themselves. As noted, Edwards was far from a fire and brimstone preacher in the tradition of the Great Awakening, but he did try, in the early 1770s, to alert his congregation to the dangers of spiritual complacency, especially in light of the ominous tone of God's recent "language" of discord and judgment. "The shortness of life" is a theme sounded in a 1770 sermon whose closing exhortation sets forth, after a litany of questions, the following fragmentary catalogue of sober observations:

> The shortness of life
> a vapour
> a moment
> yet things of infinite importance to [be] done
> Now another year gone
> O that all would hear & redeem
> now the accepted time

We may imagine the preacher pausing after each fleeting phrase, almost objectifying the theme of evanescence itself.[20]

The following year Edwards, starting with Genesis 19:17 ("And it came to pass," etc.), explored the cautionary tale of Lot and his curious wife, "the most remarkable event next to the flood," in his view. What follows is Edwards's attempt to "rivet" (to recall Robbins's sermonic ideal) the congregation to the appalling fate awaiting rebellious unbelievers. "Suppose," he speculates, as he invokes a particular spatial context, "any of the towns in this colony—as Milford . . . in sight of all . . . turned into a lake—

> not remarkable?
> not memorable?"

The rhetoric builds on the remarkable and memorable historical precedents of God's fulfilling prophecies of judgment and doom awaken sinners to the precariousness of their condition:

> God will do as says
> trace from the beginning [a private directive?] always did
> So to the old world
> when very corrupt told Noah
> gen. 6.17
> fulfilled
> So Sodom
> the very day/not delayed for a day
> So the destruction of Jerusalem/foretold long before/
> both to pass . . .
> So also with you if you hearken not
> in this season

> Because time short & uncertain
> so to Lot
> Very short at longest
> What 70 years?
> seems long to children
> But compared to Eternity nothing
> Uncertain
> even this uncertain[21]

If you hearken not. The rhetoric of conditional judgment, riveted through the authority of biblical example, recalls the congregation to the historical ambiguity and political uncertainty of the present "season." True to the awakening mode, Edwards leaves his auditors with a vision of the necessity of immediate conviction, the sinner's decision to choose faith this very moment or else languish for eternity in Hell. "Do this today put not off . . . every day's delay contempt of the warning . . .

> Now stands ready to receive—
> Behold—& know
> Now the accepted time
> Else may know how dreadful to die/in despair
>   die in sin
> see hell before you."[22]

From its opening image of local towns engulfed by God's wrathful waters to the allusive, figural sequence of God's prophecies of collective destruction to the urgent, personal summons that sinners imagine "Hell before you" and repent ("look not behind"), Edwards's sermon everywhere registers the language and form of the rhetorical modes fashioned during the Awakening: its fragmentary spatial arrangement, its tonic phrases, its "familiar" style aimed at the hearts of auditors, its call to faith in the face of uncertainty. Moreover, Edwards the Younger's preaching clearly is *not* metaphysical, cut off from the social world he addressed and sought to affect. As the Revolution loomed he used the pulpit to sound, not only the Awakening's urgent pleas of repentance, but its attendant socio-political message: people must act in history, *now,* save themselves and the community, *now,* for the times signaled the imminence of some judgment, whether apocalyptic or millennial, which the Protestant clergy, along with everyone else, waited to discover.

The rehabilitation of the figure of Edwards may not issue in a wholesale recovery—no one ever claimed that the son imbibed what William Gordon described as "a double portion of his father's spirit and abilities."[23] Nevertheless, while the son edited and transcribed the father's papers he formulated his own response to the Revolution. Indeed, the sermonic legacy installs Edwards the Younger in the pantheon of patriot preachers; at the same time it reveals how the father's historical vision shaped that of the son. If Edwards the Younger did spend his life in his father's writings, then we may gauge the nature and extent of that filial immersion by glossing the son's reading of God's providences to America using the grammar provided by the *History of the Work of Redemption.*

Before describing that influence, however, we must note an important thematic shift in Edwards's sermonic tone, a change from the imprecatory rhetoric of 1770–1771 to the more soothing, comforting style perhaps best characterized by his most frequently preached oration of the revolutionary era, a sermon delivered at least eight times, at home in October 1773 and then in various New England pulpits in 1775 and 1776 (including Bellamy's Bethlehem church in early September 1776). The sermon, let me reemphasize, is not a splendid performance; Edwards's contextual opening, drawn from the figure of Elijah captive in Dathan by the King of Syria, simply repeats the prophet's assurances, "Fear not, for they that be with us are more than they that be with them," (2 Kings 6:16) and then, in his own voice, the preacher reads aloud the doctrine to be extracted: "I think I may observe the following proposition to be plainly contained in" the example of Elijah: "The children of God have no reason to fear, tho they appear to be in the greatest danger." Elijah's bewildered servant, Elisha, could only see mere appearances, but the Lord "open[ed] his eyes that he might see," despite "disappointments in providence as to . . . ⊙ly [worldly] affairs," God's design of deliverance and redemption.[24]

Yet the sermon contains some of Edwards's most compelling rhetoric, offering a kind of rhetorical solace "in this day of darkness and discouragement" (note the purposeful temporal ambiguity of "this"). Resummoning the biblical prophet's soothing explanation, Edwards's prose captures the rhythmic cadences of the Old Testament as it adopts the mode of refrain (although in linear, not vertical form) characteristic of the Awakening pulpit:

> however now things may look dark & gloomy; how[ever—*Edwards's insert*] Satan
> & his emissaries may now rage & rave, & seem ready to

swallow em up at once, as the whale did Jonah; however
they may be persecuted, stript of all their ⊙ly
enjoyments,
& reduced to shame & contempt; however they may be
seized,
imprisoned, tormented, put to death in the most violent &
excruciating ways: yet admist all these dangers and
trials,
they need not be afraid . . . but have reason to rejoice
& be
exceedingly glad . . . however it may fall with em as
individuals,
yet the cause of the church in general shall be safely
defended, & shall finally be made triumphant.

Note how the sequence of "however . . . may" phrases limns a disturbing, "dark & gloomy" present reality that gives way, "in due time,"
to the assurances sounded by the speaker's voice. Still, the immediate
afflictive moment may not be dispelled easily, even by the hopeful "yet"
fixed at the virtual midpoint of the passage; the vivid language depicting
the country's current plight in many ways overwhelms the conjunction's
teleological promise. Edwards, of course, did not utter these words in
bad faith; "I have endeavored," he explained to his audience in the next
sentence, "to illustrate & enforce the words of my text." To "enforce"
neatly registers the social aspect of Edwards's linguistic authority; his
voicing of eventual triumph ("shall finally," "in due time") amounts to
a kind of oral correlative to the perseverance of the saints against political and spiritual trials. To "enforce" recalls as well Robbins's sermonic
ideal of "to rivet"—the dynamic transaction between preacher and audi-
tor that (in this case) displaces anxiety with assurance, or, better, *draws*
assurance out of anxiety, by exchanging the somber meaning of "mere"
political appearances for the true designs of providence.

Fittingly, Edwards's rhetoric moves toward prophecy, first by em-
boldening his listeners with a refrain of "shall we" questions ("Shall we
be discouraged? Shall we despond & sink . . . Shall we give up all for
lost?") His answer? "No m[y] b[rethren] such a conclusion would be
rash & groundless"; and then by *reversing* the subject of another sequence of "however" phrases, replacing the earlier "However *they* . . .
may" construction with "However *we* may" [emphasis added]—in effect
shifting the semantic emphasis from plotting, external agents (i.e.,
"they," Satan) to the collective strength (and will) of his colonial
auditors: "however we may be hated and reviled for the truth; however

we may suffer in the cause of X [Christ] . . . yea . . . yet we have the comforting & animating consideration to support us." What animates Edwards's closing vision is an image drawn from the book of Daniel (that favorite prophetic text of Puritan exegetes) of the stone "cut out of the mountain without hands"; the stone "will grow & become a great mountain, & at last fill the earth." The stone will, in time, smite "Satan's kingdom" in this world, scattering his minions to the wind.[25]

Edwards continued the theme of God's monument to His chosen people in a Thanksgiving oration of November 1774 drawn from the 1 Samuel text on the Ebenezer stone, the physical emblem marking Israel's victory over the Philistines. The providential deliverances of an earlier time prompt Edwards to offer a brief lesson in English monarchical history from the Reformation ("a remarkable work of God . . . particularly in our nation"—Edwards's ambiguity is fascinating; does he refer to America or to England?) through Henry VIII ("a most bigoted papist—never a real friend"), Edward VI, Mary, and Charles I. Edwards pauses over Charles's reign, highlighting the "tyranny both church & state" that, in retrospect, anticipates "just as they [the British parliament] to us." Indeed, that "doleful state" spurred God to raise up "men to assert their rights." "Had it not been for these struggles," the preacher speculates in fragments, "been under—/at this day." (Here I believe Edwards indirectly implies that the earlier tyranny would have prevailed to his own time.)

The lesson continues, with Edwards tracing the pattern of papist designing and the people's impassioned response: James II "intended to bring over the notion of popery" but the Lord "stirred up the nation in general to seek relief" from the "deep laid scheme to introduce popery—arbitrary power" plotted during the reign of Queen Anne. Arriving finally at a recent juncture of threat and affliction, Edwards invokes the collective memory of the Stamp Act ("when . . . act passed—struck dumb—dare not say nay") and the even more subtle designs of the tax on paper and tea—in each case God "aroused the country" to action.[26] Now, however, Edwards rebukes his congregation for the current (spiritually) dead time. "Now the country a great measure asleep," he warns in 1774, the populace immobilized "between surprize & fear—know not what to do." What was the answer? In reply, Edwards turned to the diastole/systole patterns of providential history, the alternating rhythms of oppressive civil tyranny and the quickenings of spiritual renewal as the mobilizing agent against current inertia.

By the end of the sermon the preacher erects what might be called his own Ebenezer, his own rhetorical monument to the precursor mo-

ments of awakening when God "excited the minds of the people remarkably united." Thus Edwards's attempt at mobilizing rhetoric *relies*
on the memory of the Great Awakening as a spur to ritual renewal.
The compendium of historical *exempla* together form a sequence of
latter-day Ebenezers, a collective *oral* memory of popular union in the
face of crisis. It is surely amazing, observes Edwards, that a "people
remarkably united . . . agreed in sending [representatives] to a general
congress." "Such unionism & resolution [are] hardly to have been expected."[27] With this nod to secular history and current political affairs,
Edwards might have added the first Continental Congress to his continuum of key moments; he even might have helped build the Ebenezer
then being fashioned in Philadelphia.

If the younger Edwards was keenly attentive to the world of political
conventions, versed in the troubled history (and legacy) of English
liberty to the New World, he was also immersed in his father's writings,
especially during the revolutionary era. We know that, with Samuel
Hopkins, Edwards, Jr. was instrumental in recovering Jonathan Edwards's literary corpus; he transcribed and edited (among other works)
the long-awaited *History of the Work of Redemption,* eventually published in Scotland in 1774. Indeed, the son's perhaps overzealous editorial activities may have played a role in his later expulsion from
White Haven church. (The fundamental dispute was doctrinal, yet in a
1790 letter to Edwards's influential supporter Roger Sherman, a detrac-
tor speaks in exasperation over Edwards's genealogical priorities: "Has
he not imployed himself in transcribing a volume of his father's sermons
& printing them at Hartford? . . . and lately a volume of 33 sermons
of his father's study and preaching? and has he not likewise been imployed a great part of his time for two years in writing against Dr.
Chauncey" [*sic*].) Edwards himself confessed to a consuming attention
with extrapastoral obligations; apologizing to his New Haven colleague
Benjamin Trumbull, Edwards explained his recent (in 1772) lack of
pulpit etiquette: "I have not exchanged with anybody since the Election
nor within some time before. I am pretty much hurried in transcribing
the work of my father." The son did more than transcribe, however. As
the following brief excursion into the father's historical vision suggests,
Edwards the Younger's political stance in 1774 drew *heavily* on the
Redemption papers—a seasonable application of "father's ideas" for the
times.[28]

Contrary to prevailing accounts, which (following Ezra Stiles) depict

Jonathan Edwards as immune from history, the original type of New Divinity otherworldliness, the manuscript evidence clearly shows Edwards attuned to contemporary events, absorbed by even the smallest details of world affairs. Indeed, Edwards interpreted political events in language that, in a later period, would be characteristic of the Protestant clergy in general. Exhorting (for example) his Northampton congregation in support of the 1746 "expedition to Canada," Edwards speaks of God's armies as "not only . . . the instruments of such good to their land and nation but . . . the instruments of the overthrow of a considerable part of mystic Bab[ylon]," Antichrist, in Edwards's scenario, had a foothold in North America, and he viewed the Canadian campaign as a holy effort in the "quelling down [of] the reign of Satan" and "setting up [of the] kingdom of Christ in America." Pursuing a theme he had developed privately in *Apocalyptic Notebooks* (where by recording world events Edwards noted the progress of secular history as forecasts of the penultimate battle with Satan's kingdom) Edwards asserted that these victories "will weaken the kingdom of France, the greatest power that supports antichrist."[29] Of course Edwards's method of interpretation drew from his own model of historical progress (and process), the *History of the Work of Redemption,* a sermon series preached in 1739, and a major treatise worked on with renewed intensity at the end of his life. A Thanksgiving sermon of 1745 (delivered again in 1757) builds on Edwards's theory of historical "pulsations"—or, as he describes the temporal motion in the manuscript notebooks for the *Work of Redemption:* "in each period there has been a gradual increase and diminution, like the waxing and waning of the moon"—as he recalls to his auditors how God's "wonderful and remarkable providences delivered the nation from the Popish yoke and blessed it with the light of the Reformation." (In this case Edwards is reviewing the history of England, a frequent subject of the revolutionary pulpit, as his son's sermons testify.) Yet, as every clergyman knew—in 1745 and 1775—England fell. "The nation began very much to depart from the purity of doctrine," the preacher reminded his audience, and this betrayal propelled a saving remnant to settle a new world.[30]

Thus the manuscript notebooks for the envisioned *Work of Redemption* reveal that a good measure of Edwards's antiquarian fascination with cataloguing those "Episodes in the history of the church" (including a detailed chronology of papal reigns) involved the place of New England in the scheme of redemptive history. He even planned sections "concerning the settlement of New England as the most special introduction of the gospel in America." As late as the 1750s, then, Edwards continued to mark the origins of America "as one great thing done to prepare the way" for the millennium.[31]

From this perspective, the influence of the father's historical imagination on the son's pulpit vision—at least in November 1774—seems unmistakable. Keeping the faith, Edwards the younger rehearsed the providential patterns of English history in the effort to summon his own congregation to the cause of liberty. Significantly, that call meant spiritual renewal and a return of that (revival) spirit displayed "in remarkable times in your remembrance";[32] only the heart-quickening pulsations proffered by a religious "stir" could awaken a sleepy, immobilized nation.

Of course I am not arguing for the *direct* influence of the Awakening on the revolutionary pulpit; rather, I suggest that the much debated links between Revival and Revolution may reside in neither the realm of abstract theology—pure, inert ideas, whether religious or political, cannot, without the compelling weight of ideology, help people act in history—nor in the opposing political stances that determined religious allegiance after Edwards's death in 1758. Instead, the continuities between Awakening and Revolution may finally exist, most suggestively and provocatively, on the level of rhetoric itself.

Seen in this light, Edwards, Jr.'s military sermon of December 1775 exemplifies how the rhetoric of the Awakening was fashioned to fit a new social and political reality. Working from a Judges 12 passage concerning the "enslaved & sorely oppressed" children of Israel, Edwards retells in clear, straightforward prose, the story of heroic Jephthah, deliverer of the saving remnant (a leader who "restored to his countrymen [of Gilead] peace & liberty") and the figure who devised the test that might distinguish faithful warriors from the lukewarm soldiers of Ephraim (who had refused to join the fight against oppression) by demanding that they utter the word "Shibboleth." An Ephraimite soldier, the Book of Judges tells us (12:6), "could not frame to pronounce it right," and thus, Edwards tells *his* audience in 1775, "the Gidionites . . . distinguished their pretended from their real friends." The context established, Edwards moves to the sermon's doctrine, "that in time of War there ought to be a plain line of distinction drawn between us & our enemies." After enumerating the practical measures involved in military strategy, Edwards proceeds to his real subject, the need "to fortify & prepare" this winter "for the warm struggle which there will be next summer which we may suppose will decide the fate of America."[33]

And upon whom will the important fate descend? Surely not those latter-day Ephraimites who pretend to be of both sides—of those who endeavor to bring into contempt the continental currency—of those who pretend to be of neither side, but perfectly neuter—of those who are silent, & will say nothing on the subject of the present contest, or if they speak, do it with such caution, yet there is no telling which side they favour—of those who appear to be zealous in the cause of the country but act from merely selfish motives.

The passage recalls in general the litanies of Philemon Robbins and in particular his Stamp Act sermon decrying the "feigned" piety of would-be guardians of liberty. In 1775 Edwards was less anxious about social unrest than in separating wheat from chaff, the appearance of patriotism from its authentic incarnation. "There is no such thing as any neuters in this cause," he cautioned; "They that do not appear to be engaged on the side of their country as suspected to be opposite of its interests." Indeed, "they that are silent & will not speak boldly in vindication of the rights of their country" convict themselves by their very silence; "they are not to be perfectly distinguished by any mark, but must be known & determined as evidence may happen to appear." Thus neutral silence "serves as so many *Shibboleths* to distinguish between us & our enemies"—the oxymoronic silent "utterance" that, in effect, tests the patriotic spirit of a verbally immobilized generation.[34]

Again, although the nature of direct influence may be tenuous, Edwards's persistent invocation of "distinguishing marks" nevertheless alludes to his father's famous address of that name: the Yale Commencement oration of 1741 (later the foundation of *Religious Affections*) which sought to defend the revival in progress against its detractors and to find (in the very act of defense) a systematic way to distinguish the true work of the spirit from the latent antinomianism that the contentious times seemed to have nourished. Of course the revolutionary clergy worried, especially in the afterglow of Independence, about American liberty falling into French license (Edwards the Younger would at the end of his preaching career join in the collective Federalist lament over infidelity). In 1775, however, he "wish[ed] to see every true son of liberty, as much distinguished by the purity of his life & manner, as by his wise zeal in the cause of his country."[35]

In the juxtaposition of "distinguishing marks" with "sons of liberty" we may observe the blurring of republican discourse with a culturally dynamic religious rhetoric, effecting an interchange of ideological and affective meanings—which symbolic anthropologists call the ritual process. We might even say that the language of the revolutionary pulpit had a "multivocal" dimension: an ability to mediate the claims of residual yet still potent Puritan vocabularies and emergent political language to forge an enabling rhetoric that helped people act in history.[36] For now, however, we might say more simply that Edwards perceived the moment as a remarkable, long-prophesied season demanding authentic, not feigned response. The rhetoric of the Great Awakening provided an enabling discourse that helped him make sense of revolutionary experience; it offered (in effect) the terms that explained the perplexities of neutrality and thus resolve the ambiguities of patriotic action.

Increasingly, however, the times seemed more perplexing and ambiguous than "plotable" along the axis of providential history. Of course Edwards continued to guide his flock but, like his fellow minister just northeast of New Haven in Branford, he tried to prod his auditors out of the easy confidences bestowed by the patterns of historical design. "To expect to be prospered because [we] have been," Edwards warned in mid-January 1776 on a fast day, "on account of the civil war," is misguided; (note that now, on the threshold of collectively declared independence, Edwards can actually *pen* the once unutterable, tragic adjective "civil"; by 1776, that is, he could accept the various severings, psychic and political, inscribed in the phrase "civil war.") Instead, the preacher reminds that "past events no sure signs/providence various." But rather than a wholesale rejection of the doctrine of providence, Edwards's curious nod toward a notion of contingency might be more likely viewed as a ministerial gambit designed to recover (or maintain) the oracular office. If events are indeed "various," if there is, as Edwards asserts, "no established course," then (to recall an image from Philemon Robbins) the buffeted nation needs a patriotic helmsman steering the ship; or, as this, the most moving of Edwards's revolutionary sermons implicitly represents him, an anxious watchman for the millennium.[37]

Anxiety, of course, characterizes the tone of the revolutionary pulpit; all Protestant ministers were burdened with justifying the disturbing political realities of colonial revolt as they assuaged the emotional affect with respect to the repeated charge of filial rebellion. In the face of temporal buffeting Philemon Robbins steered Branford along a sacred course of geographic predestination; faced with explaining the times, in the wake of Lexington, to the White Haven assembly, Edwards taught a "way to avoid calamities of the night" by attending to the prophecies of Isaiah and listening to their preacher's own reply to the famous question (a question "common to ask," Edwards notes), "Watchman, what of the night?"[38]

The sermon, from Isaiah 21, is a great example of how secular events could fuel the apocalyptic imagination. Edwards begins by glossing the watchman's paradoxical answer, "The morning cometh, and also the night" (verse 12). Edwards's exegesis: "The answer—the morning & also the night—/—relief—but trouble—preceeding or succeeding—." Will the night *follow* the morning? Will night calamities *yet* appear? Edwards resolved the temporal ambiguity by choosing the night season as a time of trial *before* the dawn, thus reading the ominous moment as a kind of ritual passage before the arrival of the millennial day. We are sensible, the preacher acknowledged, of "a dark time," an atmosphere "of thick darkness" enveloping the country—"but the night first."[39]

Edwards next considers the numerous signs that have made the nation sensible of its blackness by enumerating virtually all the political woes to beset the still dependent colony ("British parliament claims a right of making laws for us & taxing in all cases; & hath acted upon this claim," and so forth). At the end of each section's catalogue of moral and civic ills, the preacher closes with the formulaic refrain, "Now the night cometh as these [the various secular afflictions] like to remain," culminating in a crescendo of urgent, fragmentary questions:

> As is, & seems like to be, so dark as to religion—
> a very dull, dead time—
> how few awakened—?engineering—?
> converted—?
> reformed?
> No appearance
> like to be otherwise
> Thus the night cometh in a spiritual sense
> G[od] is indeed calling—
> especially in these troubles—
> loudly—
> but who hears—?

Indeed. Like his revival forebears, Edwards the Younger saw his task as that of awakener, listening attentively to God's message (as embodied in both its temporal and spiritual forms) and speaking loudly himself, rousing his deaf audience to its historic task of (as he calls it) engineering for the millennium.[40]

Shifting next to the signs of the approaching morning, Edwards highlights the moral and spiritual benefits of current economic strictures and calls (as Edmund Morgan explained years ago) for a revival of the Puritan ethic of self-denial and native self-sufficiency: "Why go to the east Indies?," Edwards asks, rebuking the worldly tastes and appetites of his audience; we "can live as well on other foods."[41] But the oration, delivered and redelivered in the wake of Lexington, does not linger in conventional decrying of colonial luxury and creeping cosmopolitanism; instead, it tries to effect a transition from night to day, affliction to promise, through a rhetoric that imbibes (as it invokes) the logic of revolutionary ideology:

> The morning cometh as reason to hope we shall be successful
> in our present contest—
> Several reasons
> We, but a young country
> they an old
> States & Kings like persons—
> have infancy—youth—maturity—old age
> A young man contending with an old—good reason to hope . . .
> We contend for all—they only for mastery.

Thus Edwards blends the strains of biblical prophecy with Lockean argument (as recently described by Jay Fliegelman), the watchman's ambiguous answer with the language of the Country Party (Edwards echoes as well Tom Paine, noting that the British are "at so remote a distance . . . must convey everything 3000 miles/great disadvantage/ we have all our strength near").[42]

Yet in the end, the office of the preacher was that of reader and discerner of the signs of the times. "Calamities," Edwards advised, "are the calls of God," and we must heed them, not merely to "inquire . . . as to the times" but more importantly "to attend" to the divine voices. Are you "at least so attentive as the Edomite in the text?," the latter-day watchman asks. Calling (again) for a revival of religion, Edwards's processual rhetoric effects a kind of psychic passage by voicing a litany of "this the way to" phrases—the rhetorical equivalent of the social and spiritual journey being enacted—closing with language that, in its hopeful yet tempered optimism, neatly reflects the revolutionary watchman's dual role as comforter *and* prodder. In the end, Edwards commingles assurance with anxiety as he verbally enacts the historical passage:

> This the way to be ready for whatever—called to war or peace—
> prosperity or adversity—

life or death
O that this* [Edwards's insert] may be the happy day, when we
shall all come & return to God—
fast change into a thanksgiving
the beginning of days—the most joyful

Edwards asterisked an insertion, perhaps upon redelivering the sermon
a few days later, on 23 April, when news of battle would surely have
reached New Haven. "*but if not," Edwards amended his preaching
text, "how ill prepared for either? . . . God against—who/for you?"[43]

Before the remnant could enact the transition from fasting to celebration it would have to pass through the wilderness of trial and affliction,
and so Edwards opened his sermon for mid-January 1776 with a text
from Exodus: "And the Lord said unto Moses, Wherefore criest tho
[sic] unto me? Speak unto the children of Israel that they go forward."
As Michael Walzer's recent book on revolutionary rhetoric describes,
the myth of Exodus has throughout history served as a model for the
psychological and political impulse to break away from (received)
authority, providing the very language by which that collective desire
may be sanctioned.[44] Walzer's point is aptly demonstrated by Edwards,
especially in the conscious invocation of "that they go forward" (from
the textual opening) throughout the oration, as if the preacher himself
were voicing, along with his antitypic forebear Moses, God's verbal
command to press on with the historic journey to Canaan. Setting the
context, Edwards quickly sketches a vivid portrait of the fleeing Jews:
"pursued after/overtook by the red sea . . . the sea before/sur-
rounded with the wilderness/as some say impassable mountains."
These spatial terrors—looming sea, towering mountains—the physical
correlative to the spiritual afflictions that beset the chosen people—apply
as well to their American descendents who, "in course of providence
brot into a similar state—of great danger." We, too, Edwards reminds,
have our murmurers in the wilderness, those who lament "our own
obstinacy" in not seeking "redress" from Great Britain "in a proper
way." In reply, Edwards marshalls the evidence of recent political history, recalling for his audience England's stiff-necked refusal to acknowledge the "conciliatory," even "humble" petitions from "several
assemblies separately"; indeed, Britain was deaf to "the petition of the
Congress" where "the sense of the people better known." In short, the
plight of Israel looks forward to that of America; in each example, the
people were compelled to complete their mission with the divine injunction "yet must go forward." "If [we] give up our claims," Edwards
cautions, "[we are] undone—are slaves forever."[45]

Seen from this perspective, Edwards's rhetoric amounts to a charged response to this perceived plight. The summons to "go forward"—physically, spatially, spiritually—through the agency of Moses' voice is recapitulated on a higher level of redemptive history by the latter-day lawgiver. Be not "backward," Edwards admonishes those who hesitate to embrace their military duty: "this ruinous. . . . To be backward brings to disgrace on yourself." Indeed, to be backward is to *retreat* from beckoning prophecy:

> Neither can stop where we are—
> worse than if never begun . . .
> proceed
> no other way—
> if stop—here ruined
> if recede
> if accommodate
> no other way than to go forward

Edwards's progressivist injunction (with its litany of cautionary "ifs") hinges, of course, on the fear of the abyss of *political* accommodation; from this extract of mobilizing rhetoric we may observe how even the self-appointed guardian of the Edwardsean tradition tried to instill revolutionary ardor, a zeal for the *completion* of Exodus. We might even say that Edwards's summoning refrain moves the congregation forward in history through an undertone of apocalyptic anxiety that issues from the oracular authority of the prophet–preacher himself. We *must* move forward, historically, is Edwards's message; to regress is to be enslaved (again). "If give up our claims—undone—are slaves forever." That cautionary "if" highlights the jeremiadic strain of the rhetoric. Imbibing that long tradition in colonial preaching, Edwards moved his White Haven flock from Exodus to Revolution through a mobilizing strategy of anxiety. "If fail now," he prophesied on the eve of Independence, "lose all."[46]

Thus Jonathan Edwards, Jr. shared with his fellow ministers the belief that the American Revolution signaled the ultimate battle for the moral future of the country; and with his Protestant brethren he saw his task as explanatory: to translate events into a language that might spur people to enlist in the sacred cause yet contain the lurking, anarchic impulse implicit in the act of breaking away. The patriot ministers were made uneasy by the charge of rebellion voiced by Loyalists and the British Parliament. Edwards's preaching after Independence joined in the ministerial effort to legitimize the new form of government; in effect, he *designed* his rhetoric to sanction the revolutionary scheme of political association, republicanism.

I emphasize design, for it suggests the authorizing process itself. For example, in a Thanksgiving sermon of 1778 Edwards rehearses the familiar homiletic notion that God's designs in history very often swerve from man's assumptions and expectations; our ability to fathom the "true" meanings of events is necessarily partial. Joseph's brothers, Edwards recounts, had a "design"—"to bury him in obscurity, disgrace, suffering—not so God." The preacher continues to relate the pattern of providential swerving and disjunction from Pharaoh to Bablyon to the Crucifixion: in every case the presumed "designs" of historical actors were flouted by the Lord's overarching and *overruling* vision—especially, as Edwards works through his sequence of exempla, in "the present war," a war "begun by the King of G.B." But "God makes use of the British King & court"; he makes them the unknowing agents of *His* design. What was Edwards's message at this betwixt and between moment in revolutionary history? "So far as events have taken place [Edwards will later use the astonishing phrase "real events" in the same sermon; did he distinguish biblical *figurae* from the "hard" facts of political experience?] or possibly about to," he announces, "may tell what God's were—how contrary to theirs." His own vision of the country's future is not so hesitant or hedging, however; although he refrains from equating his watchman's status with that of the biblical oracle, Edwards nevertheless speaks of how

> God about to establish—
> erect a large, free commonwealth
> an assylum
> under greater advantages for enjoying good—peace & liberty
> than any kingdom on earth—

Thus the designs of history are still in process, still awaiting fulfillment; and Edwards's rhetoric inscribes that processual movement in a vision of America as asylum, a "free state" where "free liberty of inquiry may be "erect[ed] . . . so the truth may come out." By 1778, then, Edwards preached in a kind of liminal language—in a subjunctive mood which guaranteed the future.[47]

Yet (as noted earlier) Edwards also assumed the office of guardian of the social order. The evangelical clergy were well aware of the abuses that newly declared liberty could bring, and Edwards preached on

behalf of authority of government, most interestingly in addressing the
Society of Freemen in 1784. With Samuel Hopkins and Levi Hart, Edwards belonged to the first generation of reformers, laboring for the
abolition of slavery throughout his career. Earlier, in a less cautious
mood in 1775 (Edwards styled the moment "this critical juncture"),
Edwards had warned the assembly of the dangers of passive obedience
and nonresistance, notions that could not be authorized in scripture.
"The truth is," Edwards claimed (echoing Jonathan Mayhew), "that
rulers are bound to rule in the fear of God and for the good of the
people; and if they do not, then in resisting them we are doing God
service." Edwards's message was emphatic: "He that is not willing, if
need be, to defend his liberty, deserves to be a slave." With that ominous
warning, perhaps stirring his audience with a reminder of their once
and potential future state, Edwards called for a spirit of harmony in the
face of crisis; "so much depends," he confessed in 1775, "upon our
unanimity."[48]

In 1784, however, Edwards returned to the theme of division and
union in a sermon before the Freemen's Society which, in its anxiety
over discord and factionalism, reveals how the clergy tried to mediate
the latent threat of *unfettered* liberty with the *American* liberty sanctioned by republican ideology. The result is a history lesson in the perils
of civil disunity together with a defense of republican government—"our
government," Edwards declared, "the best form in the ⊙ [world]." Intriguingly, the defense builds (and perhaps consciously borrows) from
the famous distinction between natural and civil liberty as set forth by
John Winthrop. "What then is liberty in a state of Society?," Edwards
inquires. "Not," he replies immediately, "to do as will." This liberty is
the freedom "to rob/plunder others with impunity—/to have no government";[49] but "the true idea of liberty," Edwards continues, in an
updated version of Winthrop's, "is when a people make own constitution
choose own rulers/subjecting to laws made by them." Moreover, the
"facts" of history are testimony to the validity of the doctrine: ancient
Greece, Rome ("the factions under . . . Pompey & Caesar"), Egypt,
England (although after the civil wars she was "an excellent republic"),
and more recently Poland (whose troubled history issued in the tragedy
of internal separation). The long tale of political woe concludes, of
course, with the example of the new American republic:

> We lately been involved in a dangerous—burdensome—distressing war—
> shudder when reflect by the smiles of providence delivered in
>   wonderful manner

Eight years after the Declaration of Independence Edwards could only "shudder" at the remarkable deliverances bestowed upon the country. Indeed, shuddering may have been the only appropriate response in recognition of how history *might have* swerved from design, or betrayed the original ideal. We might, then, have been merely another somber example of woeful political descent into factional discord; instead, we "became an independent nation," smiled upon by the blessings of prophecy.[50]

Still, in 1784 Edwards remained haunted by the doomsday fear of abject judgment (recall the mentality reflected in "if fail now, lose all"). In yet another intertextual echo of Winthrop, Edwards warned the assembly of Freemen of their political obligation not to promote division. Our power depends on our union," he explained; "if fall—we shall appear to be destitute . . . contemptible . . . thus our national character lost—

> a shame to be an American
> a by word—history"[51]

Thus we have Edwards's rendering of the American fear of historical exposure, the self-consciousness that, if the experiment in republican harmony should fail, then the ensuing shame would result in an "unimaginable" history that would insert the nation within the entropic secular narrative of factionalism and infidelity.

We know, of course, that many Federalist clergymen, including Edwards, soon adopted that bleak scenario, especially in the wake of the French Revolution; in this oration, however, we may observe Edwards effecting, like Winthrop for the first generation, a transition between national identities. In the Arbella sermon Winthrop set forth the colony's social ideals on the literal threshold of a new country; so too with Edwards the younger: his jeremiad is a response to the liminal dangers attending the passage from dependence to independence. By 1784 the passage was still uncompleted, still in process, the nation still moving forward. But in looking back, Edwards imagined himself shuddering at the prospect of failure. Perhaps he reinvoked the rhetoric of the first passage to link the Revolution historically with the great Migration (it was, after all, a standard pulpit theme in his own time, especially at the turn of the century); in any event, his rhetoric, filled with the warning echoes of a Winthrop, refracts the anxious, worried psyche of post-revolutionary America, a world where the initial beauties of republican liberty were giving way to the judgment of division and discord.

The attempt to recreate the mental world of Jonathan Edwards, Jr. must, of course, remain partial, though with the wealth of extant manuscript evidence we can now perhaps reject the formulaic epithet of "the meta-physical Edwards" or the descriptive refrain about his "abstract" preaching as untrue, a too easy acceptance of slanted contemporaneous accounts of the New Divinity.[52] Still, Edwards, in his own time, was no great revivalist, and if we follow Ezra Stiles's chronicle of the New Divinity—a vast, sprawling document that, despite its biases, is an evoc-ative portrait of the (theological) climate—we sense that the younger Edwards often refused to bend in the face of perceived laxity in doc-trine, ecclesiastical and theological. Edwards was dismissed from White Haven for a variety of reasons, among them a refusal to acknowledge neighboring Fair Haven Church's desire to settle the liberal James Dana in its pulpit. Edwards "looks upon Dr. Dana as a Heretick," Stiles recorded in his *Diary*—perhaps Edwards was adamant because Dana had attacked the father's *Freedom of the Will*. As for relations with his own congregation Stiles tells us that Edwards's "people are exceedingly alienated from him."[53]

It may be, as Morgan argues, that the high-level discourse of New Divinity doctrinal squabbling did indeed compel the laity to reject the world of theology; certainly Edwards embraced his identity as guardian and spent most of his intellectual career vindicating his father's posi-tions. Nevertheless, the filial act of faith-keeping inspired his pulpit rhetoric; in the end his revolutionary visions were also acts of genera-tional rededication. Still, the younger Edwards may never escape the shadow of Stiles. The portrait offered here does not seek to soften Ed-wards's own harsh confession of psychological rigidity and social aloof-ness—his evangelical temperament most likely did not help him in his pastoral labors.[54] The point, however, is that Edwards did not respond to crisis by retreating into an otherworldly theology; nor did he preach away his audience by ignoring their emotional needs. Rather, Edward's rhetoric was a response to cultural crisis, a brave effort to mediate the often bewildering reality of war and rebellion and the complex of emo-tions that followed in their wake. Edwards may have lost his congrega-tion by the 1790s and, like his father, tried to make the best of his fate in the wilderness, but from the 1760s through the War to Washington's presidency Edwards was White Haven's foremost expounder of the meaning of unfolding history, both secular and sacred.[55]

A neat emblem for the blurring of those realms is found in a sermon of December 1781, a Thanksgiving oration on the capture of Corn-wallis's army. "God never gives up his church here," Edwards asserted;

"in covenant / a pious race." Recounting the details of "various battles / mostly in our favour"—giving in one instance the exact date of
battle, and thus adding weight to historian Richard Brown's view that
much of the people's news of war issued from revolutionary pulpits[56]—
the preacher closes with the familiar linkage between Israel and the
colonists. After listing the happy testament of recent naval victories
Edwards recalls for his flock how the Lord "led us thro the wilderness
& darkness in which we were involved / bro't us out from under tyranny." In fact, recent triumphs everywhere reveal the hand of God, who

> With a strong hand & outstretched arm
> hath divided the B[ritish] force into parts . . .
> smote great Generals
> slew famous generals
> overthrew Burgoine & host—afterwards Cornwallis & host—
> & gave the land claimed by the master for a heritage—
> even a heritage to his American Israel—

In its conflation of biblical rhetoric ("smote," "& host") with the "facts"
of recent military history, the passage reveals how the multivocal language of the revolutionary pulpit could invest the secular world with the
aura of redemptive history. Edwards's imagination renders the British
generals as latter-day Pharaohs (replete with evil "hosts" in train);
moreover, as in the Old Testament, there is a swerving from the wicked
designs and desire of the enemy who, seeking enslavement, are themselves divided (an ominous fate for any nation). Finally, Britain's
would-be "heritage" now becomes a sacred heritage transplanted onto
God's "American Israel."[57]

Heritage, of course, is the key word, for in its multiplicity of meanings
it registers the various cultural offices performed by the patriot pulpit: to
authorize, to sanction; to legitimate; above all, to invest contemporary
experience with the weight of myth. If Edwards now emerges as a major figure among those who sanctified secular history as they invented
tradition and bequeathed a legendary heritage, he rises because of a sensibility profoundly attuned to, and not turned off from, the sensibility of
the times.

3

The Dialectic of Public
and Private: The Example of
Levi Hart of Preston

If the example of Jonathan Edwards the Younger lets us follow, in some detail, the public efforts of a major guardian of the Edwardsean tradition keeping the faith, the next figure offers yet another variation on the New Light response to civic crisis leading up to and through the Revolution. In Levi Hart (Yale 1760) we examine the relationship between diary and sermon, the connections between private and public modes of discourse. Thus this chapter describes how the evangelical mind moved from the silently confessed anxieties of diary inscriptions to publicly declaimed—and proclaimed—sermonic utterances. The example of Hart, then, offers a case study of the religious imagination as it strove, along with the generation of patriot preachers, to make sense of revolutionary experience and, in the process, comfort their congregations in the midst of strange and perplexing times.

As a historical actor Levi Hart comes down to us, along with Jonathan Edwards, Jr. and Samuel Hopkins, as a major voice in the early abolitionist movement. Hart wielded the strict tenets of New Divinity Calvinism to rebuke the conscience of slaveholding eighteenth-century America. "To enslave men," Hart admonished in perhaps his most famous sermon, a 1775 discourse on (from our perspective) the multivocal dimensions of "liberty," religious, spiritual, and political, "is a most atrocious violation of one of the first laws of nature—I mean the general union for the common good." Hart's rebuke, we might say, was, in its brave democratic gesturing, the political correlative to Edwardsean theology, the drawing out of Edwards's "humble attempt" to promote "union" and "harmony" as a social reflection of God's visible saints. Of course the social and political aspects of Edwards's metaphysics remain subject to much debate.[1] My concern, in any case, is not the vexed question of whether Edwards's theology translates into political ideology; rather, my subject is Hart's literary response to what he perceived as the dark, ominous curve of God's providences.

Still, we should note how thoroughly immersed, how completely saturated Hart was in the writings of Jonathan Edwards. Within three weeks of his arrival at Bellamy's school of the prophets, in October 1760, Hart began reading "the great Mr. Edwards on religious affections" and graduated, early the following year, to *Freedom of the Will* (begun and finished in a five-day burst of reading); by March Hart had ingested Edwards's "Account of his Suspension" and may have even seen a manuscript draft of either the early "Diary" or perhaps the *Personal Narrative* itself: "Last Night felt uncommon————[?] in reading a part of Mr. Edwards' life. O tis worth all that we can desire, to be truly Religious. Before he was as old as I be now [Hart was 23 in March 1761] he had made great Advances in Holiness and lived in great Nearness to God, while I live in a stupid lazy state [a] great part of my Time."[2]

Thus long before Hopkins's 1765 hagiography fixed our image of Edwards, Bellamy's rising generation of spiritual sons cut their doctrinal teeth on the exemplary piety of the father. (That shadow lingered through the eighteenth century; on the back of a 1786 letter he received from Jonathan Edwards, Jr., Hart inscribed, "one of [our] most distinguished divines—son of the great Edwards.")[3] Indeed, the Bellamy household nurtured a nostalgia for those wondrous days of revival, that millennial moment when the imminent redemption of the country seemed at hand. "Delightful converse this Eve with Dear Mrs. Bellamy," Hart recalled in his Diary for the Lord's Day, June 6, 1761; they had spoken of "vital piety & the awakening in the land some years ago—O for the outpouring of the spirit on this stupid land again."[4] Bellamy kept the faith, it seems, not only by assigning Edwards's treatises for intellectual sustenance but also by a continuous restoking of historical embers, acts of Edwardsean rededication designed to instill and secure a sense of the past.

Young Levi Hart's education at Bethlehem was not purely doctrinal, of course; Bellamy's rural seminary trained scores of New Light preachers, many of whom went on to vocally assert the patriot cause. Not surprisingly, the major subject of Hart's Diary concerns his approaching confirmation as licensed preacher, his growing awareness of the oral aspect of his chosen profession. The Diary is filled, initially, with his response to and evaluation of local preachers which in turn remind him of his own impending task; in March 1762: "I don't expect it will be above 12 Sabbaths more before I shall be examined [over?] preaching." In early April: "a few Sabbaths more and tis most likely that I shall have done learning preaching in a constant way." When Hart did finally cross the professional threshold, accepting a call to minister in Preston, Connecticut in 1762, and receiving the ritual, formulaic "charge" by Benjamin Lord—"to preach the word, be instant in season, and out of season; reprove, rebuke, exhort, with all long-suffering and doctrine"—we may assume that the young preacher (age twenty-four) arrived in his first and, like so many of his generation, only pastorate armed with both the lofty theology and high moral vision of Edwardsean Calvinism and a preaching style honed by and formed from the example of Joseph Bellamy, the acknowledged pulpit master of the time.[5]

From the early 1760s through 1770 Hart's various diaries record the effect and relative "ease" or "freedom" attendant with his various pulpit performances. "Had not so much freedom as at some other times," he confessed in July 1764; "Thought there was not so much attention." The flow returned the following month, however, before a crowded assembly who seemed to be attentive; indeed, on this occasion Hart "had considerable freedom, especially in describing Zion."[6] The point, of course, is the almost obsessive preoccupation with pulpit image, with the ever-shifting dynamic between preacher and audience. There is virtually no allusion to temporal events in these early entries; no direct reference, say, to the looming imperial crisis over taxation, no overt invocation of the Stamp Act. Yet it would be a mistake to imagine that Hart was aloof from the political history or abstracted from contemporary issues by an airy theology; embedded within the ritual chronicle of the daily sequence of pastoral obligations—baptisms, consociation meetings—or the divine lessons to be gleaned from a parishioner's "sudden death" lies this entry for June 26, 1766: "This day attended the Thanksgiving & Spoke all day from Psalm 97:1. O! that this days sins of [crossed out] me & the people in this govenment may be pardoned."[7] The passage is curious, not only in the ambiguity of "this government" (England? New England?) but the omission of the most likely (if not self-evident) generating event of the Thanksgiving occasion, the Repeal of the Stamp Act. What sins, we might ask, had this government's representatives committed to be in need of pardon?

In fact, the sermon preached that day survives to tell us that Hart seized the colony—authorized Thanksgiving in Preston as the moment to reveal "the special hand of your exalted Redeemer . . . in the late

happy event which is the occasion of our being called together this day."
(Again, as in the Diary entry, the specific context is assumed, not announced.) These orations, we should recall, were among the social rituals of the community; to be "called together" during the course of the
secular week gave political import to the weighty message about to be issued from the oracular pastor and highlighted the town's communal en-
terprise itself. Hart opened his oration by setting forth the context of the
textual opening from Psalms, where the psalmist celebrates the arrival of
the sacred ark in Jerusalem. (Immediately there follows a brief typological exegesis of the passage, linking the historical ark to Paul and eventually to Christ, "so that the words of our text are an annulation on the
reign of Christ & a call to universal Joy"—note Hart's theologically precise use of "annul"; he is not speaking *over* his congregation's intellectual capacities; rather, he assumes *some* familiarity with the language of
typology on the part of his auditors.)[8]

The subject of the Thanksgiving oration concerns the nature and tendency of monarchical government—another nod to the contemporary
scene. Before analyzing Hart's discourse in detail, however, it will be
helpful to glance briefly at one of Hart's student exercises, penned while
at Yale in August 1759—an uninspired response to the standard scholas-
tic dispute, "Whether Monarchical Government is the best form."

Not surprisingly, the college student of twenty-one chose to argue for
monarchy, despite the tone (established immediately) of self-effacing ignorance. "Truly I am no politician," he confesses at once, but agrees
nevertheless to go on with the exercise if only "for method sake and to
keep up a good custom." That mildly ironic tone becomes even more
self-effacing toward the end when, after arguing rather unimpressively
that conscience or right reason is the "vice regent in the soul" and thus
"by a parity of reason" kings "are to be obeyed also" (the figures of
Adam and Moses are also invoked as early examples of monarchical
reign), Hart concludes by pleading insufficient knowledge and authority
(not an uncommon gambit among students who recognize the lameness
of their efforts): "and now if I was a Sufficient politician I would next
prove that the right of power is not originally in the people as some
vainly imagine, but this I must leave for some penetrating Genius Skilled
in the deep Recesses of civil and politic Science."[9]

Seven years later, in the wake of the Stamp Act, Hart contrasts the
pure, absolute monarchy of "Christ's Government" with the temporal
afflictions visited by "greedy Monarchs" who would sacrifice thousands
in quest of a "royal Diadem." "Whereas other kingdoms are frequently
encroaching on the rights of their subjects & one another," Hart in-

structed his Thanksgiving audience, Christ's government "bring[s] the greatest Liberty to all who submit." What is the social and political import of Hart's comparison? What was his reading of the "late happy event" to which the people have been summoned to sanctify (and, in effect, sanction) by their presence? By reminding his congregation of the joys of obedience in their proper form of expression—"not in carnal mirth . . . spiritual joy should be expressed in a spiritual manner"— the logic of Hart's sermon argues the necessity of sweet submission to Christ and, "by a parity of reason," to that of political deference to Great Britain. Revoicing the Psalmist's exhortation from the sermon's textual opening, Hart *extends* spiritually and geographically the Biblical song of praise and rejoicing: "With regard to this event we may say— the Lord reigneth, let the earth rejoice & the Multitude of isles (from east to west Indies the Isles of great Britain not excepted [)] be glad."[10] Hart's imitation of the biblical singer's cadenced vision blurs sacred and secular landscapes, incorporating the isles of *this* world with those of the Bible; indeed, the uncompleted bracketing of temporal-geographic entities highlights the preacher's conscious effort at imaginative incorporation, of linguistically inserting "even Great Britain" within the scheme of redemptive history.

Of course Hart's rhetorical move issues in a cautious pulpit stance in response (however indirect) to the incendiary aspect of colonial New England before the heralded Repeal. If Philemon Robbins's anguished reaction to the Stamp Act riots is representative, then Hart's refusal to name in public the political occasion for Thanksgiving reflects how (perceived) social upheaval in prerevolutionary America troubled, indeed unsettled the evangelical ministry. In 1766 Hart could not imagine leaving Britain out of God's providential design; and, by a parity of reasoning, as long as Britain remained incorporated, as long as the Mother country could be read (or discovered) in the gospel text, then Hart (echoing his 1759 exercise) could intone, together with his fellow pastors: "let us yield a most cordial submission to the good King whom He has set over great Britain & her colonies & show in every proper Method our [meekness?] in yielding obedience to the Law,—be subject to Magistrates."[11]

Clearly, Hart was no agitator for the republican beauties of American liberty, at least not during the summer of 1766. With Robbins (with whose son Hart had studied under Bellamy)[12] Hart called for obedience and submission to the Christ-sanctioned government represented by Great Britain. From this perspective, the ambiguity of the Diary entry for June 26 may be resolved. After speaking "all day" from his chosen text, Hart prayed that "the people of this government may be pardoned." Although the sermon never specifies the source of the collective guilt (at least Robbins *named* the sons of liberty as he chastised their misguided zeal) it seems clear that Hart prayed that a guilty *America* be pardoned for her sins. He would, of course (to recall the ministerial charge upon ordination), continue to rebuke and exhort his congregation, especially during the Revolution, yet by 1775 England would no longer be excepted on the basis of biblical authority. Perhaps the most intriguing sign of this displacement is Hart's orthographic reduction of "Britain" to "britain" in later sermons. The lexical shift is telling, for as Hart lowered England to the merely worldly, he elevated America as the vanguard of the approaching millennium. Both in private and public realms, Hart's millennial fervor was a response to the distressing events of revolutionary history *and* a strategy of comfort and assurance, both for himself and to his "dear people" living through those distressing times in Preston.

Before examining the connections between Hart's revolutionary rhetoric and his private inscriptions, let me sketch briefly the shape of the Diary, for its shifting narrative rhythms are expressive of evangelical mentality. As noted, the earliest entries draw on Hart's initial exposure, under Bellamy's faithful eye, to the writings of Jonathan Edwards together with Hart's growing concern over his professional passage into the pulpit. In general, the entries through 1769 consider and evaluate the continuous stream of oratorical performances—their quality, whether uttered under a spirit of "freedom," the character and response of auditors, and so on. Indeed, one senses the thoroughly imbued oral dimension of colonial New England culture, at least within the pastoral world. Hart records the occasions of his preaching, various pulpit exchanges, and his ministering to the afflictive needs of the congregation. By 1770, however, the entries tend to shift from accounts of pastoral and domestic obligations to the loftier world of religious controversy and debate. Passages now open with "wrote" or "received," in reference to the high-level discourse and theological wranglings of the New Light defenders of strict Calvinism. This new tone may reflect Hart's enlarged role in what Joseph Conforti calls the "paper war" among the Edwardseans and their more liberal detractors (from surviving correspondence it is clear how *deeply* sensitive by the 1770s the guardians had become to *any* charge against the Master); the shift may also reflect that, by 1770, what Hart deemed his "real life" was linked more to the world of polemic and defense than with the domestic world of the parish.[13] Collectively, these 1770–73 entries highlight a world of growing self-enclosure, of increasing isolation from the demands of associated life. Of course this sketchy, extrapolated portrait does not mean that Hart ignored his pastoral obligations or was socially aloof; nevertheless, the Diary for the early 1770s gives the indelible impression of a self *turning* from recording daily concerns to matters of infinite theology, adding a measure of weight to Stiles and Morgan's portrait of the New Divinity men enmeshed in airy metaphysics, fervidly dreaming of the approaching millennium.

Seen from this perspective, the events leading up to the American Revolution shook Hart loose from the atemporal world of pamphlets into a scene of psychic and social crises, political rhetoric, and divine judgment. Perhaps the clearest index to the transition lies in the return to Diary entries about preaching; indeed, after 1773 there is a veritable *explosion* of preaching events, as if the times demanded that the minister leave off his polemical obsessions and resume his oracular office as defender of the faith, interpreter of signs, and watchman for the impending glory—or doom. Hart donned all these mantles before his Preston congregation; in the process of assuming those public identities his Diary no longer became the place to gauge his own spiritual progress or the space upon which he reinscribed the current epistolary state of evangelical controversy. In the example of Levi Hart we discover a blurring of public and private discourses during the years he was expected to explain the Revolution to his people. Like Edwards the Younger, Hart could never quite name the looming upheaval as rebellion; he too lived amidst the confusion attendant with what, in vague language, he called the "present dark state of public affairs." Whatever his private anxieties or fears may finally have been, he voiced his apprehensions in formulaic modes, rarely charging his entries with the immediacy of particular crises or private confessionals. "May we be accepted & blessed," Hart prayed in November 1775. By the end of that year he preached with the voice of a hopeful prophet, but would not dare (or perhaps could not attempt) to predict the future. "The year 1776, which is now about to commence," Hart hesitantly prophesied, "will probably be distinguished by the most important events which America ever saw—If so it will be for the Redemption of God's Church & overthrow of its enemies, though we may not, immediately see how."[14]

In 1774, however, Hart could not yet discern the import of events. Historians of the American Revolution often cite the spring and especially the summer of 1774 as the turning point in a series of exemplary junctures leading to Independence. For Levi Hart, the times that summer everywhere recalled to him the history of Mordecai—the favorite typological text for the revolutionary pulpit—from whose story may be discovered how the "great things of the plan of redemption are fitly represented." Hart drew on the Book of Esther almost continuously during June 1774: on the same fast day ("on account of publick calamities") in Newport he preached in the morning for Ezra Stiles from Proverbs 28:13 and for Samuel Hopkins in the afternoon from Esther 4:3—a sermon he would repeat at least six times that summer, including at the colony-wide fast on August 31 (Esther 4:3 was also Robbins's text that same day).[15] Some ten days before that collective outpouring Hart preached "all day" from Amos 4:12, a text which voices God's entreaty to a sinful people to "prepare to meet thy God."[16] Although the preacher never explicitly mentions contemporary events (as in the 1766 oration alluding to the Repeal), the sermon is filled with a tone of anxious expectancy, as if Hart wished to alert his congregation to the ultimate, momentous aspect of current affairs yet could only invoke the biblical trope of captivity in order to jolt his audience into conviction and consciousness.

Hart's rhetorical gambit, after numerous scriptural citations fixing the image of the Israelites fallen into an "exceeding great sinfulness as represented by their oppression," is to recreate the prophet's "very pungent reproof" to the "wicked" Jews of the Old Testament by a vivid rendering of a God on the threshold of wrathful judgment. Using the catechismic mode—asking questions and then immediately supplying the appropriate response—Hart ominously speaks of "What God [is] about to do," "Why he [is] about to do thus," and repeats the "about to" refrain continuously through the sequence of question and answer. The shade of Jonathan Edwards even appears in reply, as a reminder to those "hell-deserving sinners . . . in the hands of an angry God" (recall Hart's early nourishment in Edwards's writings) who "are brought to a hearty, free acknowledgment of God's perfect righteousness in their condemnation." The point, of course, is that "hell-deserving sinners" need desperately to repent—immediately—for "it is a fearful thing to fall into the hands of the living God!"[17] Again, although the political context is never made explicit, the sermon's message, that the impending threat may reach ultimate fulfillment, captures the troubled, restive mood of revolutionary America.

A week later, speaking on the text from Jeremiah on the balm of Gilead, the preacher turned from the healing aspect of "the sanctifying influences of the holy spirit" to their "application—to our nation & Land at this day (1774)." The parenthetical tag is intriguing. Did Hart need to remind his auditors what year it was? Or did he amend his thought with a temporal sign to link the community to the continuum of redemptive history from Jeremiah to Preston circa 1774? Conscious of the exceptional nature of recent history, Hart heralded God's predestinating vision: "The work of redemption," he reminded his audience, "wonderfully compleats & perfects God's other works—shows them to be parts of a great & most beautiful system."[18]

Of course the Revolution ultimately challenged this entrenched providential mentality as it, in the long run, subverted ministerial authority in general. Yet what makes Hart's revolutionary rhetoric compelling is its effort to mediate that secular challenge by accommodating Whig ideology to the demands (and assumptions) of the evangelical vision. Hart's extant sermons do not reveal him to have uttered incendiary rhetoric in the face of British tyranny, yet Bellamy's son-in-law still offers a vivid portrait of faith-keeping during cultural crisis. How did Hart, the elder Robbins, Edwards the Younger, together with the generation of New Lights, labor "to comfort the hearts of God's people & persuade others" (as Hart's Diary puts it) of America's sacred cause?[19] In response, we might say that from evangelical pulpits there issued a kind of rhetorical balm, a soothing stream of words that ministered to the collective souls gathered on these ritual occasions designed to explain the course of history.[20] If Hart reminded his people over and again that "now is the last & perhaps your only time"[21] to repent of sins, his soul-hooking gambit was not simply to argue for the necessity of conviction; Hart also sought to awaken through anxiety a *historical* consciousness as well.

On April 19, 1775, in the wake of Lexington (yet one day before Hart recorded news of the fighting in his Diary), Hart hurriedly (and uncharacteristically) omitted the textual inscription (from Isaiah 22) and went directly to his doctrinal gloss: "God at this time called the people to mourn for sin." *At this time.* The ambiguity of the phrase registers the multivocal dimension of Hart's ritual language. Rather than dilating on textual origins or context, Hart assumes familiarity with the Bible ("God called them [again, note the ambiguity] to this by his Judgment for their sins. . . . See context") and seems eager to arrive at the requisite observation, "our case is like that of these people"—indeed, "too much like those mentioned in our text."[22]

The rebuking comparison—a familiar theme sounded in the pulpit from the seventeenth century on—is the ministerial response to the seeming "fact" of colonial existence: our "disaffection to divine government—

practically calling God a hard master" has issued in divine judgment; "we are threatened with tyrannical government from men." We are a rebellious nation, Hart admonished, "too much" like that of God's ungrateful people in the Old Testament. But proper repentance would not only bring about individual salvation; more important, if the people of Preston offered true conviction, that behavior "might be a means of saving your dear country from the iron yoke of tyranny—your children & children's children from being slaves." Thus repentance has an individual and collective, patriotic and generational aspect: the call to spiritual and political deliverance amounts to a generational injunction to deliver the future to the children. (Hart would soon be preaching, à la Samuel Sherwood, in the "pregnant" language of birthing and travailing associated with the Book of Revelation.) "Our fathers left us the enjoyment of liberty by opposing tyranny," Hart preached a month later, "we should do by our children as we desire [our] fathers did by us."[23]

At the afternoon portion of the April 19 performance Hart returned to his favorite revolutionary text, the Book of Esther, for the subject of his fast sermon. This one-page sermon (how long it would have taken to deliver or to what extent he embellished as he spoke is difficult to say) briefly limns the "perplexed" temper in biblical Shushan where the "subtle, selfish, proud tyrant" Haman, "who governed the King & made him do what he pleased," sought "to gratify his own haughty will" through the destruction of the Jews. Haman's "fatal councils," Hart contextually remarks ("fatal" in the sense that Haman was fated to be the victim of his own political machinations), "filled the capital with perplexity— *infer*" (emphasis added). Of course we do not know if Hart uttered "infer" aloud that afternoon. It is more likely that the word signaled the requisite sermonic shift from Old Testament scene to its current application; Hart's reminder to "infer" seems (like Robbins's shorthand, "amp") a private notation recalling the speaker to his oracular office. In any case, Hart's series of inferences reveals a blossoming of Whig rhetoric:

> The fatal tendency of monarchical government whether open or covered [?] or that people should be governed in any other way than by their own representatives—officers of their own making, & who have a common interest with them—the good of the people is the end of government—& they the proper judges of their own good. The perplexity of this Kingdom & triumph of administration at this time is for want of a just representation—describe the present state—Bless god we suffer no more—humble ourselves under this great judgment & look to him to restore english liberty.[24]

The lament to "restore english liberty" (more about the implications of Hart's orthography later) was, to be sure, standard pulpit fare in pre-revolutionary New England. What is interesting is the (ostensible) authority that Hart bequeaths "the people" in this brief disquisition on the ominous tendencies of monarchy. By the spring of 1775 Hart allows for a self-determining agency—the people can and should fashion "officers of their own making" as well as decide upon the "proper judges of their own good." Here is a full-blown Real Whig position that dramatically departs from the political philosophy implicit in (say) 1766, let alone Hart's Yale exercise of 1759. Of course Hart's republican-inflected discourse emerges from biblical exemplum—the figure of Haman became the archetypal "designing" minister for the revolutionary clergy—but its power (assuming that the Diary entry faithfully records an occasion of *affecting* "freedom" in Hart's performance)[25] derives from the linguistic ambiguity signaled in the typological parallels: "the perplexity of this kingdom"; "at this time." Hart's (perhaps) private note to now "infer" amounts to a crossing of textual thresholds, a turning to the contemporaneous crisis that could be explained only through the rhetoric of emergent republican idioms. We are, sadly, *too much* like the Jews, Hart admonished his audience in the morning; in the afternoon the perplexity of Mordecai's city shadows forth the current plight of America; yet the fated (and fatal) telos of monarchies looks forward (nevertheless) to the longed-for restoration of "english liberty."

The perplexities of April 1775, then, sent Hart back to the Old Testament for appropriate exempla for the country's spiritual malaise and political plight. News from Lexington, which he recorded in the Diary for Thursday, April 20, issued the next Lord's Day in two orations drawn from the most popular texts of the revolutionary era, Isaiah and Revelations. The afternoon portion, based on Revelations 21:4, is particularly telling, for it contains the vision of the spiritual Jerusalem that follows the Lord's soothing promise of "no more death, neither sorrow, nor crying . . . for the former things are passed away." About his Sunday performance Hart glossed in his Diary: "I endeavored to show the excellent state of the church in the millennium & in the upper world after the Day of Judgment, from those passages . . . in order to comfort the hearts of God's people & persuade others."[26] The sermon itself no longer survives, yet Hart's private account of his response to political crisis reveals how he adapted the public ritual of the Sunday sermon to allay the collective fears of the moment. Hart did *not* retreat, let me emphasize, from history in the wake of the judgment of Lexington; nor should his formulaic response be termed "apolitical millennialism," a phrase suggestive of an otherworldly stance toward current events.[27] Rather, Hart summoned the "comforting" vision inspired by Revelation as a response *to* events; his rhetoric in this case served as a personal balm to mediate the trauma of battle.

Still, there is at times in Hart a private urge to escape from the mires of civil war and the implicit judgment inscribed in "the present dark day." A heavy percentage of his preaching texts during the latter half of 1775 call on the books of Isaiah and Revelation, indicative of a desire to imagine publicly the millennial prophecies foretold in the Bible. Yet privately there is a moving refrain penned during these weeks, a telling phrase that offers a tender counterpoint to the public optimism. "May our sins be blotted out," Hart prayed (from Isaiah) on the Lord's Day April 30, "& salvation come to our land."[28] The words are touching in their plea to alter the text of human history. Sin leaves an indelible imprint, every Puritan preacher knew; without the transforming agency of grace its stain could never be erased. Franklin, of course, in his *Autobiography* would speak, perhaps ironically, of sins as mere "errata," printer's errors that might be corrected in later editions of the self. Hart's metaphor is not unlike Franklin's notion in this respect; privately he longed for a new beginning for the nation's collective self—the erasure of past sins, the blotting out of recent history to form a new slate upon which God might reinscribe the nations's providential destiny.

Hart shared this hermeneutic dilemma with his patriot brethren: how can one plot an unbroken arc in the face of the contingency of recent history? "Public affairs," Hart reflected, "remain, so far as we know, as they were."[29] *So far as we know.* Thus Hart's confession of interpretive inertia, the admission of a limited perspective. In general, the Protestant clergy tried, at least publicly, to impose a telos upon the often intractable events of revolutionary America; privately, at least in the example of Levi Hart, public affairs remained, so far as *he* could tell, uncertain.

Perhaps the most poignant rendering of that uncertainty is captured in Hart's sermon delivered on the last day of 1775, on the threshold of a new year, applying the prophecies of Isaiah 63:4—a passage that blends threat of chastisement with the promise of redemption: "For the day of vengeance is in my heart, and the year of my redeemed is come." What follows amounts to a sweeping recapitulation of Old Testament history, limned in fragmentary portraits of those occasions when God poured out "his wrath on his finally obstinate enemies":

Noah & the old world flood & ark—Lot & Sodom—Egypt & Israel in plagues, & at red sea—Joshua's passage over Jordan & possession of

Canaan, & the destruction of the Canaanites—
Destruction of Saul & exaltation of David—
Destruction of Babylon by the persians . . . redemption of the Jews
by Cyrus—Destruction of the finally obstinate Jews, by the Romans.

The preacher next moves from biblical–historic episode to the figure of Christ, and then shifts to Revelation—Hart invokes the famous millennial vision of chapters 20 and 21 (note again how the books of Isaiah and Revelation were continually linked in his imagination, one generating its redemptive completion in the other). Finally, Hart arrives at the contemporaneous moment, citing the temporal as the culmination of the sacred. "The events which have taken place in America in the year past," he intoned, "once ordered by God for his Church's good and the overthrow of his grand enemy . . . his name is wonderfully displayed in protecting America." Thus does God shape events, His decree creating historical design, His voice verbally "ordering" the scheme of redemptive history into being. But from his Preston pulpit on the last day of 1775 Hart could not claim an equivalent oracular vision of the country's future. "The year 1776, which is now about to commence," he declared, "will, probably be distinguished by the most important events which America ever saw—If so it will be for the Redemption of God's church & overthrow of its enemies though we may not immediately see how."[30]

On the threshold of a momentous year Hart could only guarantee the future in hesitant tones. The ordering design of events may not be self-evident, he confessed, even to the community's Isaiah-like watchman for the millennium. Nevertheless, he urged "a hearty compliance" from his audience at the end, and recorded in his Diary that the text of that day afforded "a very affecting subject" in the pulpit.[31] Privately, Hart sought to blot out collective sin, to wash clean the sullied soul of the nation; publicly, although at times he confessed to an interpretive helplessness, Hart continued to preach and chart the gradual yet steady movement of sacred history contained in secular experience. He continued, even though its reflections remained obscure, to look forward to the arrival of the Messiah.

A sermon of May 1776 makes clear how temporal history was infused with the urgency of biblical prophecy in the revolutionary pulpit. Preaching on a "Continental Fast" day (the ritual occasion appointed by the Congress) Hart turned to Revelation 12:16, a text that describes how the woman in the wilderness swallowed the floodwaters unleashed by the heinous dragon. In perhaps the most extemporaneously delivered of all his sermons, Hart set forth a series of fragmentary images that re-creates the bizarre world of Revelation: "Explain the chapter," begins the first line of the sermon (perhaps a private directive to the orator), "woman, means the church of Christ—his son—true converts—time spoken of, from the woman flying into wilderness . . . the woman flying with eagles wings—her safety under divine protection, compare Exod 19:4." The allusion to Exodus refers to God's redemptive promise to Moses, "Ye have seen what I did unto the Egyptians, and how I bare you on eagles' wings, and brought you unto myself."[32] Neatly demonstrating the typological parallels between Old Testament captivity/deliverance and the later assurances of the prophet, Hart assumed that his audience would have an easy acquaintance with the opening and concluding chapters of the Bible and their rhetorical continuities. The invocation of Exodus links the preacher as well with the oracular continuum from Moses to John to Levi of Preston, as the living embodiment of the assuaging Word spoken to a languishing people.

A sequence of ministerial textual glossings follows next, each metaphor receiving its proper exegesis: "The Dragon means . . . the wilderness, an emblem taken from the case of Moses," and so forth. The fantastic figures of Revelation are the fulfillment of previous historical "Instances," as Hart styles the series of secular antecedents, beginning with "Constantine the Great, Henry 8, Cromwell & the parliament against Charles & the popish Queen" (recall a similar history lesson from Edwards the Younger) to "the british government & forces in the reduction of Canada in the last war" and most recently, "The American Congress . . . in the present ~~war~~ defense against tyranny and popery.[33] All parties took a heroic, oppositional stance against enslaving popery; each episode looks forward to the woman of Revelation and the ultimate battle with the forces of Antichrist. Note Hart's intriguing orthography and word substitutions. To alter *"war* against" to *"defense* against tyranny" suggests a dramatic shift in Hart's sense of moral and military agency: "war against" summons an image of mutually aggressive parties, battling from equal moral planes, whereas "defense" connotes America as "victim," fighting the necessary moral fight against the designing plotters of tyranny.

More intriguing still is the lower case "b" wherever Hart represents Great Britain: "American Congress & powers against british & popish tyranny"; "it is very affecting . . . to behold Christ at the head of affairs, directing the storms & ruling all things in britain & America."[34] Of course the orthographic impulse may simply be idiosyncratic, but the "reduction" of Britain to lower case status still seems significant, in light

of Hart's 1766 political sermon which included the British Isles within
the sacred telos. By 1776 the mother country could no longer be incorporated; now perceived as an agent of Popish tyranny, she forfeited both
the moral and historical position as "capital" nation. It is as if Hart
could not bring his pen to elevate the English nation; instead, he could
only inscribe her with the sign of her lost eminence. In any case, the juxtaposition of "britain" and "America" in 1776 bespeaks the tragedy the
Protestant clergy perceived in the fall of England, from redeemer nation
to a popishly-inclined, profane country.

Thus the testament of Levi Hart's public and private rhetoric reveals the
following dynamic: in his Diary he could voice his personal disquiet, his
fears for himself, and for the nation at large: "Sept. 15, 1776: Our Land
is now on the point of being soaked with the blood of its inhabitants, &
of being brought into subjection. We are expecting to hear of another
battle which may issue in the subjection of America." The entry conveys
the sense of looming threat and fear of collective captivity; above all, it
registers the apocalyptic mentality, immobilized, awaiting the fall into
the abyss. Yet publicly, on those ritual occasions when Hart was obliged
to sort out and give shape to the bloody battles and doleful expectations
of revolutionary experience, he turned to the language and prophecies
of Revelation (and its Old Testament *figurae*) to explain history. Perhaps he fixed on the exotic rhetoric and visionary comfort of that book
to mediate his own privately confessed fears for the future. We might
even say that Levi Hart discovered his preaching office in the effort to
allay his own anxiety over the fate of America. "This is a day of darkness," he lamented in September 1776, "Let me not be afraid of what
man can do to me."[35]

By the late 1770s Hart's public orations highlight what might be
called (from a ritual perspective) the processual aspect of colonial experience, at least as viewed from his pulpit. A 1777 sermon drawn from
the messianic text of Ezekiel 21:27 extends the prophet's refrain "I will
overturn, overturn, overturn it" into a discourse on the upwardly spiraling pattern of political transformations "all designed by God to prepare
the way for the coming of the Messiah." Speaking from a condition of
captivity, Ezekiel prophesies (in Hart's words) "the turning over or
transferring of that government [Israel] from one to another," culminating, after the preacher summons a flurry of textual citations (from
Daniel, Isaiah, Luke, and 2 Samuel), in "the present war," which, despite "all the attending wickedness & misery, will issue for the good of

the Messiah's Kingdom." Although Hart's oration concludes, formula-ically, on the necessity of reformation—"let us remember that except we repent we shall all perish"—the emphasis remains on "those overturnings under old testament & new": on the ongoing process of God's "wonder-ful works . . . in those overturnings," which find their ultimate expres-sion in the (political) fulfillment of the Revolution.[36]

The theme of "advancing" history is made even more explicit in a Thanksgiving sermon for 1779, which moves almost immediately from its official text from Romans 8 to the famous "Watchman, what of the night?" utterance of Isaiah (Hart cannot seem to leave Isaiah alone). As before, the country is *figured* in midpassage, in transition; even though "the war has been attended with calamities . . . & the time of [its] end can not even now be ascertained with certainty," the signs of the times still point toward America as "a rising empire in the Western world." From a strictly temporal perspective, there have been military triumphs and disappointments tallied on both sides: "if American army have re-treated from before the walls of Savannah" (note how Hart's pulpit in-cludes newsy accounts of skirmishes, maneuvers, etc.), Hart reports, "the british have done no less at Charlestown." Nevertheless, the coun-try "is advancing with a rapidity hardly equaled . . . in history, ancient or modern."

And with that passage through history Hart explicitly links the proph-ecies of Revelation—above all the figure of the woman in the wilderness in midlabor, pregnant with the predestined body of the true church, ready "to effect this happy birth & glorious liberty of the sons of God." Together with Samuel Sherwood and other patriot preachers Hart ap-plied what might be called a rhetoric of liminality inspired by the sub-junctive language of Revelation (its emphasis on process, potential, the future). In a rare moment of clerical self-consciousness, Hart spoke to his auditors

> in reference to a well known Metaphor, it may be said that the whole creations groneth & travaileth in pains together until now, for the ob-taining the manifestations, & glorious liberty of the Sons of God.

Eventually Hart's language takes on a processual dimension, envisioning the country's "animating prospect of final success." All events are "tend-ing" toward "the perfections of the Messiah's Kingdom," Hart's teleo-logical imagination assures, "the whole of creation is travailing in pain—struggling for this mighty birth . . . O how great and glorious is the object for who so much has been done & is doing! The whole creations has been in travail for it ever since the fall of man."[37]

In its ejaculatory style, its emphasis on events still in progress, Hart's language literally enacts the vision of history sounded from his pulpit. "Travailing," "struggling," "is doing"—together they highlight the processual nature of the rhetoric as well as reveal how potent the visionary last chapter of the New Testament became for the patriot clergy. To limn a world on the threshold of a new birth—"the travail pains of the mother," Hart explained to his auditors, extending their own biblical facility with a "well known metaphor," are analogous "to providential events in the natural world"—contrasts sharply with the anxious Diary confessions of abject subjection and bloody judgment. Before his Preston audience Hart translated his private fears, through well-known metaphors, into a language of assurance and prophecy. When he crossed the professional line from chamber to pulpit he discovered in the language of Revelation a rhetorical balm to sooth both his own fearful soul and that of his congregation. In this respect, Levi Hart may indeed be deemed representative of the ministerial office during the Revolution, for his example reveals the *human* side of the "otherworldly" New Divinity clergymen, whose collective soul-affecting orations sought to help people through a bewildering juncture of historical self-consciousness and ambiguity.

4

The Discovery of Whig Ideology: The Example of Stephen West of Stockbridge

Philemon Robbins's coastal village of Branford, Jonathan Edwards, Jr.'s more cosmopolitan White Haven, and even Levi Hart's obscure Preston hamlet—all three Connecticut communities seem to have been alert to the agitations and arguments for independence, at least as sounded from the pulpits of their respective pastors. Viewed together, these ministerial sketches limn a variety of responses to impending upheaval: from Robbins's dramatic shifts in narrative mode in response to the Stamp Act to the anxiety voiced in the privacy of Hart's diary inscriptions, the preceding portraits offer a series of revealing episodes in the dynamic interaction between evangelical mentality and insurgent political discourse. That complex dialectic, as Ruth Bloch and other historians of eighteenth-century American thought have shown, did not issue in the ascendency of a purely Whig-inflected rhetoric over antedated or obsolescent religious idioms; rather, the rhetoric of the patriot clergy "infused political debate with sacred meaning that inhered in . . . religious vocabulary." The examples of Robbins, Edwards the Younger, and Hart support (as they demonstrate) Bloch's observation through an exegesis that, following Pocock, draws out the multivocal character of ministerial rhetoric—in both its agency as ideological spur, infusing the rhetoric of "liberty" with religious and political overtones, *and* its office as guardian of the social order.[1] As noted earlier, most patriot ministers remained wary of the so-called beauties of liberty and often perceived antinomian threat instead of republican millennium in the socially fractious world emergent in revolutionary America. Thus the cultural fix of the Protestant clergy: to what uses, religious and political, should the latent powers of incendiary rhetoric be employed? To what extremes may the affective (and affecting) rhetoric of sensation—as "rivetingly" codified in Robbins's ordination sermon for the younger Edwards—be put, if the costs of collective arousal be jangling controversy or the rending of the once seamless social fabric?

The cases of Robbins and Edwards, Jr. attest powerfully to these dilemmas; and as for Levi Hart, he sought the comforting vision of the millennial reign of saints in (public) response to God's judgments upon *his* (private) American Zion. The next figure, the Reverend Stephen West of Stockbridge, Massachusetts, in Berkshire County, offers a study of the transmission or, more accurately, the *discovery* of Whig ideology, at least in one western Massachusetts pulpit during the Revolution. To enter the mental world of Stephen West, to follow the arc of his response to events, is to witness how the American Revolution transformed the consciousness of even the most aloof, distanced (geographically *and* politically) religious spokesman examined thus far.

A staunch Calvinist in doctrine and temperament, especially after imbibing the stricter aspects of the creed from his Great Barrington neighbor, Samuel Hopkins, a defender of the Edwardsean heritage (although West followed Jonathan Edwards in the Stockbridge mission, there are no extant reflections of West's thoughts about inheriting that weighty mantle), West was allied with the politically powerful families of that frontier region and, after the Revolution, opposed both the Berkshire Constitutionalists (led by the incendiary Thomas Allen) and Shays's Rebellion. "I dreaded him," confessed a scion of the Stockbridge oligarchy, Catherine Sedgwick; in her memory West loomed (in lines that recall Harriet Beecher Stowe's *Oldtown Folks*) as "the dry, sapless embodiment of polemical divinity." His Yale biographer softens that harsh estimate, asserting that "in the Revolutionary struggle" West's "great influence was unrestrainedly put forth on the patriot side."[2]

Yet the manuscript evidence yields not so much a portrait of unrestrained patriotic zeal as an image of evangelical fear and perplexity—West was at once fearful of the dark signs of God's displeasure (to be read and applied to Stockbridge) and perplexed at what a people might do (if anything) to avert judgment. His foremost desire, preached over and over again on the eve of revolution, was to implore his congregation to escape impending doom, to secure safe hiding from the tremors and shocks of history. But the charge of abstraction, voiced in a recent monograph on Berkshire County, that "Stephen West, we know, tried to divorce himself from worldly concerns," too easily assumes that West succeeded in his separatist impulse. What concerns me in this chapter is West's continuing *struggle* to divorce himself temporally, and the literary reflections of the "trying" effort itself. "In the charged atmosphere of Revolutionary Berkshire," the social historian continues, West "could not easily have escaped exposure" to Enlightenment thought.[3] As part of a study of the dynamic between rhetoric and history in revolutionary New England, the story of Stephen West lets us measure the amplitude of that charge and calibrate how Whig ideology, radiating out from Boston, came to register (and sound) in the hills of Stockbridge.

The geographic context is important for an understanding of Stephen West's preaching, for unlike the more radical east, the backwater of western Massachusetts was slow to embrace the cause of liberty. Before 1774, historians tell us, Whig sentiments were opposed. By the summer of 1774, however, there was a veritable "explosion of local political activity"; indeed, "the lethargy of non-participation," observes historian Richard Brown, gave way to "a local activism which promised committment to Whig ideals."[4] Of course West was not unaffected by the political ferment of that summer, but before examining his response to and participation in that eventful season we need a clearer sense of his preaching concerns from the summer of 1759, when he was installed in the Stockbridge mission (some eighteen months after Edwards had left to assume the presidency of Princeton) up to July 14, 1774, the occasion of the County-wide Fast and, significantly, West's own passage from airy theology into the polemical atmosphere saturated with politics and the ambiguities of history.

I exaggerate that cultural passage, of course. Sermonically speaking, there was no *dramatic* disjunction between West's pre-1774 orations and his performance on that county-appointed ritual gathering in mid-July. Still, there are notable shifts, but visible (and audible) only within the wider compass of West's preaching career. In general, West's earliest extant sermons (beginning in 1764, five years after arriving in Stockbridge) are fully written out, and are rarely concerned overtly with the political fate of New England (let alone America) in the wake of perceived British oppression. Unlike Robbins, for example, West seems not to have preached on the Stamp Act or on its Repeal; nor did he later interpret, as did Edwards, Jr., the various crises leading to Independence as the glorious victories signaled by the series of British military defeats in the early 1780s. For the most part West's sermonic output addressed purely theological issues; more interesting are those early sermons preached specifically to the Indian congregation. For *that* audience West departs from the cramped, minute handwriting sequencing the list of religious doctrines to be expounded in great detail and thoroughness—to the white parishioners of Stockbridge West's early sermons must have been hard going (and listening), even with the clearly announced expository transitions from doctrinal point to point—to sermons penned in a larger script, much shorter in length, often employing the rhetorical catalogues and litanies characteristic of the "familiar" preaching of the Awakening. Perhaps in recognition of the Indians' limited theological capacity (did West preach more simply, even more slowly, to accommodate an adjacent translator?) or perhaps in the hope of awakening conviction, West adjusted his preaching style and rhetoric to meet the needs of his native audience.[5]

Still, West's early sermons register powerfully the ministerial imagination in the performance of its key office: to guide his flock through the wilderness of the world to the heavenly glory awaiting those saved in the next. A sermon of December 1764 (preached, uncharacteristically for West, again the following December), for example, explores the familiar scriptural trope of light shining in a dark place (from 2 Peter). "There are discoveries," he announces in direct, complete sentences, "which the light of natural reason never would have enabled us to make, and mankind must ever have remained in the dark about them, had not God of his mere goodness seen fit to reveal them." That biblical light illuminated as well "the gradual opening of divine Revelation and the progress it has made in . . . various stages" of church history. Most important, God's light "shine[s] in this dark place"; He "manifests a kind design" to all those—temporally, in Stockbridge and universally, in *this* world—"lost and bewildered in the darkness of the night."[6]

Of course West's poignant evocation of wandering pilgrims in need of scriptural illumination may reflect little of the civic world of prerevolutionary Berkshire, even if West's temporal nod to "this dark place" refers to Stockbridge itself. And similarly, when West, speaking under the mantle of the prophet Isaiah, alludes in 1766 to the comforting designs of providence as a way of mediating "the doubtful aspect and apparent uncertainty of things" ("Let us not be discouraged by the apparent darkness & uncertainty of things," he repeats in exhortative strains at the close), we should not rush to equate pulpit vision with social reality.[7] Yet for all its apparent disregard of (say) the political ferment of the Stamp Act, West's rhetoric nevertheless offers a fair representation of colonial mentality: bewilderment, the sense of a looming unknown, the experience (however tentatively voiced) of historical contingency—all these prerevolutionary realities are inscribed in West's memorable "lost & bewildered in the darkness of the night." Despite his backwater status, and the oft-noted lag in the arrival of Whig ideology to the western provinces, West's career provides a startling case study of the ministerial effort to forge a path through the dark passage of Independence. Significantly, as he assumed his office as beacon illuminating that way, West became more alert to—indeed, immersed in—the political rhetoric of the times; yet in the process West's own discourse became *less* syntactically complete and coherent, more fragmentary. In the end, sermonic fragments may well be the most profound reflection of the evangelical minister's engagement with revolutionary history.

An index to the shift in West's habit of imagination is found in comparing a Thanksgiving sermon of December 1772 with a sequence of Lord's Day orations during the spring of 1774—just before the mobilization of Stockbridge in mid-July. The Thanksgiving performance adheres to the established formulas of the genre: we ought to thank God for his bounties of the harvest as well as our good health, in both personal and civil realms. "It is God that strings our bodies with sinews and nerves," West reminds his audience, "and moistens our bones with marrow." God also bequeaths peace to the body politic, the rare gift of "civil liberty." "There is no people under heaven," West intones,

> so highly favoured in this respect, as we in this land. How many nations are groaning under the iron hand of oppression & tyranny; who have no security of anything; nothing that they can call their own & whose liberties and property at the mercy of some despotic wretch who has no notion that his subjects were made for anything but to serve and obey his will. How thankful should we be for the blessings of peace, and for the blessings of our civil government![8]

Together with his ministerial brethren throughout New England, West joined in the collective hymn to English liberty: the standard, deferential paean to Great Britain's celebrated tradition of liberty and its happy incarnation in the New World.

By March 1774, however, West's rhetoric betrays a distinctively different tone. Two orations delivered that month treat the religious and social aspects and obligations of "peace." A sermon of March 13 (from Jeremiah 8:11) builds on a vivid application of, in West's own words, "the metaphor—from the unskillfulness or unfaithfulness of a surgeon in his management of a wound, either in giving some stupefying potion to make the patient insensible to pain, or endeavouring to heal it over while it is yet putrid at bottom." Such partial measures endanger the patient, West observes, "but how much more dangerous is it to cry peace, peace to sinners, when God says there is no peace."[9] The "dangerous" glossing over of deep-seated iniquity (disease) has a multiplicity of reflections, from the welfare of society and church to those souls in need of spiritual healing. By the close, West's sermon on the "danger—healing hurts slightly" shifts into an awakening key, invoking both the central theme *and* stylistic mode of revival preaching:

> And how short & uncertain are your lives. You must have a view of yourselves as infinitely guilty in everything—and as being called by God immediately repent—love—believe, or pain—eternal—or undone. Don't, then, wish for anyone to cry peace— no peace.[10]

"Repent—love—believe, or pain—eternal—or undone"—the syntactic foreshortening recalls the cataloguing characteristic of awakening rhetoric, as does the litany of injunctions issuing in conditional threat. By the spring of 1774, that is, West's sermonic language, his very habit of composition, appear hurried; he seems less concerned with semantic coherence and more with transcribing the essence of his thoughts in the rush of pulpit preparation. And significantly, too, the break in narrative flow inaugurates what might be called the onset of temporal imagination, for as West's syntax loses fluidity he becomes more alert to secular history; he achieves, we might say, a sense of the present.

"What a promising appearance, as to religion—last summer—Since [then] we have been contending—how the concern gone— we are sunk into stupidity." Thus does the sermon close, in woeful rebuke and anxious entreaty. "Where are the feeling [*sic*] you had last summer! What became—promises. Are you not in the hands—same angry God—& are you not the same guilty sinners. O awake from your stupidity or—undone forever."[11] Both in form and content this mid-March 1774 oration signals a break from the less impassioned, but narratively more fluid style of West's early sermons. Although the connections between imaginative shifts in sermonic art and social experience remain tenuous, West's preaching registers, perhaps even contains, an increment of pre-revolutionary social reality in colonial Stockbridge. If new ideas were indeed stirring in the western countryside (as historians tell us), then perhaps the most telling gauge to the emergent mentality lies in the preaching career of the region's major intellectual figure.[12]

A sermon delivered a fortnight later reinforces that speculative assertion as it displays the Reverend West's encounter with Whig rhetoric.

Continuing the preaching theme of "peace," in this instance working from a passage in Romans on the fruits of social concord—"If it be possible as much as lieth in you, live peaceably with all men"—West sets forth the Christian obligation "of living peaceably with all." Remarkably, in the oration's early moments West seemingly invokes Whig logic to explain the relative limits, in secular terms, of Paul's injunction. "Living at peace must not consider as—*highest end,*" the minister advised; in fact, "We are not obliged for the sake of peace, to sacrifice *all* our common natural rights as men. *Every*thing is not to be given up, to gratify the humours & caprices of men" (West's emphases). And furthermore, West continues, "We are not obliged to give up the real rights of conscience to please men."[13]

In another context West might have assumed the oppositional stance of those eastern conscience patriots in Boston who refused to recognize the unsanctioned, merely temporal authority of the British Parliament and argued, in familiar Lockean language, for their "real rights," their "natural rights as men." From *that* perspective West's rhetoric resounds with the high strains of Country ideology. But we know, despite his Yale biographer's efforts (and desire) to elevate him to the revolutionary pantheon, that Parson West was not overly zealous for the cause—at least not as of March 1774. The balance of the sermon issues not in an affecting summons on behalf of "natural rights" but in a cautionary tale against the perfidy of "contention," of social discord. "In order to peace," West reasoned, in tones that the Sons of Liberty would have found irksome, "I see not but that Christians are obliged cheerfully to give up their estates when the civil magistrate & the community calls for it." "Religion and quarrelling never go together," he admonished, and in every case "Pride breaks the peace of society." Perhaps in direct response to fractious Stockbridge, perhaps in sentient reaction to looming unrest, West read "contention" as a reflection of God's dark judgment on the community: "certain proof—want of the power of religion." In a telling reversal West spoke instead of those happy souls "who truly contend for Christ . . . they will not be selfish, self-willed."[14]

To be "self-willed" was of course the latent horror embedded in the rhetoric of natural rights, a psychic stance inimical to the Protestant clergy's vision of an ordered, harmonious society. From this perspective, we may observe the multivocal aspect of the rhetoric; the blurring of the Lockean language of resistance with the conservative impulse of West's closing refrain: "we see how ready [we] —should be to sacrifice our own interests . . . to peace, for the sake of God's cause."[15] The interpretative ambiguity symbolizes the rhetorical dilemma of the patriot ministers. Philemon Robbins, we recall, was appalled at the Liberty Sons' self-appointed license to unsettle the social equilibrium, yet on the eve of the Revolution he invoked Mordecai as *figural* patriot, refusing deference to a King's minister. (Curiously, West was never moved to retell the Book of Esther from his pulpit; the scores of his sermons which survive from 1774 through 1777 reveal that West, unlike his patriot brethren, was not much interested in the seasonable application of Old Testament *figurae* for the times.)[16] Thus in the spring of 1774, before the ideological "explosion" in Berkshire County, West's sermons mingled both religious and political overtones, blending the language of Whig opposition with that of religious anxiety in the face of social upheaval. If Stockbridge shortly was to embrace the cause of liberty, that political allegiance did not arise from the patriotic strains of the minister. Of course the people may have *preferred* to listen more attentively to the first part of West's discourse rather than adhere to its cautionary, indeed retrograde (viewed politically) closing admonition. As for West himself, he sought to escape from the ideological ferment in his midst. As summer approached, he read everywhere "the face of divine providence wearing a very threatening aspect toward us in this land." "We are threatened," he warned in early June; "Everything seems to betoken calamity—clouds gathering on every side."[17]

Thus we have a vivid evocation of the mental world of Stephen West on the threshold of political explosion. Rather than patriotic exertion (or confrontation) West did indeed shrink from the dark, "threatening" events he perceived closing in; but as we follow, in some detail, the saga of his sermonic response to revolution, we shall discover that, with the rest of the Protestant clergy, even the otherworldly Parson West had to descend from his metaphysical pulpit, despite his continuous urge to flee. That descent records, in effect, a fall into history.

On July 14, on the occasion of the general public Fast in Stockbridge, West sought refuge from the history being enacted.[18] His text, from Isaiah 26, neatly captures his own psychic mood: "Come, my people," the voice of the biblical prophet implores, "enter into thy chambers and shut thy doors about thee: hide thyself as it were for a little moment, until the indignation be overpast." We live at an omnious juncture of history, West's text implies, a frightening interval metaphorically betokened by "clouds gathering thick and fast, storms just breaking," signs which propel us inside our "chambers" (West later recalls for his audience the various typological levels of the image) like the Old Testament Jews waiting out God's wrath before *their* exodus. Passover allusions abound in this sermon: "blood—lintel—doorposts, as it were, sealed fast the children of Israel within—houses." (Did West, upon declaiming, reconstruct the fragments imaging these familiar scenes into narrative?) In West's mind, latter-day variations on the biblical plagues were on the verge of recommencing, and the only safe ground lay within, behind the spiritual doors marked with the sign of redemption. Or *within* the comforting language of the sermon itself, the rhetorical correlative of (spatial) communal retreat. As the embodiment of the prophet, revoicing Isaiah's words of solace, West performed his mediating office, guaranteeing his auditors "that when God is about to bring judgments upon the earth, he is careful to provide for the safety of his own peculiar people. He never forgets them."[19]

Of course the blessings conferred by God's promise were conditional, a function of religious and civil adherence to His law. What was problematic for Stockbridge's fate, as West surveyed the biblically imbued landscape from his pulpit, was the polemical atmosphere that filled the town with the jangling noise of political rhetoric. Storms and clouds may be about to engulf our little world, West feared, because people are too much concerned with all the noise about "liberty"; "Let such as think that they feel their own liberties invaded, let me ask you to inquire whether you are not servants [in] sin, slaves—satan—in his interest, friends to his cause. O be concerned to be the free men of Christ."[20]

Thus Stockbridge (and perhaps the County in general) was astir with ideological debate during the eventful summer of 1774, but through an admonishing rhetoric West tried to avoid its secular taint. "To declaim on the sins of the times, I know—popular—And at this day, it is a very copious theme—fruitful subject," he noted; and he joined in the popular lament by cautioning against purely political "endeavours" (his word), dissociating them from the realm of the spirit. "Trusting in God doth not exclude the necessity of prudent endeavors to preserve our privelidges. What these methods are, considered in a political light, don't belong to ministers of the gospel to point out. Others know better"[21]—a confession of ministerial hesitancy in the face of *realpolitick*. Still, it is just as apparent that West's Fast oration is a response to the very "commotions" (again, West's term) that his sermon swerves from addressing. The injunction to flee to a sheltering, otherworldly chamber in effect gives way to an engagement with contemporaneous, secular convulsions, compelling the preacher to interpret, to *read* the meaning behind political agitations. Thus West's sermon conjoins the human desire to hide in traumatic reaction to upheaval with the (equally) human desire to explain, to impose *some* meaning upon the "open," unfolding narrative in progress. In 1774 West could respond to the emergent Whig rhetoric of liberty only with its other, atemporal referential valence—the spiritual liberty proffered to Christ's free saints.[22] Soon, however, West would begin to accommodate—or mediate—the multivocal, ritual levels of Puritan and Whig languages to empower his own rhetoric and, in the process, to help propel Stockbridge toward Revolution.

By December of that year, when West surveyed the times, reading "the language of divine providence" for (and to) his congregants, he again discovered "storms . . . now gathering oer America," but precisely "where the storm is to break," he cautioned, "don't become us to presume to foretell." Still, the hermeneutic impulse marked West's habit of mind; his own response to a "world this day peculiarly in tumult, full of action" issued, especially during the mid-1770s, in a continuous application of the Book of Revelation as perhaps the *key* to the meaning of those "events crowding fast, one on the back of another."[23] Secular commotions at turns immobilized and liberated the evangelical imagination: immobilization, for the psychic shock of military-political threat prophesied God's heavy judgment and fiery rebuke which only passive prayer and chamber repentance could appease; liberation, for tumultuous events needed to be ordered and shaped by the active, narrative-imposing office of evangelical mentality. Above all else, the Revolution prodded as it inspired the clergy to "foretell," despite the dangers of exegetical presumption latent in the interpretive act itself.

Thus by December 1774 West sensed "something great" inscribed in the rumblings of current affairs and urged his congregation to give thanks.

> God—now pouring out—or about to pour out [note West's hesitancy to clarify the ambiguities of Stockbridge experience]—sixth vial—the 7th mean[s] 7 periods time—7 judgments or plagues brought on the enemies—church—generally agreed fifth poured out—reformation—now time—6th make great musterings [note the militia rhetoric]—convulsions in the nations . . . Prepare O ye christians, for trying times.

Was history spiraling out of control? Or, by the consensus of apocalyptic scribes, were the times unfolding according to predestined patterns? Although he feared the convulsions of history, West tried to assure his auditors of divine design. Still, he could only lament the current apostasy from the spiritual glories of the previous summer, when the town was blessed with awakenings. "How different state from what a year ago—How wonderful the mercy—enjoy such peace among ourselfes."

"O Lament your deadness," West exhorted at the close, "O then awake & arise—gird up—& stand up for the Lord."[24]

By the following spring, in May 1775, the times still offered no stable reading, though West betrayed an uneasy confidence in the act of decoding the meaning of events: "Since—canon of revelation compleated . . . We are now able to interpret the language of providence." But the vision of "calamities . . . gathering thicker over our heads"—note again the anthropomorphic tendency, as well as the apocalyptic tones of "thick*er*"— did not result in a call to retreat but rather in a striking engagement with contemporary events (striking, for until now there is virtually no *overt* allusion to secular affairs in West's rhetoric). "Think of poor fellow creatures/Boston—may we not learn something from them?," West asks, most likely in reference to the blockade of Boston harbor by British troops. The afflictions signaled by Boston's plight, however, pale before the insidious distractions of political debate. "We don't seem to consider that heaven has any controversy with us," West began, before indicting his auditors with the testimony of *their* current rhetorical obsessions:

> we consider Britain—but not God. . . . See our wicked partiality in our resentments against those whom we call tories when we discover little or none against those who are still maintaining the controversy against God. These are worst tories, most to be abhorred. Therefore raise up, & direct your opposition against them.[25]

In this startling passage we sense more than just the ideological embers still glowing from the political fires of the previous summer; we also hear the conservative oligarch deconstructing the fictions of political labels, exposing the human, and therefore arbitrary dimension of "mere" political identity implicit in the astonishing phrase "those whom we call tories." Of course from one perspective West challenged the legitimacy of the accusatory epithet to rebuke those who, in "wicked partiality," claimed a holier than thou stance; more numerous, however, were those lost souls, "maintaining the controversy against God." In time West's rhetoric would more deeply imbibe the idiomatic currents of Whig thought, but his sermons rarely match in tone the exertions of patriotic zeal, or the poetic rendering of the psychic and human costs of toryism found in Philemon Robbins. In any event, the charge against self-righteous political labeling bespeaks West's own political plight in Stockbridge, circa 1775. For all his exhortations from his pulpit to hide, there was no chamber for any public figure to flee to on the eve of Independence, not even in geographically obscure western Massachusetts.

West continued to offer visions of collective spiritual redemption in his week-to-week sequence of regular preaching (we can follow that pastoral office in the rich, voluminous series of extant sermons), but when called upon on public occasions to address the nature and course of current events his rhetorical stance shifts distinctively—by mid-1775 West becomes more attuned to history, more engaged with revolutionary affairs. Preaching from the book of Jonah in July 1775 ("You all, probably, remember the story," he assumes at the outset), West turns in the "Improvement" toward recent affairs so that we may "more sensibly feel the importance" of repentance:

> a great & powerful nation—against us—strongly resolved—& probably verily thinking—right to subject us—Many now rejoycing to hear—bloodshed— . . . now lives may be taken—estates forfeit—now find . . . now . . . to provide. . . . If they conquer us—we brought very low—civil religion priviledges taken away—the common people be despised . . . men in a temporal & spiritual capacity to Lord it over us—with a train of evils.[26]

With its cascade of "nows" introducing each new evil that will beset a "subjected" nation, the passage inaugurates a new tone in West's revolutionary pulpit. To make his audience "more sensibly feel" their dangerous condition, West's imagination launches into a hurried, nervous rhetorical style which, in its fragmentary syntax and litany of "nows" (Robbins might have set off each phrase separately, in a vertical column of "now . . ." lines), recalls the Awakening mode of preaching. Intriguingly, West's first truly "affective" oratory appropriates that earlier style as it strives to awaken his Stockbridge audience to Britain's "capacity to Lord it over us." It is as if West discovered the antiauthoritarian impulse of the Awakening (the one revival characteristic that survived into the revolutionary era, according to most scholars),[27] its oppositional stance toward all forms of unsanctioned authority to be "seasonable" for the times. I am not arguing that West *consciously* returned to a revivalistic style, but rather that his oracular desire to stir his audience to sensibility required a complementary form, and that the rhetorical modes of the Great Awakening met the requirements of West's hesitant revolutionary imagination.

Yet true to the generation of evangelical clergy who could never fully assent—at least not in the still dependent year of 1775—to the discordant implications of absolute separation, West closed his performance with a rebuking reminder of the dangers of disunion and the need for what he calls (in Edwardsean language) "union and love [which] are the strength and beauty of every society—without this we are an undone people." That frightening image, with its suggestion of a nation unmoored, shorn of a future *in* history (either secular or redemptive), compels the preacher to another evocation of the country's current dilemma, a brief but sharply focused history of declension:

> When we view the present state of the land, is there no encouragement in the promises of the word of God, which we take hold of to hope for relief—no, not the least [note the invocation of the catechismic mode, as well as the image of a nation falling out of time, groping for ballast] British Court—against us, because they think we N. England possessed that old puritan spirit which—forefathers—God because we are not puritans. In England's view we wont reform—nor in God's. . . . We are mostly become apostates from the true doctrines—

In a time of abject apostasy, a time when even God offers no comforting words, a time of pronounced "enmity—opposition to order, & real government," West could only helplessly decry, Jonah-like, "these public judgments [which] loudly call sinners to repentance."[28] Of course we do not know whether Stephen West mounted his pulpit as a veritable son of thunder (to use the favorite phrase of the Awakening clergy); we do know that his response to the revolution in progress was conflicted: he sought the atemporal realm of Christ's chamber at the same time he exposed the British threat to America. When in a more optative mood, as in a Thanksgiving sermon some four months later, in November 1775, West could read "all these calamities" as tokens of a "greater good," signs that God continued "to prepare the way for the enlargement, peace & glory of the Redeemer's kingdom—*even in this land*" (emphasis added). But the darker, contrapuntal rhythm of his rhetoric ritually returns, hedging the "prophecies & promises" of events with a cautionary tone. "O my people," West warned that Thanksgiving assembly, "fear and tremble, amist [*sic*] the awful, terrible things in righteousness which God is doing—O *see* the hand of God . . . and pray that you may be hid, til the indignation be overpast."[29]

After 1776 and Independence, however, West would "see" more and more the apocalyptic scenario in the "text" of events, and that clarified vision enabled him to "come out," so to speak, from within the otherworldly chamber marked like the lintels and posts of Egyptian bondage and join (however timidly) in the historical exodus already in process.

The journey out was not a literal passage, of course; unlike Philemon Robbins's zealous sons, West did not serve as military chaplain on the battlefront; and unlike John Cleaveland of Ipswich, West did not urge his congregation to leave their pews, pick up arms against the British, and then (according to legend) lead the aroused procession himself into battle.[30] West experienced the American Revolution from within his study and from his pulpit, where he translated the language of events in the effort to order and contain the fissive tendencies of the Revolution itself. Throughout 1776 he wavered (characteristically) in pulpit mood, from the somber observation of February that "the noise and tumult of war . . . drown[s] the voice of God. . . . He can hardly be heard" to (by mid-December) an eclectic array of allusions drawn from Ezekiel and Revelation designed to prove how "we, in this land" are to expect the fulfillment of those prophetical books, gradually, in time, in America.[31] What is telling about West's rhetoric during 1776 is its *increasingly* fragmentary form, the syntactic breakdown of narrative flow, especially when the language strives to represent visionary scenes.

In mid-May, for example, preaching on a Fast Day from Ephesians 1:11, where Paul speaks of the "predestinated" nature of all things— how (in West's own words) "God's heart is . . . for the advancement of the good of this kingdom"—West first limns a figural portrait of current plight with a nod toward Exodus: "troubles—present day, all brought by hand—God. Kings heart—hard. God—turned it against us." And then, as if answering the question most frequently posed in the revolutionary pulpit, "events crowd . . . What do—this land—know not," West hedgingly offers an apocalyptic timetable to make sense out of a world too "full of events":

> Some great event—expect—divine providence—truth advances—Zion's kingdom comes—and, as mountains shook—old—Jehovah came—so nations shake all around. Now the period, Rev. 16.12 Euphrates—support strength Babylon—may be dried—here. Can't be positive.

Thus does West blur sacred and secular geography, investing his backwater outpost with the aura of redemptive history. *Now* is the prophesied period, West intones on the eve of the Declaration, yet we "can't be positive." The grammatically compressed question, "What do[?]" could not be answered in a world where even the assurances of biblical prophecy were made ambiguous by the experience of contingency. Still, only an unshakable, indelible belief in God's predestinated design could help people act in history. "Know—all things ordered right," West concluded, perhaps trying to address collective anxiety, "it can't be comforted in this,—no comfort for us."[32]

By the summer of Independence West found yet more comfort in the words of the Old Testament prophet Zephron, who "before the babylonish captivity . . . foretold heavy & severe judgments . . . coming on the jewish nation." Despite the ominous context and message of biblical history West records a continuum of remarkable deliverances: "He delivered Lot 'See the uses which Peter makes of this, 2 Pet. 2.4' [West can't resist a quick lesson in typology] Israel—red sea—young men furnace—Daniel—den." From these linked images of salvation West works toward an assuaging application of biblical design to current affairs: "the present commotions—world—our land are all ordered—evidence to promote interest Zion—is there not much comfort and consolation—people of God, under present troubles?" How can troubles be at times afflictive and at times comforting? The answer depends in part along which visionary axis the preacher aligns himself. "Present commotions" activated in West a retrospective imagination—a historical frame of mind—which issued, according to mood and occasion, in a rebuking comparison of an apostate generation with a race of Puritan giants or, as the sermonic testament begins to reveal, a tempered yet essentially optimistic reading of the signs of the times *in light of* the book of Revelation.[33]

From this perspective, the evangelical mind often welcomed the news of heavy, doleful battles as signs (in West's language) of "overturnings great"—ultimate transformations which might inaugurate the millennial reign of peace.[34] "From a variety—considerations," West declaimed in August 1776, "[we have] reason to think that this is one of those grand periods particularly foretold—spirit prophecy. see Rev. 16.12. The fifth was—reformation—about 250 years back—now time for sixth—If so, now a time of peculiar joy in heaven—God's language to his people." The nature and meaning of that language preoccupied the revolutionary ministers throughout the war; in the case of West, God's holy idioms opened up long familiar episodes in redemptive history that filled the preacher with the excitement of original discovery and the obligation of interpretation. The tumultuous times wrought a new text, with "every page presenting new & bright scenes" to be read and incorporated within the divine telos. We might even say that the very *act* of interpretation answered West's rhetorical question, "What—do?"[35] Thus the hermeneutic impulse had its own kind of socio-political agency; certainly West's ministerial office as guide and comforter drew on the collective event of public reading, the weekly ritual of charting the community's journey along the horizontal line of providences and, simultaneously, on the vertical axis extending up to millennial redemption. West's rhetoric graphically incorporates the idioms of both realms, the secular and sacred, and blends them to forge a charged language that *translates* its listeners from one plane to another, or enables the historical to resonate with the reverberations of the sacred.

Thus by the end of 1776 West's sermons continuously gloss the prophecies as authorizing texts of the country's historical progress. Ezekiel merges with the visions of Revelation to offer, again in the fragmentary mode, the exotic images and metaphors of those visionary books as almost palpable foreshadowings of revolutionary experience—of the collective fate of "we, in this land":

> As all God's providential government tends uniformly to this great—glorious end ["the beauty & glory of Zion"] . . . So his government is most universal. . . . This extent of government & uniformity of design in divine providence is admirably represented in the vision which Ezekiel had—glory—god—Israel . . . So whirlwind, cloud—lightening—vengeance—rainbow—mercy—4 faces—every way, 4 corners—earth—. . . wheel in a wheel—cross wise—interpret might go this or [that] way . . . Present calamities all brought—Diety—stirred up—king—Britain—makes laws—people—this land to refuse submission—him—levy wages on—to oppose this all the work—wonderful providences. . . . Now probably period, 6th vial . . . antichristian against true religion—But God means the salvation of his people—for gathered—battle—great day.[36]

What an amazing collage of biblical allusions! Of course we can no longer recover fully the meanings, let alone the affective responses, that such disjointed, unhinged language might have ignited and aroused in colonial Stockbridge; at best we can only imagine that West's December 1776 Thanksgiving address warmed the hearts of its winter audience with the glow of the familiar prophecies.[37] But lest his audience become too complacent in their pastor's assuring strains, West, in familiar contrapuntal rhythm, cautioned against any easy confidences:

> Everything seems ~~yet~~ still/yet to threaten and announce farther trouble—God, in his providence, seems to encourage both sides by turns & that, to keep up & prolong the Contest God, in his righteous anger, is taking Britain & America, & dashing their heads together. Oh! what evils are coming on both, on all God's enemies. Do feel the importance of reforming, escaping.[38]

This rhetoric of "seeming" signals a return to ambiguity, most tellingly inscribed by the preacher's rare textual emendation, of "still/yet" as an unresolved choice of conjunctions. "Yet" enhances the tone of nervous anticipation, of looming threats; "still" registers less anxiously through its connotative overtones of inevitability. In any event, West's refusal to choose in the text suggests a return to the metaphor of spatial and hermeneutic immobilization—"interpret might go this or [that] way". For all the heady confidences inspired by his oracular office, West still (yet) sought an escape from the noise of clashing armies, the thunder rumbling in the wake of God-dashed nations.

After 1776, however, the impulse to retreat recedes in the apparent design of military victories and the optimism such providences inspired. In addition, West's sermons appear more fully enmeshed with the textures of history itself—that is, West's rhetoric becomes more alert to and mediated by the language and issues of contemporary political discourse. Examples of this transformation occur at the beginning and end of 1777, a key psychic interval wherein West's own lukewarm inclinations toward revolution (relative, that is, to other, more fiery New Lights) gives way to fervid embrace.

Even the logic and concerns of these sermons reflect this new attentiveness. "Enemies, such as used to be our friends," West remarked in late January, working his text from the Book of Job, "have risen up against us. The subjects—debate—hath been labored by reasoning, by expostulation: They have finally made the appeal—sword; which is in some peculiar sense—appealing to God, we have joined them in the appeal." With Edwards the Younger West could not bring himself to name this enemy, yet the passage is notable for its conscious demarcation of parties (us versus them) as well as its indirect allusion to the long history of prerevolutionary arguments, petitions, "reasoned appeals," and so on, which has ended in an "appeal" to swords that even God himself finds "appealing." (Edwards the Younger also rehearsed that polemical history of petitioning for his White Haven congregation; West assumes familiarity with those politically inspired "labored . . . expostulations.") Now "the cause itself," West opines, "we trust, on our side is just & righteous." But more significant than the new tone of partnership is West's brief soliloquy on the fate of "civil liberty" for the "increase—enlargement—Kingdom." Earlier, in 1774, West dissociated the rhetoric of secular, civil liberty from the purer (spiritual) Christian; by 1777 West had to consider how the experience of Stockbridge and the fate of "liberty" were enjoined:

> Tyranny—oppression fitted to keep people—ignorance—ignorance op-
> posed—kingdom—for this a kingdom—light—liberty.—devil always loved
> tyranny—by this means held his dominion—light—truth will increase
> only in proportion—liberty.[39]

Light will increase only in proportion to the increase of liberty. Returning to an earlier pulpit theme, West *supplants* scripture as the source of
light to a darkened world with the power of liberty *as agent;* "civil
liberty," West declares, not only irradiates the shrouded landscape with
truth but its "increase"—that is, its progress *in history*—acts as a bulwark
against the ominous, conspiratorial design of ignorance. "If our enemies
conquer," he worries, there will follow a suppression of free inquiry—
"Episcopy probably established; perhaps conformity enforced; dissenting interest discouraged, perhaps put down—by authority."[40] Shades of
Hawthorne's John Endicott! The dire utterance marks West's recognition of the political ferment outside the missionary outpost; it also
reveals how the multivocal overtones of liberty could blend in the
mingling of religious and political vocabularies of revolutionary discourse. If Stockbridge and pockets of western Massachusetts embraced
the cause of liberty by 1777, that social assent followed from the ideological spur, the enabling office of ritual symbols.

Perhaps the most telling illustration of that social–linguistic dynamic
occurs in a Thanksgiving oration of November 1777 which opens with
an image of "babylonish captivity" and ends with a febrile vision of the
approaching millennium. On this particular occasion of collective historical reading, when the watchman/preacher was obliged to acknowledge "those great things which God—done—people this land, wherein
his hand remarkable visible" (note again the foreshortened, staccato
syntax), West singles out the astonishing testament of recent military
victories, highlighting "how remarkably—God wrought for us—north-
ward." Such spatial specificity is rare in West's sermons, yet the nod
toward local geography is of a piece with the emergence of a general
historical acuity. Only with divine aid could "a raw, undisciplined mili-
tia" achieve victory. Admittedly, West recalls, "at one time—whole
country in panic," but suddenly "a spirit—courage—military prowess,
flew, as it were like lightening thro whole land—and a great powerful
army wholly delivered up . . . such a thing scarce ever known." Such
inspiring scenes were among the distinguishing marks of providence to
be read aloud in revolutionary Stockbridge.

But the national excitement ignited by British defeat paled before the
recognition of the Lord's "further deliverances," the "still grander

things" to be fulfilled. "This God," West reminded his hearers, "can revive religion—bind satan—subdue sinners hearts." And then, after uttering the jeremiadic ritual phrase "Things now very dark—light may be near," West launches into an inspired, impassioned biblical and rhetorical exegesis of the times that offers, in its weaving of religious metaphor and political overtones, perhaps the clearest example of the evocative, suasive powers of the revolutionary clergy and the ritual process in general:

> not amiss [to] attend—little aspects divine providence—respect future events, as held up—spirit prophecy . . . seven seals—seven trumpets— seven vials—history—seven seals—to Constantine—about 300 years [West continues to explain the sequence of seals through the sixth, the river Euphrates] . . . can only conjecture events—river is anything which . . . will open a way—destruction—civil tyranny—particularly—satan loves this; now kings—setting one another—by & by, when rights mankind come to be understood (tho men now averse to proper authority)— unite to see if can bring mankind subjection—This occasion—great battle . . . [yet] world . . . not destroyed—look round—find ourselves— without government, in a new state. Then prince—peace—came—set up his own government—satan bound—what glorious period this . . . blessed holy he who has part—present scenes—opening to this. Let Zion's friends rejoyce—glad.[41]

If in 1774 West separated politics and piety ("We consider Britain but not God") by the end of 1777 and the onset of war his rhetoric reflected, indeed answered, a new perception of social and political reality. The language of Revelation blurred with that of Republicanism; in the process, the familiar tropes of that prophetic portion of the New Testament yield a nascent Whig rhetoric: the pouring of the vials, the opening of the seals, resound with "civil tyranny" and "rights—mankind."

Yet the passage portrays more than an enactment of the ritual process. I refer to West's astonishing confession of interpretive subjectivity; the minister's (almost casual) "conjecture" that the spiritual Euphrates, the reservoir of Antichrist's wicked waters, that "river is anything" validated by—or discovered in—rummaging secular history. Thus West's apocalyptic scenario for revolutionary Stockbridge exemplifies the hermeneutic shift from Biblical allegory to a proto-modern symbolism—the temptation (or need) to order the world from within the self. In effect, West's conjectural reading of the times inscribes the gradual loosening of scriptural authority in revolutionary America and, as Hans Frei has taught us, in eighteenth-century religious culture generally.[42]

Of course West's congregation heard their pastor represent recent events as *figurae* of cosmic battles at the threshold of millennial reign; they also heard him, conservatively inclined citizen of the emergent republic that he was, admonish the insidious aversion to "proper authority"—it is not surprising that West surfaced later as a leading Berkshire Federalist. Still, the movement of the Thanksgiving rhetoric is progressivist in vision, optimistic in tone. Like his Stockbridge predecessor, Parson West understood the historical moment of 1777 as a passage to "a glorious period . . . present scenes—opening to this." And like Jonathan Edwards, even the otherworldly Parson West could, at times, descend and speak to his congregation's emotional needs at a juncture of historical crisis and divine deliverance.

The fragmentary mode of the long passage quoted above verbally approximates the disjunctive, dizzying encounter with revolution, at least as one minister experienced the upheaval and rhetorically tried to order its meaning. The revolution in progress was grammatically intractable, if West's efforts at verbal representation can be said to bear witness to the experience. It is as if his pen, omitting connective words and phrases, could not keep pace with events; West's hurried rhetoric thus bespeaks a view of intractable history as well. From this perspective, his Thanksgiving sermon of December 1783 marks a key moment in the turnings of his pulpit imagination.

Based on the celebratory ecstatic hymn from Psalms 78, "O sing unto the Lord a new song, for he hath done marvellous things," the preacher surveys those "marvellous things" revealed in the recent American victory and, in a distinctively different form and tone, sings his own paean to Independence. Assuming what he himself calls "the retrospective view," West now examines and distills the scene of secular history with a clear, sustained linear narrative. And with that return to narrative, West's rhetoric rings with the idioms characteristic of Whig ideology. Of course the return may be linked to a retrospective stance itself; in any case, it seems clear that by embracing the logic of Whig thought, West (in 1783) achieved an ordering vision of those late perplexing events that had earlier left him in the opaque realm of conjecture: "What—do."

How did West come to understand the meaning of "the late distressing War," as he styled the Revolution in 1783? Like most historians of the American Revolution, West recognized that the psychic and emotional ties between England and America had been sundered:

How did we pride ourselves heretofore in our conviction. We imbibed
her sentiments; we emulated her wisdom & her Spirit; and, to our shame,
we adopted her vices, and made them our own . . . & whenever British blood ran, America bled at every vein. But, now the connexion is
dissolved, and a line of separation drawn that will probably be eternal.

The break from such weighty, internalized cultural authority would
result, as Jack Greene has shown, in a troubled search for identity in the
new republic.[43] West, however, was absorbed more by the retrospective
habit than by the vexed question of American selfhood. In 1783 he
could only marvel (with the Psalmist) at how "a people . . . divided
in sentiments, manners, customs, both in interest & affection . . . all at
once burying prejudices and abolishing local distinction, and to the
astonishment of the world, consorting in a bond of perpetual union and
friendship" could "repel a force which hitherto been deemed invinci-
ble" (note in this passage and the one above the unimpeded syntax, the
linguistic fluidity). From our own perspective, we might say that West's
astonishment at the leveling of disparate parties (especially among
various religious affiliations) remains as a question to perplex and inspire the pens of numerous cultural historians; according to West's, the
American success lay (of course) in the hands of a benevolent diety
who took "these united States[,] established in the profession of their
liberty and independence," and supplied them "with every advantage
for being the most happy and flourishing people on earth."

The confidence of 1783 contrasts sharply with the edgy tone of the
mid-1770s, most dramatically verified by the narrative facility of the
later rhetoric. Earlier, West refused to listen to the jangling noise over
"liberty": his strict distinction between religion and politics would not
accommodate secular idioms. After the Revolution, however, not only
does West become more attuned to "this world," but as he takes the
longer view he joins the patriot consensus (perhaps his *pre*-Berkshire
Federalist phase), inserting the War within (to us) familiar ideological
matrices:

> Designs have long been forming and ripening in the British Court, un-
> friendly to Liberty and the rights of mankind; unfriendly to free in-
> quiry and the increase of knowledge; and, therefore, in that nature, un-
> propitious to the religion kingdom of Christ. The late revolution has
> given a blow to these designs, which it is to be hoped that they will
> never recover. The snare broken—we escaped.[44]

The passage reverberates with intertextual echoes of Paine and Mayhew;
"rights of mankind" is re-presented, removed from an apocalyptic time-

table and refashioned to support the logic of rebellion as described by Bernard Bailyn. To be sure, West probably did not imbibe a Whig rhetoric of liberty through a conversion experience to the softer theology of a Mayhew, nor would he ever espouse the rebellious implications of Paine's insurgent (literary) style. However, West did stray long enough from his metaphysical chamber to breathe in the currents of eighteenth-century political culture; to demand a discrete *source* for his new tone (was he perhaps re-reading Mayhew in 1783?) overlooks the multi-vocal aspect of eighteenth-century discourse. Indeed, the example of Stephen West may offer the richest, clearest case study of the dynamic interaction of religious and political languages in the revolutionary pulpit.

5

The Rationalist Vision:
The Example of
Samuel Cooper of Boston

The four preceding case studies of ministerial rhetoric and revolutionary history amount to a collective portrait of the evangelical mentality drawn from the pulpit visions of those rural congregational clergymen who identified with the New Divinity style—in both theological doctrine and sermonic message—fashioned from the charismatic aura and legacy of Jonathan Edwards and Joseph Bellamy. Together, the studies follow the ministers' uneasy transition from private speculation to the problematic world of politics as they mounted the public platform and spoke to their audience of the hopeful course of events and voiced their anxious prayers for the direction of the country's millennial future. What is perhaps most striking about the evangelical response to war (and social discord in general) is the profound filial claims that the mother country exacted on her "dependent" progeny, the psychological weight of England as the astonished and injured parent in the face of American rebellion. Even the most ardent of patriot clergy could not, without much psychic and textual labor, embrace absolutely the cause of the colonies against the nurturing parent.[1] Above all else, the evangelical mind struggled to reconcile, or justify, its guilty desire to break free from the burdens of cultural and political authority by the effort to tell its own story, to narrate its own history. That struggle, I suggest, is inscribed in the often fragmentary jottings, the rhetorical shiftings and turnings characteristic of so much ministerial discourse.

The issue of cultural identification with England is important, especially for the last profile in revolutionary commitment, the Reverend

113

Samuel Cooper of Boston. I conclude with the example of Cooper for he offers a telling contrast to the array of Congregationalist spokesmen assembled above. Minister to the affluent Brattle Street Church, Cooper was virtually hand-picked by its famous leader Benjamin Colman (after William Cooper, Samuel's father and Colman's co-pastor, died in December 1743) as heir apparent to the prestigious pulpit. By all accounts, Cooper is probably the most familiar figure in this clerical canvas, easily the most significant and influential minister at the hub of Boston's Whig resistance during the Revolution. We learn from his Harvard biographer that "it was a standing joke for two decades that Dr. Cooper neglected his pulpit for politics"—Cooper, that is, chose to agitate for independence from behind the scene, in various covert political maneuvers, rather than from the Brattle Street podium. Indeed, Cooper's most recent biographer tells us that "Unlike the noisy patriot preachers, the Brattle Street pastor kept his pulpit free of political controversy."[2] (Of course the manuscript evidence shows, among other things, that patriot preachers were more self-conscious and hesitant than noisy when it came to pulpit practice.) We are told, moreover, that Cooper "left behind no inflammatory printed sermons"; nevertheless he remains, in Nathan Hatch's formulation, a "clerical colleague in Boston radicalism." Even Richard Bushman, in his recent study of political ideology in revolutionary Massachusetts, speaks of Cooper (along with the more well-known liberal Calvinist, Jonathan Mayhew) as a "well-placed, articulate spokes[man] who argued libertarian causes not as an incidental, but as a central theme of [his life]."[3] This final patriot portrait places Cooper among his more noisy evangelical brethren and describes his sermonic output in light of the preaching habits of the New Divinity.

As an urban-based minister to an upper-class congregation Cooper resembles perfectly the moderate Old Light intellectual of Alan Heimert's taxonomy—the liberal Protestant who proved less zealous for the Revolution than the fiery heirs of Jonathan Edwards.[4] (Cooper, in this respect, is a younger version of Charles Chauncy, at whose Old Brick Church Cooper was often invited to preach.) Heimert, however, did not invent the figure of Cooper as lukewarm; nor has recent scholarship dispelled early accounts which assert how "Brattle street men were charmed into the ways of wisdom by the eloquent, the graceful Doctor Samuel Cooper." Even John Adams, who rarely refrained from announcing a point of view, remarked in his Diary:

> The Doctor's air and action are not graceful; they are not natural and
> easy. His motions with his head, body, and hands, are a little stiff and

affected; his style is not simple enough for the pulpit; it is too flowery, too figurative.[5]

Most recently, Akers, deferring to the authority of previous judgment, speaks of Cooper's "self-image as a man of peace," "the bland orthodoxy of his pragmatic Calvinism," and "his soothing ministry of reassurance." In short, Samuel Cooper of Brattle Street remained at ease with his "undemanding and unexamined Calvinism," a model Old Light who "had no patience with Jonathan Edwards."[6]

But rather than abstracting Cooper as an exemplary liberal preacher, it is more instructive if we view him as an intellectual who joined with his fellow Protestant ministers of varying shades of Calvinism in explaining the course of events to his people. Cooper may not have been as "fiery" as, for instance, New Light Philemon Robbins, nor did Cooper, from his urban (and then, during the siege of Boston, displaced) seat dwell obsessively on the apocalyptic import of contemporary history, as did Berkshire oligarch Stephen West, nor is Cooper's Diary filled with the manic musings over the collective fate of the country, as is Levi Hart's, nor did he revoice the rhetoric of the Great Awakening as a mode of interpretation, as did Jonathan Edwards, Jr. Despite these clear differences in theological style and temperament, however, Cooper's revolutionary stance proves more similar than distinct in comparison to his evangelical cohort; with them, Cooper struggled in his preaching toward what might be called linguistic-rhetorical autonomy—an effort to utter safely, to name without verbal indirection, the agent of New England's current afflictions.

What is distinctive about Cooper's revolutionary pulpit is his habit of redelivering a number of earlier sermons penned during the Indian wars of the 1750s. "He dusted off his election sermon of 1756," Akers observes, "and repreached it," exchanging England for France as the latest form of colonial oppression. "With a change of only four manuscript pages," Akers continues, "he leaped the twenty years from the Anglo-French war, when colonials clung desperately for protection to the skirts of mother Britain, to the glorious day of independence, when he could proclaim to heaven the justice and righteousness of repudiating that same mother country."[7] But a careful scrutiny of Cooper's manuscript sermons yields an alternative reading: the strategy of political repudiation proved to be a risky venture; indeed, it turns out that the habit of geographic substitution (England for France) was not Cooper's revisionary method. Rather than textual exchange, the evidence of Cooper's manuscript sermons discloses the psychic burdens shared by virtually all patriot orators on the eve of and during the Revolution. In Richard Bushman's succinct formulation: "Before Massachusetts could declare its independence and form a republic, the imposing moral authority of the monarch had to be encountered and overcome."[8] The rhetoric of Samuel Cooper offers a rich, revealing testament to one minister's effort to overcome the weight of cultural authority.

Before discussing Cooper's preaching record, we should keep in mind that the theologically liberal world of the Brattle Street Church provides an important context for Cooper's preaching, especially at the outset of his career. Formed by a group of wealthy merchants who sought a less doctrinally rigorous atmosphere in which to pursue their economic interests, the Brattle Street Church had been led for years by Colman, whom they had virtually appointed.[9] A decade before Cooper assumed full pastoral duties, Colman had been a sympathetic recipient to an account of revival in western Massachusetts as narrated by Jonathan Edwards in his famous letter describing the surprising conversions at Northampton. The Great Awakening of the early 1740s had little impact on Brattle Street; on his second tour through New England Whitefield was banned from most Boston pulpits for denouncing the "dead" men at Harvard who preached a "dead" religion. In response to the fractious effects of the Awakening in Boston, Cooper elected to attend his father's congregation. (Interestingly, in this respect, Cooper's older brother William seems to have been more evangelically minded, at least in the pages of his manuscript Diary, which read like any number of New Light diaries of the early to mid-eighteenth century. For Samuel's revolutionary Diary see below.)[10] Perhaps this is why the aged Colman assumed that young Samuel would join him after his co-pastor died (December 1743).

Cooper spent a year after his father's death apprenticing under Colman and continuing his education at Harvard. One of his earliest extant sermons belongs to this early phase, when he preached from Luke on the parable of Lazarus and the rich man before the Brattle Street congregation. Delivered a year after the elder Cooper's death, Samuel inscribed on the sermon's opening page, "Preach'ed at Dr. Coleman's on probation," which suggests that the acknowledged heir to Colman's office had been invited to show off (so to speak) his sermonic stuff before his future audience. And what did the fledgling preacher of nineteen have to say about the parable, which concerns the lamentations of a rich man who, after he dies, bewails his earthly hard-heartedness from amidst the fires of Hell? As the revival flames died away, in Boston and elsewhere in New England, Cooper admonished his wealthy auditors, "a person that has pass'd his days in sensuality here, and goes out of the World surfeited with earthly Enjoyments, can have no Relish for the Entertainments of Heaven." Of course the young preacher retreated (early in the sermon) with respect to material acquisition per se; "our Lord did not blame this man ['the man clothed in purple & fine linen' of the parable] for being rich; nor for dessing well, and faring deliciously—those things being proportioned to his Rank and Fortunes." Indeed, Cooper reasons, "there was no sin in all this." Still, the rich man's sin amounted to a failure of compassion; "feeling no want of his own, he could/would [?] not learn to feel for others."[11]

Beginning with the theme of the hardened soul deaf to the entreaties of poor Lazarus, Cooper's "probation" sermon attempts to sketch the sinner's psychic and physical state from within the regions of Hell—his own effort at brimstone rhetoric made (in)famous during the Awakening. His rhetorical and literary achievements, we should note, pale before the lurid representations of Jonathan Edwards; Cooper struggled to an Edwardsean rendering of "sensible" hellfire, but his effort falls short of sulfurous preaching. "As fire is of all the most active nature in itself," Cooper observes, "and produces in us the most terrible sensations, Nothing, it seems, can give a more lively and striking representation of the torments of hell"—except, perhaps, the memorable scene in Nathan Cole's conversion narrative, where the curious would-be sinner inserts his finger into a glowing pipe to see how long the mortal body can tolerate the heat of tobacco embers. This is the characteristic revivalist trope expressive of what Perry Miller called the rhetoric of sensation.

The point, of course, is not to compare the nineteen-year-old orator to the figure of Edwards the hellfire artist but to note that, despite the denominational leveling effects of the Revolution later in the century, there *are* substantive differences, theological and rhetorical, between the New Lights and moderate Calvinists.[12] Cooper summons the image of the rich man in agony, pleading with the once-spurned Lazarus to "dip the tip of his finger in water & cool my tongue"—at this moment Cooper demonstrates considerable rhetorical skill in this apprentice sermon—to gently remind Brattle Street that riches in this life can lead to despair, hardness of heart, and a tragic reversal of fortune in the afterlife. Yet God did not condemn the rich; He afflicts all those who lack compassion. The Brattle Street Church was gathered, after all, to hear just such mild excoriations; neophyte preacher that he was, about to don his father's ministerial mantle, Cooper simply told his audience what they wanted to hear.[13] A decade later, however, Cooper would mount the pulpit with complete authority (Colman died in 1747) to perform the more urgent and timely office of explaining and interpreting the meaning and judgment of the frontier Indian wars to those less physically exposed yet no doubt concerned parishioners of Boston.

The war sermons of the mid-1750s are crucial for locating Cooper's place in the pantheon of revolutionary ministers and gauging the impact of the Revolution on his literary-sermonic imagination, for as Akers, Hatch, and Buchanan have all noted, Cooper emerged twenty years later as perhaps the key clerical agitator for Independence in the urban crucible of Boston by revoicing the orations delivered a generation earlier. "Cooper repeated sermon after sermon first written and preached two decades earlier to arouse his hearers against the Gallic peril," Akers observes; "At most he added a few pages of adaptation to the new war." Thus the Indian wars amounted to "a spiritual preparation for the American Revolution."[14] But Cooper's habits of textual emendation and preaching additions for later contexts and audiences reveal a more psychologically complex process at work. Rather than considering the evidence of repreaching as Cooper's rehearsal for revolution (the reflexive reuttering of previous sermons does suggest, however, that Cooper's implicit cyclical view of the historical moment contrasts sharply with the Edwardsean progressivist vision inherited by the New Light revolutionaries), the revisionary process of the 1770s betrays the cultural anxiety, the keen self-consciousness shared by most clerical partisans of American liberty. In effect, the continuous textual layering characteristic of Cooper's revolutionary discourse does not issue simply in the substitution of England for France as the enemy (as in Akers's reading) but rather in the historical and psychic ambiguities of filial affection and parental judgment that caused conflicts among the patriot ministers throughout the struggle for Independence.

This alternative interpretation is illustrated by a reexamination of the textual proof Akers presents in his argument. In transcribing a key Fast sermon of July 1755, which Cooper repreached on another Fast Day occasion on August 8, 1777, Akers quotes from the original manuscript as follows:

> In time of profound Peace, and without the least provocation given on our part, our Territories have been treacherously invaded, by our inveterate and powerful Enemies . . . who seem to aim at Nothing less than dispossessing us of the fair Inheritance left us by our Fathers.[15]

What, we may ask, has been omitted by the ellipsis? For Akers, the passage presents the telling textual evidence of Cooper's repeatedly "applicable" vision: *we* are meant, that is, to fill in the ellipsis (Akers's, not Cooper's) with the political and geographical entity "England," as a sign of Cooper's substituting impulse. But no such substitution or erasure takes place in the manuscript itself; in fact, Akers's ellipsis leaves out Cooper's *un*canceled phrase, "the French"—there is no textual proof that in public delivery Cooper substituted England for France as the latest form of treachery to the nation. Indeed, the same sermon 'blesses . . . our gracious King & his ministers; that they have already afforded as such seasonable & powerful success: so that we are not like to feel the whole of that force which was sent from France to be employed again" and then admonishes against "a vain confidence in our own power and a neglect of God & his Providence. This is what we are in great Danger of: and a Temper which I am afraid too much prevails in the British Nation."[16]

Did Cooper leave "the French" in when repreaching a generation later? Did he omit the grateful nod to the British King? Did he orally replace "British Nation" with "American colonies" in rebuking the too easy confidence in human agency (both in 1755 and 1777)? Of course we can never know unequivocally what Cooper chose to revoice in August 1777; but the sustained, linear narrative of *all* his extant sermons suggests that Cooper rarely refashioned his manuscript pages (at least textually) to allow for ex tempore preaching (no fragments, private directives, and so on). Stylistically speaking, that is, Cooper was no New Light. There are, to be sure, a number of telling crossings out and substitutions (more on those later), but Akers's assertion that Cooper actually "exchanged" Britain for France in 1777 is belied by the evidence of the text.

We are left, therefore, not with a case of reflexive substitution but rather with the literary sign of ambiguity and our own retrospective supposition. To cite another example that inscribes this interpretive, indeed performative dilemma, did Cooper repeat *verbatim* a sermon of July 1758 (delivered again in 1762, 1776, and twice in 1780), which, after cautiously observing "Our hopes are still suspended upon future events," goes on to express the hesitant hope that "God has been pleased in former times to defend his British Israel against the proud attempts of their enemies"?[17] Would the epithet "his British Israel" have been seasonable in 1776 or 1780? Again, there is nothing to suggest that Cooper, except perhaps only at the very moment of delivery, revised his original text. My point, however, is not the issue of Cooper's patriotism, although

Akers himself avers that "even after the Tea Party . . . the Brattle Street pulpit did not resound with denunciations of British tyranny,"[18] but that historical actors like Samuel Cooper did not cross easily over the historical divide separating 1755 and the Revolution by some oratorical sleight of hand; instead, the break from England loomed as a kind of psychic taboo which for the most part could not be sermonically uttered. With Protestants of all Calvinist hues, Cooper's orations are filled with professions of colonial love and allegiance; they remain indelible sermonic traces of longstanding filiation that could not be blotted out—not even, it seems, after Independence.

From this perspective, the various and subtle complexities of Cooper's revolutionary mentality are most evocatively described in his major fast sermon of April 1754 and repreached in 1759, 1768 (with an addition occasioned "upon the coming of the troops"), and in early and mid-1777. The sermon stands apart, not only for its uncharacteristic typological opening (uncharacteristic, that is, within the span of Cooper's performances) but for the telling textual emendations that enable us to follow the revising impulse which opens up the mental world of the rational minister. Through the sermonic layering and the movement of the preacher's shifting visions, we can observe, in effect, how the Old Light mind of Samuel Cooper swayed alternately between spiritual and historical vistas, otherworldly and social realms, as he sought to accommodate the text of 1777 to the context of former times.

After considering the duties and obligations of pious magistrates whose generous political character will be met with "ardent affections" and "have all due respect & veneration return'd 'em by a religious people," the sermon moves quickly to Cooper's vision of the fruits of such a "happy" community where "internal Disorder & Confusion is banish't." In this economic paradise, "commerse . . . must be freed of a Thousand Encumbrances with which it is now clogged"; indeed, "when religion prevails," Cooper explained in 1754, "industry also flourish[es]." But when a society betrays the religious ideal, what follows is a kind of social entropy, the Brattle Street nightmare of the spiritual–economic void: "Without [religion] communities must languish & decay, and finally come to nothing."[19]

The rhetoric, of course, highlights the laissez-faire assumptions of Cooper's audience; and in this respect we might say that Cooper's cautionary tones of 1754 were a direct response to and reflection of Brattle Street ideology. Even the invocation of biblical parallels—the conditional promises of assurance God made to his ancient people—serves not to locate the congregation within the unfolding spiral of redemptive history but to give historical weight to the minister's complementary vision of property, prosperity, and piety. The very flow of the preacher's narrative confirms the course of God's designs: "They were led victorious into the land of Canaan; success attended their armies wherever they came, and they took possession of wells which they had not digged, of Houses which they did not built, and of vineyards which they had not planted." Still, in 1754 Cooper sought to challenge the creeping complacency of his congregation, their too easy enjoyment of prosperity through un-earned virtue. Instead of guaranteeing the future, Cooper announced, in a passage later bracketed by the preacher himself as the essence of his message: "that we enjoy peace now is no argument that we shall enjoy it long; if our affairs should be prosperous & happy at present, this gives us no security against a melancholy change." Thus in its first phase the sermon moves from the social reflections of collective piety to the opaque realm of determining God's providences. "Futurity is dark," Cooper warned, "& the Events of it are hid from us by a cloud impene-trable to mortal eyes."[20]

In repreaching the Fast sermon to the troops fourteen years later, Cooper added a long section that builds on the ambiguities of temporal history announced toward the close of the 1754 performance. On this political–military occasion Cooper's rhetoric shifts to what Jackson Cope has styled the "incantatory mode" characteristic of Quaker preaching: in Cooper's example, "It is indeed Time, my hearers, it is high Time, for us to be earnestly engag'd in this Search to seek the Lord."[21] The incan-tatory tone of 1768 highlights a psychic landscape marked by the con-tingencies of shrouded prophecy and the neglect of proper filiation:

It is indeed Time, my Hearers, it is high Time, for us to be earnestly engag'd in this Search. Are we affected with the Darkness and Per-plexity, in which the Affairs of our Nation, of British America, are at this Day involved? Do we regard with deep Concern the Cloud that hangs over us; Do we notice the Blessings of that Political Constitution which has so long been the glory of our nation, the admiration of its Neighbors, & the envy of its Enemies. Are we sollicitous, not only to enjoy these Blessings ourselves in their full extent but to transmit them undiminish'd to Posterity as the fairest Inheritance they can possess this side [of] Heaven of a temporal nature, that we can bequeath.

Note the sequence of interrogative refrains ("Are we . . . ; "Do we . . .") which moves the speaker from the realm of providential shadows to the collective rebuke embedded in the tradition of British liberty. Note, too, the mutually sustaining rhetorical and political merger

of Britain and America in Cooper's imagination. "The interests of G. Britain & their colonies is really one," Cooper reminded his 1768 audience
toward the close; "Let us directly implore the divine Blessing on our
Sovereign; on the British Nation; & that large part of it that is now
planted on this western continent."[22] Even after the unsettling imposi-
tion of the Stamp Act Cooper could perceive in 1768 no moral or spiritual disjunction between the British nation and her planted colonies,
claims of allegiance and affection bonded Britain and America. The
apocalyptic clouds that perplexed the nation in 1768 would be dispelled
if America acknowledged her rightful (political) inheritance.

By 1777, however, Cooper's final preaching revisions dramatically reveal the change of heart, the affective shift, in his own historical imagination. A small leaf tipped in as the penultimate page of the bound sermon pamphlet voices the hopes and anxieties of the transitional moment.
"We all, I trust are disposed to cultivate this union," Cooper prayed
(here I believe Cooper means the newly autonomous "this governement
& the United States" to which he refers in another addition to the 1754
sermon); "we esteem it our honor & Felicity, to be a part of the greatest
and freest Nation upon Earth. We only wish & pray, that our Brethren
in ~~Britain~~ separated from us by the ocean would cherish a fellow
feeling for us; and allow us to enjoy those Rights of such they justly
boast . . ." Cooper's astonishing syntactic circumlocution—the erasure
of Britain—amounts to the rhetorical correlative to the psychology of
repression and displacement which so often affected the generation of
patriot ministers who, faced with the accusation of rebellion, could not
utter that taboo sign of their cultural dependence, "Britain." (Recall,
in this respect, the textual swervings of Jonathan Edwards, Jr.) Cooper,
it would seem, could not directly acknowledge the reality of separation,
both psychic and geographic; he could hope, at the end, "by the im-
mutable Rule of Equity," that America be granted her "Rights . . .
constituted by human compact."

Still, Cooper closed his last occasional emendations of 1777 with a
series of behavioral injunctions that portray, by their very *inclusion,*
what had been dangerously imperiled by the Revolution:

> In every step we may take for the Preservations of these Rights, may
> we be calm, prudent, & steady & united [inserted later by Cooper] loyal
> to our Sovereign, obedient to our God, & observant of his will, & con-
> fiding in his care & Protection. Then we may upon the best grounds
> commit our cause to Heaven.

Thus do Cooper's social prescriptions register the social discord unleashed by the Revolution, at least in the imagination of the liberal Protestant clergy. Let us be "calm, prudent, steady"—and, perhaps as an immediate afterthought to the cautious litany of urgent directives that needed voicing, especially in 1777, the preacher inserted "united," the communal hope devoutly to be wished in the face of political rupture. In the wake of the Declaration, Cooper called for obedience and loyalty; he wished, above all else, that Britain still "would cherish a fellow feeling for us"[23]—a poignant evocation of the affective costs of overturning authority.

Another revision in the 1754 sermon links its original typological stance with the series of behavioral cautions appended later in 1777. Speaking of God's relation to his chosen people during their wilderness trials, Cooper recalls that God "treated them in a manner exactly answerable to those solemn Declarations. For after they had ~~in a good measure~~ repented of their ~~rebellious~~ undutiful behavior in the wilderness; and were reduced to a better Temper & conduct; They were led victorious into the Land of Canaan." It is impossible, of course, to determine when Cooper translated "rebellious" into "undutiful behavior" (most likely at the time of composition and not at a later moment of repreaching), but the conscious effort to soften the social implications of "rebellious" to a function of more proper modes of communal conduct—indeed, to speak of the Israelites' necessary *reduction* "to a better temper," or temperament, bespeaks (again) the need to deflect, to displace social fractiousness with a less challenging stance toward authority. Cooper's habit of literary circumlocution thus reached a logical (and necessary) fulfillment when he exchanged "rebellious" with "undutiful" and crossed out "Britain" for the psychologically safer indirection of "brethren separated from us by the ocean."[24]

From this perspective, Cooper's practice of repreaching sermons during the revolutionary era complicates the view that he read the Indian Wars of the 1750s as a "spiritual preparation" for the Revolution; instead, the layers of textual additions and revisions limn the clerical mind in process, not simply as a reapplication of an original vision to a later historical event but rather as a rhetorical effort to bridge the separate moments and *impose* historical continuity in the face of political rupture and spiritual–geographic chasm. The summons to union and obedience, the call for a proper temper, the habit of textual swerving from the literary signs of authority betray Cooper's uneasy response to history perceived, to recall his vision of the economic void, entropically spinning toward "decay, and finally come to nothing." Cooper, we might say, joined in the collective effort to resist decline by advocating a behavioral approach to the problem of piety and prosperity.

Yet he could never sanction unbridled rebellion, as the textual blotting out vividly shows; Cooper was not, contrary to Akers, "an early and fervent advocate of separation from Britain."[25] When he returned to his sermon file during the Revolution, searching for seasonable subjects for the momentous times, he continued to speak of the colony's stance toward the mother country "with Hearts truely loyal, & affections entirely British"; indeed, the trans-Atlantic allegiance continued to be "formed by affection, & not merely a forced submission." Again, it is not clear from the surviving text whether Cooper included such formulaic gestures in his 1777 and 1782 repreachings; in one instance Cooper replaced "the British nation" with "our nation" in revoicing a Thanksgiving sermon of November 1757 "thro all the States" in 1782.[26] In general, however, Cooper was less fervent in espousing the cause of liberty when drawing upon previous sermons; only when Cooper *abandoned* the habit of sermonic rummaging did his rhetoric, now unmoored from the constraints of earlier contexts, answer to the challenge of revolutionary events. Still, Cooper's pulpit did pour out what Akers calls a "soothing ministry of reassurance," but the Brattle Street minister's assauging message for 1776 was neverthless tinged with worry, as Cooper himself expressed in the voice of David, the biblical poet whose psalms ring with "the language of mournfull Israelites in their Captivity," the faithful shepherd who lamented, "How can we sing the Lord's songs in a strange Land?"[27] The American Revolution displaced a pious generation of ministers who sang of a strange, unfamiliar, transfigured territory where human will and reason no longer seemed accountable to the ways of Providence.

Throughout 1776, Cooper preached on the subject of human agency and divine order from various Boston area pulpits, including those of Charles Chauncy and the genteel Mather Byles. British troops occupied the capital between 1775 and 1776, and while in exile from Brattle Street Cooper received invitations from a host of surrounding churches and kept a Diary of his daily activities. Cooper's Diary, it should be noted, contrasts sharply with the evangelical style of private inscription in, for instance, the example of Philemon Robbins or Levi Hart. There are no extended meditations on the spiritual state of the soul, no anguished, ejaculatory private summonses to humiliation or self-denial, no (as in the case of Hart) speculations on the uncertain fate of the besieged country. Except for a usually brief allusion to dates and text of a delivered sermon, Cooper refrains from any commentary on the moral or political scene he recorded from the margins of Boston. The following excerpt, dated March 26, 1776, on reentering Boston, two weeks before he returned to Brattle Street, is wholly representative: "a melancholy scene. Many houses pull'd down by the British Soldiery. The shops all shut. Marks of Rapine & Plunder ev'ry where. We din'd at Dr. Bullfinch's."[28]

I cite this passage not to indict Cooper for his seeming indifference to the ravages of military occupation, the ease with which he juxtaposes a scene of urban ravishment with the aloof shift to dining. The entry is striking because Cooper's steady stream of laconic, private reactions to the state of siege in Boston is belied by the often powerful, riveting performances of the same period when he preached, throughout 1776, of the uncertainty of events and the limits of human agency.

In public, we might say, Cooper voiced what his audience expected to hear—"the way of man is not in himself"—yet privately, in the back rooms where Sam Adams dwelled, the question of political agency and strategy must have loomed with ultimate significance. "Our hopes," Cooper intoned in December 1776, "are suspended upon future events." The phrase itself sounds with the open-ended, rhetorically subjunctive mood of the revolutionary pulpit. With other patriot clergy, Cooper ritually invoked the example of Israel to his Brattle congregation: "Everyone knows . . . in how wonderful a manner [God] delivered the Children of Israel out of the House of Bondage in Egypt: by what miracle of mercy he secur'd the passage of his own people . . . & succor those who stand up for the Freedom of their country & acquit themselves well in so noble a cause."[29] First the assumption of a shared history (biblical and secular) and then the multivocal overtones of "passage," which build on the ambiguities of "own People" and "their country"—effecting a rhetorical bridge between biblical promises and future prophecies, "suspended upon future events" yet unfulfilled.

Cooper's revolutionary rhetoric *relies* on the multiplicity of applications, despite the preacher's continual hedging tone, his refusal to assume the mantle of the prophet (in this respect Cooper again differs only *in degree* from his evangelical cohort). Only God, Cooper explained in a memorable phrase (preached some seven times in 1776) "is himself without any variableness or shadow of turning."[30] Only God's light is historically enabling, illuminating the true design of things. During the Revolution it was the preachers' oracular office to acknowledge their limited perspective yet rhetorically ease the passage through temporal ambiguities. "I cannot presume to say," Cooper reflected, but "that the present aspect of divine providence towards us, & the mixture of Light & shade in the complexion of our affairs, call for our very serious attention." The Black Regiment was perhaps the most attentive to the shifting mixtures of shadow and light in the at times obscure, at times lucid historical atmosphere (both sacred and secular) enveloping late eighteenth-century New England. To discover the pattern was the obligation of the preacher to his audience, yet "the *way* of man," (emphasis added), as Cooper cautioned through the year of Independence, "is not in himself."[31]

What, then, was Cooper's message from exile in 1776? God, he exhorted, is *invariable* in his ways; he exhibits no ambiguous shadows in his providential turnings, his "various dispensations are all ordered." Man, however, lives according to the shifting temporal rhythms as sounded in the Book of Ecclesiastes, whose contrapuntal movement Cooper appropriates for his own verbal uses in a key sermon based on Psalms 31:13 (preached, by the way, at Chauncy's Old Brick Church in July 1776). Even though it has been described as "entirely spiritual and containing no reference to public affairs," the sermon nonetheless refracts the edgy political scene of occupied Boston. "There is a time to weep," Cooper intones, "& a time to laugh; a time to mourn, & a time to dance; a time to get, & a time to loose. . . . Now we are in peace & security; and presently we are alarm'd with some threatening Danger, Now it is a time of Darkness; by & by the Day breaks & the shadows flee away; Now we are in sorrow [?], Fear, & Distress; and now we are rescued from the Danger, and the voice of Salvation is heard in our Dwellings."[32] To look for, or assume, that the minister would announce *specific* dangers, or renarrate the successive acts of recent colonial infringements, is to *overlook* those rhetorical overtones that evoke a precise mental world: the uncertain, besieged atmosphere of Boston in the spring of 1776. The rhythms of Ecclesiastes shift at the verbal transition "presently," which highlights contemporary affairs as the phrase translates the speaker from the Old Testament to 1776 ("Now we are . . . now we are . . ." Note, too, how the phrases "Now it is a time of Darkness" takes on a greater temporal urgency after the audible breakdown in the biblical cadence. In this respect, Cooper's ritually hopeful vision of fleeing shadows, unveiling, "*by & by*," the true destiny of things reflects the processual movement of the rhetoric itself as well as the preacher's sanctioned office as "the voice of salvation" prophetically sounding in "our dwelling." "By & by" is the rhetorical utterance linking those "hopes . . . suspended upon future events" with the unfolding movement of redemptive history.

For most patriot preachers future events were shrouded by the obscuring shadows, the foreboding clouds of contingency; or else (as in the example of Robbins) the providential course was difficult to steer against the variable, shifting winds. Still, the clergy labored to effect the passage through tumultuous history by encouraging and rebuking their audiences at the same time. Although Samuel Cooper emerges in this collective portrait as less temperamentally inclined to rouse through apocalyptic fear and trembling than, for example, Stephen West, he understood profoundly the psalmic injunction, "Rejoice with trembling": "For when our fear, united with joy, has carried us safe thro this state of tryal, it will have done its office." Cooper's gloss may stand as the literary and cultural formula by which the rhetorical blending of hope and anxiety—or as Sacvan Bercovitch describes this ritual process, hope *through* anxiety—helped effect the "safe" historical passage through a revolutionary "state of tryal."[33]

Still, Cooper's rhetoric never reached the impassioned nay-saying of Robbins or Edwards the Younger. For all his revolutionary zeal, especially in the few directly occasional sermons penned in 1777 and 1778 (a "rare exertion," according to Akers), Cooper could never preach a full-scale rhetoric of Antichrist; nowhere in Cooper do we find (as in Robbins) Britain luridly styled "murderous, tyrannical, cruel"; nor does Cooper ever exhibit the often vivid biblical imagination of those evangelicals who *explored* (again, as in Robbins) the typological levels of Old Testament figures and the plight of New England, blurring sacred and secular history in the process of public exegesis; nor is there ever in Cooper a call for a revival of religion to avert divine judgment (given Cooper's rejection of Edwards this observation is hardly surprising).[34] More important, Cooper's narrative *never* swerves syntactically; the manuscript evidence reveals a number of suggestive crossings out and substitutions, but throughout the whole corpus of Cooper's surviving sermonic output there are no signs of arrested narrative, no linear lapses into fragment, no extended catalogues or litanies.

But perhaps the most ironic difference between the Boston rationalist and his evangelical brethren is the striking disjunction between what Akers calls his "clandestine political ventures" and his restrained pulpit exertions.[35] For, despite Cooper's infamous role amidst Whig politicians (made infamous by Peter Oliver and other Loyalist observers) there is less of a sense of palpable *engagement* with the world of revolutionary Boston in Cooper than in the New Divinity men laboring in the rural backwaters. This is not to say that the Brattle Street minister should be ranked with the so-called otherworldly figures in Ezra Stiles's pantheon; one of the points of this study is that the rhetoric of even the most seemingly "abstracted" preacher in eighteenth-century New England (for instance, Stephen West of Stockbridge) opens up the mentality of the revolutionary times.

Indeed, the urban liberal shares more with his clerical colleague to the west than we might suppose. When called upon to mediate the experience of the Revolution to their congregations, both West and Cooper turned to Isaiah 26 and the beckoning spiritual chambers of safety proffered by the Lord. "In times of Danger & Distress," Cooper explained, in reaction to "An alarm of the Enemies['] Fleet on our coasts," "The ordinances of religion afford us a safe & happy re-treat." With Parson West of Stockbridge Cooper offered the Covenant of Grace as "the true ark to a world delug'd in Sin" and as a haven "from all the Evils of the present state." In preaching *to* the events of the Revolution, that is, Cooper emerges as more spiritually absorbed in pulpit vision, atemporal in sermonic context than the New Lights. Yet Cooper's originally composed occasional sermons of the revolutionary era, the literary evidence for his political stance during the crisis, unveils a mentality markedly *similar* to that of the evangelicals: anxiety over the recurrent charge (by the mother country) of rebellion; the ambiguities of human agency in the face of providential design; the need for piety and prayer in response to the uncertainty of events—these are some of the shared themes that reverberate, across denominational lines in the revolutionary pulpit. Cooper may not have been the "high priest to the new Israel whose spiritual capital was Boston"—Cooper's rhetoric is not, for the most part, laced with seasonable Old Testament exegesis—but his rhetoric *did* rise to the challenge of the times when, toward the end of his career, he decided not to repreach earlier sermons but, instead, to write firsthand meditations on the meaning of the Revolution.[36]

The decision not to dust off a Fast sermon from the 1750s is crucial, for the refrain from pastoral rummaging suggests that at key moments in the wake of Independence the times demanded their own narrative; unprecedented events compelled the orator to carve out new words, to give shape to *original* history. Compared to the almost inflexible narrative line of earlier sermons, these late compositions are filled with a nervous, agitated rhetoric—sequence after sequence of tonic phrasings and litanies, an almost obsessive habit of repetition. Listen, for example, to a portion of a sermon untitled by either occasion or biblical text, and prepared around 1778:

And what reason have we to adore the Goodness of our God and to celebrate it with our warmest Praises & Thanksgivings in the course of the present important content. a contest not for Trifles, not for insignificant Forms of State; not for uninteresting modes of conducting public affairs; but for those Rights that are the Foundation & Security of all civil Happiness; and without which all other temporal Blessings are given in vain. In vain do we enjoy a fruitful soil; in vain do we possess all advantages for an extended commerce.[37]

Or the following mildly apocalyptic vision, which recalls the language of New Light Philemon Robbins:

There is no other way to secure the Favor of him who governs the world, and we shall sooner or later be convinced of this. In vain is Salvation hoped for from the Hills & from the multitude of mountains—From this & from that Quarter we look for it in vain, if Heaven is affronted by us, and provoked by our sins to go on in distributing Sorrows to us—at such a Day as the present we ought indeed to guard against that Fear of Man that bringeth a Snare; that Trepidation of mind, that betrays the succors of Reason, & renders us incapable of performing to advantage the most important Duties to which we are called . . . But this implies Religion and the Fear of God, without which we have no solid support, no ark to stay us when the Rains descend, when the Floods come, & when the winds blow. If the Judgments of Heaven do not teach us Righteousness, they will roll on in such a Succession as to appall us at last, and leave us destitute of all Tranquility & Happiness.[38]

Or consider, finally, this passage linking Israel with America, after the surrender in 1777 of General Burgoyne:

There is no People whose circumstances of Settlement in the common course of divine Providence more nearly resemble those of the Israelites when they were conducted by a divine hand to canaan, than these States, & particularly, the N. England ones insomuch that a great Number of Passages in holy Writ, that have their Foundation in the state & condition of that People, may with a surprizing Propriety be adopted by ourselves; and seem as if they had been dictated with a particular view to our own circumstances. . . Like the Israelites our Fathers were led by remarkable Dispensations of divine Providence from civil & religious Tyranny, to a distant land, a goodly Heritage, where they might have Liberty to serve the God of Israel, according to what they judg'd his own appointed [?]. Like them, when they were few in Numbers, very few, & Strangers in the Land they were wonderfully ~~defended~~

preserved. Like them ~~they~~ we have surprizingly increas'd and multi-
plied in a short space of Time. Like them we have been constantly
surrounded with Enemies & in Dangers & Battles. Like them we have
been hated & despis'd by many for our Ecclesiastical & civil constitution. Like them, we have been remarkably secur'd in imminent Danger,
and supported in hard & unequal contests. Instances of this favor are
too many to be easily reckon'd up; and some of them are too recent &
important not to arrest our attention & employ our Thots.[39]

Instead of revoicing the Indian war sermons Cooper chose to engage
the historical moment; in the process, his rhetoric became *more* biblically textured, more resonant. Finding no antecedent occasion in his
drawer of sermons Cooper virtually *discovered* the verbal powers of
the evangelical preaching mode. Note, for example, the incantatory repetition of "Like them, when there were few in number, very few," or how
the key substitution of "we" for "they" inaugurates the tonic repetitions
that follow, or how the pronoun exchange foreshortens the spatial–historical distance between the example of Israel and Cooper's audience—
indeed, that verbal move symbolizes the most important rhetorical transition of the revolutionary clergy: the blurring of Old Testament exemplum
with contemporaneous fulfillment, in the process of historical identification, from "they" to "we."

In general, then, the figural language and landscape of biblical proph-
esy fill these originally penned late orations with texts drawn from the
Books of Ezekiel, Isaiah, and Revelation; even the figure of Washington
is elevated to mythic status (with every patriot preacher Cooper prayed
that "the important Life of this distinguished Leader [be] preserv'd by
a gracious providence"); and as for England, Cooper can now paint
a vivid portrait of the mother country "disheartened & disconcerted . . .
staggering under their own fruitless exertions against us alone, they
tremble at the apprehension of an European as well as American War."
Britain now can at last be named, although still indirectly; by 1778 Cooper prayed "that we may no more be at the mercy of a Nation and monarch whose tender mercies have been to us cruel." Thus did Cooper's
rhetoric achieve the verbal autonomy (and daring) to accuse; the ability
to imaginatively dissociate from Britain coincided with the *fact* of political rupture. It is as if Cooper's direct, textually *unmediated* encounter
with the meaning of the Revolution stirred his pulpit abilities, compelling him to straddle the historical divide "suspended upon future events"
(to recall the language of an earlier sermon). Rhetorically filling that
metaphysical void, Cooper's later sermons effect the passage "of these
infant states, brot up in a state of dependence" into collective selfhood.

For a time in 1777 and 1778, Cooper could no longer adapt past explanatory efforts; recent "instances" were too "important not to merit our attention"; history was not to be so "easily reckon'd up."[40]

Thus in response to the political and domestic crisis wrought by the Revolution, Cooper discovered a way to encounter and overcome the moral authority of the monarch (to paraphrase Bushman) in the rhetorical strategies of the New Light pulpit. Of course temperamentally and, so be sure, doctrinally, the Brattle Street minister could never have aligned himself with his fiery brethren in the New England backwaters; but it seems clear, at least from the literary evidence, that Cooper's sermonic effort to accommodate civic upheaval publicly (as opposed to his various political maneuverings) issued in a rhetoric that reverberates with the familiar strains of the evangelical mode. Alan Heimert speaks, correctly, of the "rhetorical division" in preaching between Old Lights and New Lights during the Awakening; the liberals perhaps did mount their pulpits "for education rather than for exhortation." But the example of Samuel Cooper attests to the political and rhetorical—indeed, even at times *hieroglyphic*—leveling power of the Revolution.[41]

It is not surprising that Cooper, moderate Calvinist that he was, called for spiritual union in the face of social and moral threat; what is startling is that his collective injunction took the literary form of a crescendo of "the spirit that shall . . ." phrases (including a summons for a "spirit that shall lead to us to act as one for the advantage of the community which we are members" and "a spirit that shall make us more concerned for Godliness than Gain"), a style emblematic of the evangelical habit of mind. We may wonder in what "faith" Cooper uttered such anticommercial sentiments to a gathering of colonial merchants worried that the Revolution might subvert their livelihoods. Still, Cooper's rebuking challenge against worldly gain, his series of staccato "we" clauses voiced "in this trying day" (to cite yet another evangelical trace), his hopeful amazement at "the union of these states—an astonishing union all circumstances considered . . . an almost unexampled spirit & courage among the Body of the people to defend their Rights[42]— these formal and ideological aspects of Cooper's language represent the rhetorical currents of the evangelical pulpit which he imbibed in the rhetorically charged atmosphere of the Revolution. Again, I do not wish to blur the clear theological and temperamental differences between strict Calvinists and liberals, but the clear *rhetorical* affinities highlight how the Protestant clergy *collectively* rose to the domestic challenge with a language that met the demands of history.

Toward the end of one of his revolutionary litanies Cooper called for "a spirit that will warm every bosom with a steady, undaunted zeal at this important day in the service of God & our Generation."[43] Never inclined to incendiary discourse, not given to privately recording the wrenching overturnings of the self recorded in evangelical conversion narratives, Cooper could only speak of the affecting spiritual agency as "warm," "steady," with "undaunted zeal." Such moderate ejaculations characterize the generation of ministers his example is meant to represent. But such "lukewarm" sentiments did not prevent him from joining the good fight against perceived tyranny, even when the psychic costs of naming the betrayer of filial affection proved difficult to overcome.[44] By avoiding the sermonic rehearsals of the past and (instead) by emulating the rhetoric of the evangelical pulpit, Cooper discovered how he might overcome the moral authority of the monarch.

6

After the Revolution:
The Evangelical Imagination
Circa 1800

The case studies of rhetoric and history sketched here record the alternating rhythms of collective hesitancy and revolutionary summons that characterize the patriot pulpit during the American Revolution. The colonists' political timidity had manifold sources, as Bernard Bailyn explains, including their profound allegiance to Great Britain (with the dire psychic costs attendant on filial rupture always looming as a potent taboo). But their hesitancy to separate was fed above all else by a generalized anxiety about the course of future history that they, by severing political and affectionate ties with England, were themselves enacting. "Their future as an independent people was a matter of doubt," observes Bailyn about the political and psychic threshold of 1774; the colonists were "full of fear of the unknown."[1] From this perspective, the resounding rhetoric that issued week after week from local pulpits powerfully confirms Bailyn's vision of reluctant revolutionaries living through a transitional (and transforming) moment reflected in the loosening of social and religious sanctions constraining the self, a historical juncture that elevated the idea of individual agency (at times, and in places) to antinomian extremes. Of course by 1794 most evangelical clergymen had come to the tragic conclusion that the glorious example of the American Revolution had degenerated into the religious infidelity and political anarchy that followed in the wake of France's internal convulsions—tragically, for in its first republican fruits most New England ministers felt that the French Revolution represented the logical, indeed providential *continuation* of their own glorious cause against tyranny.[2] But by the end of the century the French Revolution had come to symbolize the religious and social threat posed by unfettered rationalist thought, and thus was to be invoked as a cautionary tale rehearsed over and again, especially from the politically charged pulpits of Federalist clergymen.

This final chapter is a portrait of the three preachers whose pastoral careers survived to the end of the eighteenth century and the beginning of the nineteenth. What did the sermons of Jonathan Edwards, Jr. (d. 1801), Levi Hart (d. 1808), and Stephen West (d. 1819) sound like after the Revolution? How do their respective pulpit concerns, political and spiritual, clarify or perhaps enrich the prevailing scholarly consensus—that by 1800 the religious authority of the minister in American culture had given way to the social authority of the politician; indeed, that "the politician," to quote James M. Banner, "played the role of secular preacher of the early republic."[3] It is a historical commonplace that "not a single divine appears from the rank of the Founders," but the purpose of this attempt at what might be called narrative closure is not an explanation of the clergy's "loss of esteem," their sense of "estrangement" after the Revolution, or an account of their "ambiguous relationship to the new politics" that preoccupied their secular counterparts.[4] Rather, I am concerned with how the ministerial imagination translated its experience of late eighteenth-century history to the people, and with how the clergy's pulpit visions mediated the often disturbing political realities of the new republic—the meaning of the Whiskey Rebellion, for example—in light of a complex rhetorical engagement with unfolding history a generation earlier.

Perhaps the most telling observation to make about the three figures is their energetic return to the doctrinal chamber after the war. In all three cases the majority of their published theological treatises issues from the 1780s and 1790s. In Edwards the Younger, all of his sixteen titles appeared, beginning with a 1784 reply to Charles Chauncy's long-awaited defense of universal salvation to Edwards's 1799 Farewell Sermon to his Colebrook, Connecticut congregation before assuming the presidency of Union College in upstate New York.[5] Levi Hart's key 1775 sermon on liberty was followed by silence until a veritable burst of theological writings in the late 1780s; in all, twelve of Hart's sixteen published items appeared after the war.[6] And Stephen West, who penned the most important work of the three (a 1772 treatise on moral agency which entered the jangling controversy among the Congregational clergy over Jonathan Edwards's *Freedom of the Will*), published eight of twelve works between 1785 and 1801.[7] Given these publication figures it seems clear that in some sense Edwards, Jr., Hart, and West *returned* from political to religious concerns by the 1780s, often resuming doctrinal battles set aside for the moment by the Revolution. In the case of Edwards, Jr., for example, his zeal to answer Chauncy may have led to his dismissal from White Haven church in 1795; at least one parishioner charged that the pastor had neglected his flock in the filial desire to take on his father's now aged controversalist[8] Yet it would be extreme to state absolutely that the patriot clergy fled to their metaphysical chambers a decade later, relinquishing the cultural turf (so to speak) to the country's ascendant leadership. For one thing, "ceremony, celebration, and sermon remained conspicuously alive" through the end of the eighteenth century and beyond;[9] and, more important, the ritual aspect of revolutionary discourse inhered in the politicians' creative appropriation of religious language, their recognition of the "actively residual" valences of ministerial rhetoric. "This language of national creation," as Robert Ferguson aptly styles the writings of Paine, Madison, and Jefferson, drew heavily on the imagination of the patriot clergy;[10] here, however, I wish to examine the other side of that cultural dialectic: how the once socially powerful generation of ministers accommodated their pulpits to the secular American world of the 1790s, another critical period in the formation of national identity.

In the example of Jonathan Edwards, Jr. we find a representative Federalist clergyman who perceived the threat of infidelity and insurrection both at home and abroad. Along with his fellow New Haven–area ministers Timothy Dwight (Edwards's nephew) and Jedidiah Morse, Edwards worried over the meaning of France for the new republic. As early as 1792—earlier, that is, than the cascade of Federalist rebuke after 1795[11]—he announced to his White Haven congregation (and then later, in December 1795, to the people of rural Colebrook, in the northwestern part of the state) the standard moral distinction between France and America. In considering "in what respects G. hath dealt with us as a nation . . . as to our natural advantages/as to our political/as to our religious advantages," the forty-seven-year-old preacher launched into a detailed account of local providences (the quality of Connecticut produce and livestock, "no complaining in streets") and a consideration of national "advantages," including a "consistently increasing" population and (even) the country's providential geography: "at so great a distance from the great powers of ~~Europe~~ Old ☉." (Edwards's exchange of continent for symbol indirectly reveals an instance of the American myth of newness in creation.) By the end of the oration, after ritually enumerating God's favors to America, Edwards concluded with a fleeting nod toward France, already implicit as a cautionary tale. "When we consider the state of France," the preacher observed in 1792, "when we reflect on our own past troubles—how sincerely thank God."[12]

Further reflection issued two years later in another Thanksgiving sermon which specifically compares France and America and in the process sets forth the myth of America as more popularly disseminated by Paine and Crèvecoeur. Now, in 1794, it is again "useful to consider the situation of other countries," Edwards remarked, those especially "under arbitrary gov't/no liberty/no security for life/liberty or property." Indeed "some countries," he went on, conjure up "scenes of war—invaded—desolated by fire & sword"; and further: "many without the gospel—in heathenish darkness—some under Popish darkness/One under the govt of infidelity"; and further still: "In most instances inequality/Many—greater part depressed/no possibility of their rising." The new republic to the west, by contrast, offered a glorious testament to proper political and spiritual *rising*. In the old world, nations silenced "free inquiry," repressed the natural "rising" spirit of their citizens—in short, Europe languished under the weight of papist thrall. "How different our situation," asserted Edwards in 1794; here there is "no restraint on any/As great equality as men's talents—improvements—industry—usefulness admit."[13] Thus Edwards discovered and announced to Colebrook the key words of the new culture, the laissez-faire ethos of Franklin's "rising people," the "indulgent laws" of Crèvecoeur's exemplary farmer.

Of course Edwards, Jr. was no Jeffersonian apologist; like his father, who collected obscure, scattered references from around the evangelical world pointing toward the overthrow of Antichrist, the son tallied the costs of "reason" in France, where the Sabbath had been abolished ("let them see [what] it had done in France, he cried out in 1798): "th____ds imprisoned—many put to death for observing." And when news of the Whiskey Rebellion reached the western Connecticut frontier Edwards joined (not surprisingly) other Federalist clergy in denouncing "an attempt to overthrow . . . our constitution," the symbol of "a free & an independent nation." Edwards may have celebrated the myth of a rising people, but the insurgents in western Pennsylvania were not to be counted among what the preacher called, separating true believers from false, the "real subjects" of the republic.[14]

Whatever the local social and economic contexts of the Whiskey Rebellion may have been, it seems clear that the eruptions of discontent on the Pennsylvania frontier during the summer and fall of 1794 revived the rhetoric and rituals of the American Revolution: liberty poles, social criticism cast in millennialist terms, the invocation of French liberty, and so on. And it is just as clear that Edwards, "skittish Federalist" that he surely was, anxiously surmised that the rebellion "threatened the overthrow of our government."[15] In cataloguing the ominous signs of the times to Colebrook in mid-February 1795, and on at least six other preaching occasions later that year, Edwards drew out the formulaic distinctions between temporal and spiritual kingdoms to explain the political lessons offered by "the suppression of the insurrection in the western counties of Pennsylvania" (as he titled his manuscript sermon). Revoicing the prerevolutionary theme of the transience of this world, its continuous (political and social) overturnings, Edwards compared the frequent "shakings" of republics (it is "generally acknowledged," the preacher reminded, that "republics [are] liable to changes") with "this kingdom," "this government," by which he *seems* to refer to the otherworldly, perfect government of the saints in heaven. I emphasize "seems," for Edwards's rhetoric in effect blurs the lines between the political and religious, between the newly sanctioned authority of American government and the perfect polity of God's spiritual realm. In the republics of *this* world people are "changeable—liable to be wro't upon—excited into tumult" (here we might note that one of the recurrent Old Light charges against the Great Awakening revivalists was that of being "changelings," selves quick to embrace the latest winds of religious fashion, like a reed bending under the force of a directionless breeze).[16] "So that all human governments," Edwards argued, are "exposed—shaken—~~overthrown~~—dissolved." The apocalyptic imagination of the evangelicals accounts for the often tortured, always ambiguous aspect of ministerial hesitancy on the eve of revolution; even the most zealous patriot could never quell completely the nervous thought that unregulated human agency, the temporal efforts of a rising people, was, in the end, a divinely *unsanctioned* mode of selfhood. By 1795, in the wake of the Revolution and a return to order, Edwards could read the reincarnation of the strategies of liberty "lately" revived in western Pennsylvania only as "an insurrection extensive, formidable"; indeed, these would-be citizens of the secular realm may attempt to overthrow—"those who profess may apostasize—rise"—but their degenerate rising (note how the preacher conflates the spatial metaphor of the rebels' fall from grace as a result of inflated pride) avails not against "this kingdom." In effect, the Whiskey rebels were "not real, cordial subjects" of "this kingdom"; they denied the affective springs governing their hearty assent to legitimate authority; their tendency to anarchic rising, that is, lay outside the consensual vision of Edward's rising, industrious, useful generation of authentic, *cordial* subjects.[17]

Of course on one level Edwards's response to social crisis was utterly conventional; salvation comes only to those who are subjects of the heavenly kingdom that "cannot be moved," the atemporal realm of the saints who persevere against the temptations to change.[18] But the preacher's repeated invocation of the ambiguous "this kingdom" highlights the multivocal dimension of the rhetoric. From a local perspective, Edwards was addressing a small band of new citizens on the frontier, yet the notorious instability of republics made him nervous. The rhetorical defense of "this kingdom" against the social dissolution posed by the Whiskey insurrectionists relies on the necessary blurring of sacred and temporal worlds in the minds of his auditors: the implicit, political, *this*-worldly context of a kingdom whose bulwark against change is the collective deferential "heart" of its people. In exposing the Rebellion with the language of antirevival unmasking, Edwards tried to ensure the current government against *accidental* history, to prevent discord from swerving the country off course, and to equate, in effect, America the historical republic with the divine kingdom and thus fix the secular nation in sacred time. His political desires explain the necessary ambiguities of "this kingdom," of "this government" laced throughout the antipopulist sermon.[19]

In retrospect we can understand how attractive, perhaps obligatory Edwards's (and other New England guardians of the social order) conservative vision was for a clergy of disminished (and diminishing) authority. The Whiskey Rebellion and drama of French infidelity released what might be called the residual monarchical yearnings of the Federalist mind; even the typological parallels between George Washington and the biblical king David center on the shared qualities of David as figural monarch and Washington as his "great and good" fulfillment.[20] Hesitant watchman till the end of his preaching career, Edwards, Jr.'s response to the Whiskey Rebellion profoundly registers the mental world of the New Divinity men at the end of the century.

The upheavals continued, and Edwards continued to read the gloomy reports of world-wide declension and "above all [of] intrigues" through the 1790s. A Thanksgiving sermon of 1798 opens with a portrait of David—"a pious man/a friend to Zion"—and closes with another cautionary tale about France. As before, Edwards reminds his congregation to "Be thankful/that we enjoy peace, as a nation," in contrast to "most of the nations/Europe in war/more & more extensive." The country must be ever watchful, the preacher warned; America must guard against international exposure—a central theme in the rhetoric of the Critical Period, most famously voiced by Washington in his Farewell Address. "We been greatly exposed," Edwards noted, reviewing colonial history, "first—with G.B./lately France." The plots of "intrigue" lately posed by France's "unbounded ambition" toward "universal dominion over Republics" (note again the figure of limitless rising) in the past "roused the resentments of the U.S." and issued in "exertions for defense" (note too in "roused" the actively residual rhetoric of revival). Continuing the history lesson Edwards recalls that, in the past, "before—a province of France," but "now—act like an independent nation . . . we are now less exposed to their infidelity & irreligion."[21] Thus political and geographic separation girds against the threat of foreign exposure; isolation is an aid to true piety, an internal resistance to French "irreligion."

But the frontier preacher is not through until he dramatizes for his audience the ultimate challenge to Christian society posed by subverting "deism or atheism." In a remarkable passage—really an insert in the sermon—Edwards tries to characterize the skewed logic of "reason" in the voice of a deluded anarchist:

> no king in heaven*
> ~~No monarch above~~
> Reason dethrones both,
> kings of the earth, the kings of heaven—No monarchs above, if we wish
> to preserve our republic below—
> If you once admit the existence of a heavenly monarch, you introduce
> the wooden horse within your walls.
> We shall instantly see the monarchy of heaven condemned by the revolutionary tribunal of victorious reason.[22]

If the image of Great Britain and France became, after 1795, the "rhetorical symbols of the emerging Republican and Federalist parties,"[23] we can see in Edwards's reifying rhetoric how the *idea* of monarchy, the great and just moral Governor of Calvinist theology, remained a fundamental image indelibly imprinted on the Federalist imagination. The vocal gambit at rationalist casuistry betrays Edwards's unbounded fear of overturning human agency latent in Enlightenment thought. And if the American Revolution "let loose the politics" the clergy "so much deplored,"[24] the historical irony highlights the human dimension behind the fears of conspiracy of so many patriot preachers by the end of the revolutionary century: their uneasy recognition that the patterns of divine providence were becoming opaque in a world filled with regressive scenes of man reduced (as Edwards voiced in 1798) to "a mere animal," where "schools neglected/growing up in ignorance/parents not allowed to teach own children."[25] And if Edwards's lamentations sound much like a contemporary evangelical educator or parent calling for creationism in the schools to arrest the spread of secular humanist infidelity, we ought not to be surprised; in each, the complaint reveals a sensibility overwhelmed by the whirl of the modern, a fear that history is spiraling out of control. In his own time of cultural upheaval Edwards sought refuge from social entropy in a vision of a perfect monarchy safe from the hidden tyranny lurking in the Age of Reason. During the often acrimonious debates in the 1790s over which political ideology the nation should embrace, Edwards, Jr. joined in the Federalist chorus cautioning against national exposure and monitored the nation for troubling signs of domestic discord.

Like Jonathan Edwards, Jr., Stephen West tried to disengage his congregation from the stormy affairs of this world. In 1776, we recall, West perceived in revolutionary events a prophetic pouring out of the apocalyptic vials; when he opened his Bible in 1796 and read the story of Mordecai and Esther, once the key biblical trope of the patriot clergy, West now applied its well-known drama of the "fruits" of haughty ambition as a critique of the culture. Ironically, in West's version the emphasis is not on the figure of Mordecai (celebrated in the 1770s as a conscience patriot defiant of kingly invested authority), but rather on Haman himself, the self-important minister seeking to rise in the world by design and plotting.

West labored in his original Stockbridge pulpit for almost sixty years; like other long-lived clergymen, he mounted the podium on hundreds of Sundays as well as on numerous weekday preaching occasions to interpret both the meaning of scripture and the text of history to his congregation.[26] On the threshold of revolution West characteristically held back from embracing the Whig summons to resistance and the political rhetoric attendant with patriotic exertions. "We consider Britain but not God," he admonished Stockbridge, in that memorable phrase of 1775. Nonetheless, at the time of Independence West was compelled to consider both spheres in light of how the war with Britain reflected in the apocalyptic prism through which he viewed events. By the end of the century, however, West appears to have returned—rhetorically, that is—to the metaphysical chambers that always beckoned as refuge from the earlier chaotic juncture. To enter the late eighteenth-century mental world of West is to encounter a mind uneasy with an emergent ideology of self-improvement, a mind alert to any signs of religious behavior at home and abroad, and above all a mind wary of the spiritual dangers that prey upon the soul too "considerate" of political culture. In short, West's later preaching powerfully refracts evangelical hopes and fears around 1800.

As noted earlier, West's October 1796 version of the Book of Esther is in many ways a response to Crèvecoeur's America. "Pride," the preacher reminded the people, "centers everything in self. Hence we— always inclined—rise above our fellow creatures."[27] As opposed to the "faithful Mordecai," Haman sought "a station above that which belongs to us" and thus suffered the famous reversal, announced in West's sermon doctrine: "The higher pride rises, the greater will be its fall."[28]

In this respect, much late eighteenth-century social history is embedded in the preacher's public gloss on the biblical trope; in the end, West translates the Haman story into a sober homily on the dissolution of social hierarchies and the rupture of economic limits. In 1796 West called for the spirit of "true religion" as a rebuke to restlessness, as a constraint against those who seek to rise above their station. "Everyone cannot be the first, and outshine his fellow—everyone cannot have all, and the others none." Only faith, in West's view, "takes away pride"; its reducing agency levels the Haman-like impulse to transgress the boundaries of the self.[29]

In this respect, too, we can observe how the New Divinity religious imagination functioned to *contain*—in its double sense as sustenance and restriction—the emergent ideology of individualism.[30] Jonathan Edwards, Jr.'s American "rising people" defend against French infidelity; West's call for true religion betrays an anxiety over those same rising selves discontented with status and degree. Thus the antithetical meanings (and political and social uses) of "rising" in New Divinity rhetoric suggest how the New Divinity metaphysic could both sanction the late eighteenth-century laissez-faire ethos yet offer a severe critique of that shifting, grasping modern world born in the wake of revolution.[31]

Still, in Stephen West's eyes the world he surveyed from Stockbridge paled before the possibilities inscribed in the promise of personal and collective redemption of the saints in the kingdom of God. And with his fellow divines he took note of all potential religious stirrings. "The Awakening continues," Joseph Bellamy reported to West in 1785, in a phrase that resonates with ambiguity, referring to both the late-century quickenings of spirit called the Second Great Awakening and (more generally) to Bellamy's personal hope that the revival embers of 1742 might still be glowing forty years later.[32] In 1798 West reported to the aged Samuel Hopkins of "some appearance of uncommon attention, in a small number of my people"; indeed "one woman, in her 84th year has been exercis'd to a high degree, and, as I think, there is some reason to hope, has experienced a saving change."[33] West, it seems, was attentive to *every* happy instance of "saving change" around him; in his orations at the end of the century he preached the necessity of the new birth as he tried to quicken his auditors' hearts with visions of hellfire and torment.

A sermon delivered in early September 1799 is filled with the imprecatory rhetoric made famous by Jonathan Edwards and the early revivalists. Sketching the terrifying landscape of hell, West placed his congregation "in this distressed, agonizing situation . . . when they will hear the thunder of the sentence, depart." In a tour de force passage the heir to Edwards's missionary pulpit drew on fifty years of preaching to conjure the following lurid image of tormented, abandoned souls lost in hell:

> Feeling themselves left behind, and all nature trembling and dissolving, the earth on which they are left melting with fervent heat, and flames breaking out of its bowels on every side; how will they try and strive to rise with the righteous. But all in vain. There they are, held down by almighty power. Oh! what horror, what horror of thick, dreadful darkness will fill their whole souls! What awful despair will appear in every face! How will their whole hearts sink! What a dreadful sinking of the heart will it be! Such horror of mind, such an awful sinking of heart— such deep and black and dreadful despair, was never conceived before![34]

How such end-time, nuclear tones might have sounded at the end of the century we can only surmise. Perhaps to some members of West's audience his discourse was satiric grist for their parodic mill: the Quaker rhythms of the brimstone rhetoric were an anachronistic reminder of and remainder from an earlier preaching style.[35] To our own ears, the rhetoric betrays the minister's sense of displacement, his private sinking of the heart (after all, the ministers were among those "left behind," their world "dissolving," "melting"); yet given the public aspect of the ritual occasion it seems just as clear that West was trying to keep the Edwardsean faith, perhaps best revealed in the series of exclamatory "What" phrases and in the rhetorical reification of writhing souls, in telling relation to the figure of Haman, now "try[ing] to *rise* with the righteous [emphasis added]." There is prideful rising and then there is righteous rising, West's message implies, and the preaching's revoicing of the magisterial "thunder" commanding eternal expulsion reverberates with the strategy (practiced throughout the pulpits of New England) at social control through ominous threat.[36]

Yet the times, even in 1799, were not entirely abject; "The very remarkable revivals of religion at the present day," West informed his congregation in late November, at his last Thanksgiving of the eighteenth century, "are evident testimonies of the power and presence of Christ with his church." Even "this clashing & collision of interests," from which "we may probably expect a dissolution of all the governments," were "preparatory to the peaceful reign of Christ." In speaking of preparatory events, the testimony of revival both in America and abroad, the progress of "divine truth [which] shines with increasing clearness and lustre," the gradual weakening of "this tyrannical antichristian power" binding the church's progress, "the present turmoils and commotions of the nations"—all these momentous stirrings were, to West's postmillennial imagination, signs particularly "fitted to excite joy and praise"—and fitted, we might add, to the divine schema of redemptive history. Adjusting the apocalyptic timetable to this new, "promising" juncture in the history of the saints, West perceived glimmerings of the millennium in his turn of the century world, a "preparatory" light "necessary . . . toward the happy event" foretold in Daniel and Revelation.[37]

Perhaps in response to the rhetorical challenge of Stockbridge's local, contentious "lay premillennialist" Simon Hough (who styled himself in the voice of an instituted minister, in mocking, ironic self-rebuke, as "a very great talker, and [someone who] would destroy all order if you could"),[38] West preached a gradualist, unfolding correlation between scriptural prophecy and historical events which assumed that human nature required "forcible restraints . . . to preserve any considerable degree of order in society."[39] Thus did the socially sanctioned postmillennialist outlook serve the political agenda of the Berkshire oligarch. Still, as Ruth Bloch observes, "Even in the 1790s, differences between premillennialists and postmillennialists did not correspond clearly to wider progressive and fatalistic world historical outlooks." If the case of Stephen West is representative, the historical optimism and belief in human agency characteristic of postmillennial thought did not completely apply; at times he too shared the premillennial "tendency to withdraw from the world," as his impulse to hide behind the divinely marked doorposts of revolutionary Stockbridge testifies.[40] Though the

American Revolution compelled the preacher to cross spiritual thresholds and enter history-as-process, West, like most patriot preachers, could not linger on that other, politically tainted side for too long.

In the end, the Revolution did indeed *displace* the evangelical clergy, dislodging them from their routinized pastoral world into a charged scene where the power of religious discourse achieved cultural sway. But from the perspective of 1800 their earlier fall into history had its own opposing momentum of flight; after the Revolution West sought (again) a realm where God mattered more than political janglings about the meaning of liberty, a spiritual haven that might gird the would-be saint in armor—or, to alter the figure slightly, religious raiment—in defense against exposure to the world. In recreating the inward experience[41] of Stephen West at the end of his preaching career, we observe how evangelical engagement with history gave way to the fear of public exposure, a stance toward history and politics that completed, in effect, the famous displacement from minister to politician by 1800.

The return to otherworldliness is signaled in West's "concert" sermon delivered in the fall of 1805, an oration whose text (from Revelation 6:15) concerns the prophet's injunction to the believer to "watcheth and keepeth his garments"; or, as West distills the message of the biblical text: "The object of the present discourse will be to mention some things necessary to be attended to and done that we may keep our garments, not walk naked, and expose our shame."[42] It is important to note, before examining this key sermon, that the rhetoric of "filthy rags" was a commonplace among pro-revivalists some sixty-five years before. For New Lights in the 1740s, "filthy rags" symbolized the false, ineffectual works in the Arminian doctrines of their opponents. To be clothed in such ungodly garb was implicitly to admit the efficacy of works as an index to spiritual condition, to display outwardly the false fruits of unmerited atonement. (Perhaps the most famous, or infamous, New Light attack on the spiritual worth of mortal shrouds is James Davenport's literalizing of the *figura,* his demand of a New London crowd to strip and consign their filthy rags to a huge dockside bonfire.)[43]

In 1805 West appropriates the biblical trope as a defense against shame—in 1805 the self must be spiritually clothed before he would be saved. Indeed, as West draws out the implications of his text he cautions (with apocalyptic overtones) against all threat to exposure—"A small rent in a garment, if neglected," he advised, "grows larger." "To keep our garments" is the preacher's message, and to avoid potential shame "we must be watchful over our tempers——words—actions—sudden emotions of anger and passion lead to unguarded and rash expressions and actions . . . give great advantage to the unclean spirits . . . which are now gone forth to and are going about to corrupt the world." And what is the greatest threat to the tearing and sullying of the protective garment? "In these times," West explained, "christians need great care and caution . . . lest they enter too deeply into politics, and political concerns and controversy. Here will be one of Satan's snares—one of his baits to draw you off from religion . . . [whoever] devotes much of his attention to political concerns, and indulges himself therein, may expect to lose, at least some of his garments, and expose his shame."[44] This remarkable passage displays a remarkable return: in 1775 the people (in West's view) considered Britain over God, engaged the world of political discourse to which their preacher joined, revoicing (in 1783) Mayhew's *The Snare Broken;* by 1805 that famous image, which fueled the oppositional rhetoric of the Revolution, had become Satan's lure to *ensnare* the innocent, to bait the unaware into the dangers of infidelity. Moreover, by 1805 politics had become the sign of human self-indulgence which at the very least taints our garments, making them as filthy rags, stripping us naked, shaming by divine judgment. Politics thus exposes the self; true religion clothes and protects.[45]

To what extent does West's rhetoric register American anxieties in 1805? Returning to a prerevolutionary vision of self-enclosure, West preached a kind of spiritual isolationism to ward off the threat of worldly, political exposure. That dialectic, of course, between isolation and engagement, filled American discourse after Washington's Farewell Address and beyond. By the end of the century those once historically engaged clergymen who helped steer the ark of revolution were themselves overwhelmed by what West perceived as "flood gates of iniquity."[46] West himself was compelled, once again, to seek shelter above, on the higher ground afforded by his Stockbridge chambers, beneath the impervious fabric of otherworldly garb—or, as in the case of Levi Hart, within the formulaic language of diary inscription.

During the Revolution, we recall, Hart recorded sustained acts of preaching—to his Preston congregation, to the local troops off to war, at private homes, and on Fast and Thanksgiving days—a continuous chronicle of oracular performances. "The public calamities still continue," he noted in May 1775, a month after the battle of Lexington, "but blessed be god He remains the same."[47] The passage neatly highlights the profound tension in the clergyman's mind between the virtual implosion of secular events and the yearning for the timeless assurances of heavenly realms. Again, the impulse to take refuge in the history of redemption despite the moral and communal obligation to help the people through a calamitous passage is perhaps *the* key emotional dialectic informing the mental world of the evangelicals. A diary entry two years later dramatizes that disjunction: "Thursday April 24, 1777—This day was set apart by order of authority for public fasting & prayer. My health so far recovered that I attended public worship & preached (tho' with difficulty by reason of a soar throat & cough) from 2 Kings V. 26,27." The revolutionary days of fasting and thanksgiving were days set apart from the sequence of regular preaching; they were political moments that marked the clergyman's public crossing onto the platform of history. Just ten years later, however, the worried tone and apocalyptic urgency of Hart's revolutionary diary vanish, replaced by what a nineteenth-century memoirist terms "a record of the daily incidents of his ministry."[48] It is as if the Revolution's jostling agency, its power to draw the diarist into history, was replaced a decade later by the homelier narrative of pastoral life in the country. And even when Hart's entries seem uncharacteristically charged with emotion, those occasions are the aging minister's almost sacramental observance of key dates in the cycle of his life—anniversaries of parents' deaths, his original Preston ordination, his birthday, and so on. (Only news of Joseph Bellamy's death in 1790 and Washington's in 1799 are given over to sustained though still formulaic, conventional reflection.)[49]

In effect, the testimony of Hart's private meditations after the Revolution reveal, by the very absence of reference to current events, how unsettling, transforming the American crisis of 1774–1778 was for the minister. Once "public calamities" ceased, he could at last return to the world that "remains the same." Let us closely observe his world, mediated through the diary, during a three-week interval in the fall of 1785 in order to gain a sense of the life of a local pastor no longer consumed or distracted by the disjunctive "day[s] set apart."

Between October 23 and November 13, 1785 Levi Hart preached on at least ten occasions, which included the baptism of a child, a gathering in an unnamed private house, "the funeral of an aged woman," "a fast in south pasture AM," and a sacramental lecture (where he evaluated his performances as "wandering in the forenoon, but had some freedom in communion"). In addition, he rode to a new preacher's ordination examination and recorded (in opening this juncture on October 23) the thirty-first anniversary of his father's death and (on November 5) the completion of "23 years since my ordination." Finally, after the Lord's day November 13, a Sunday when "Mr. Benedict filled the pulpit for him"—Hart had complained earlier of being "fatigued with the labours of this & past days"—he noted the departure of "my dear son" setting back "out for Dartmouth College, having been at home during the vacation."[50]

For the next twenty-two years, until Hart's last recorded entry in March 1807,[51] the diary more or less follows the same pattern, with the sequence of ritual entries marking, with more and more amazement, the longevity of the pastor in his office. Perhaps the most charged passage is that of July 1802, which fills an entire two sheets to accommodate Hart's reflection on forty years of "my life at Preston." Yet, as with the responses to Bellamy and Washington, it too remains purely formulaic; only rarely does the text reveal authentic (as opposed to stylized) emotion.[52] It seems clear that the life of the pastor was richly filled by pastoral obligations, which he performed, we imagine, even when fatigued. Whatever turmoils—social, religious, or political—filled the polemical atmosphere in New England in the 1780s and 1790s—a world of factional debate, theological controversy, economic and social discord—the diary does not record the reverberations of *that* world.

What did preoccupy Levi Hart at the end of the century was the future glory of God's kingdom and its inheritance by the rising generation. Both in private treatise and public oration Hart joined in the collective New Divinity effort to discern the signs of the times with respect to the millennium. Among his numerous unpublished manuscripts is the "Dissertation" of 1797 "on the literal & figurative sense of scripture prophecy, & the return of the Jews to their own land when they shall embrace the christian faith."[53] This was a millennial subject he revoiced to the people of Preston on the first day of 1799 from the Isaiah text, "Comfort ye comfort ye my people, saith your god," a passage which the preacher glosses as "words [that] immediately follow a prediction of the babylonish capitivity & preceed a representation of the coming of the messiah." In public, then, Hart (on this particular occasion at least) took as his audience "the children of the rising age," to instruct them in how "this scripture furnishes abundant matter for consolation in the darkest times, & under the most distressing sorrows." Moreover, a careful reading of the biblical prophet "assures us that in the final issue of things" the millennium "shall be unspeakably great & glorious"; that, indeed, "we have cause to believe that the time of the church's calamity will bear no proportion to the duration of its blessedness, & that the number of the finally lost will be very small in comparison of the number of the saved in the happy millennium." Like his fellow New Divinity minister Samuel Hopkins, to whose Newport church he traveled in 1803 to deliver Hopkins's funeral oration, Hart spent his last years living his intellectual life longing for the "happy millennium," envisioning a purely spiritual utopia as compensation for the failure of history.[54]

But history, both mythic and personal, pulled him back to earth, to Preston, where for the public fast of March 1799 he spoke from the book of Judges, "to consider the case respecting the fathers of N. England & the present generation."[55] And as for the rising generation in his own family, Hart's diary movingly charts a father's anxiety for his younger son's future in entries evocative of the problems of career in postrevolutionary America. "My son Levi at College," the father recorded in July 1800, "after much discourse with him & the best warning & advice I could give him—a great burden has been on my mind for sometime respecting that child." By 1804 it appears that young Levi had resolved his vocational crisis. On Lord's day December 9 the father inscribed (uncharacteristically) two entries: "last Wednesday the solemn ordination of Mr. Nelson, an apparently pious & promising young minister at Lisbon"; and the second: "My son Levi who had been absent some time is just entering into business as an attorney [and] is come home in very bad health, the issue is in my view uncertain."[56] The contrasts in tone and emphasis could not be more revealing. The evangelical patriarch's recent witnessing of the ritual sanctioning a "promising" young minister prompts the worried reflection over young Levi, whose poor health makes even more precarious his entrance into the "business" of law.[57] A generation earlier, Hart had studied with Philemon Robbins's son Ammi under Bellamy. Perhaps in wincing, ironic recognition over the "son" who kept the faith and the son who chose not to follow the father, Hart ends the entry on the note of familial distance and vocational uncertainty.

Of course it would be interesting to discover what advice Levi gave his son over the years, and what the fatherly discourse sounded like in 1800. And how *did* young Levi arrive at the "business" of the law? The point, however, is the representative aspect of the Hart family biography, for its history limns the transition from minister to lawyer with which this chapter began. Hart's personal story provides, in effect, a kind of historical closure to this collective ministerial narrative.

The three figures whose public voices and interior worlds I have described reveal, through their preaching concerns, political—and apolitical—stances, the private hopes and fears, the shifting contours of American cultural history around 1800. As we have come to understand, the rising generation of intellectuals embraced law above theology, a vocational shift that displaced the ministerial fathers to the cultural margins. The ministers lived for their congregations' pastoral needs, and dreamed of the approaching millennium; the mythical legacy of the American Revolution seems not (as it would for the first generation of classic authors in the mid-nineteenth century) to have absorbed their imaginations. They had once *acted* in history; by 1800 their secret desire was to get out of history, to a place where all "remains the same."

But earlier, in the 1770s, the evangelical ministry did *not* retreat in the face of social upheaval, despite the judgment of later historians of religion and the American Revolution; on the contrary, their manuscript sermons bear irrefutable, eloquent witness to their secular engagement, their profoundly political voices. And if lawyers eventually came to displace ministers by 1800, religious discourse itself was not displaced. Patriot rhetoric survived long after the clergy retired to the safety of the millennial ark.

Epilogue

In closing this study I wish to highlight how these exemplary ministerial portraits both enrich and complicate current perspectives of the mental world of revolutionary New England as refracted from the pulpits of the five historical actors limned above. Of course the view is necessarily partial; it leaves out the active contribution of lay piety, the voices of those dutifully assembled people alert to the messages delivered by their communal spokesmen. Still, if we assent to the claims of recent scholarship that the colonial sermon was the "central ritual" of the culture, the key mode (and medium) of communication informing all levels of society, if we believe that the minister himself "embodied and expressed" the leading ideas of the culture, then we may observe, perhaps even enter, the world of revolutionary New England through the sermonic efforts of the patriot clergy.[1] I have offered what David Hollinger calls "a more linguistically conscious history";[2] or, from my perspective, a reading of revolutionary sermons attuned to the often bizarre shifts in literary form preserved in the voluminous testament of the original manuscripts themselves.

Since a large measure of the argument of *Rhetoric and History* concerns the social and political implications of what I term the fragmentary mode of sermonic discourse in the Great Awakening, let us return to the question of literary form and political import to suggest the ways in which revival rhetoric and its sermonic traces in various New Light ministers later in the century issued a (perceived) threat to constituted authority.

As noted in the early portions of Chapter 1, the high level disputes among the ministerial elite in the 1740s turned on the nature and means of preaching the Word. With the celebrated arrival of the itinerant George Whitefield in the colonies, those clergymen doctrinally sympathetic to Whitefield's repertoire of antistructural stances—his histrionic pulpit theatrics, his extemporaneous sermonizing—consciously appropriated the radically shortened, brief sermon outline as a "homilectic badge," a rhetorical sign of doctrinal (through stylistic) affiliation.[3] But the shift from fully penned (and therefore publicly read "word for word") orations to the inventive freedom attendant with fragmentary notes was not simply a declaration of rhetorical independence, as Philemon Robbins discovered after he preached in the new mode at Wallingford. The rejection of linear narrative had a clear political dimension, especially in the eyes (and ears) of the New Haven Consociation. The rhetorical freedom of the fragment challenged their vision of what and *how* a gospel minister might preach. In swerving from standard narrative, Robbins's unsanctioned method subverted the authority of the more logical, rigidly composed, *codified* doctrine inscribed in unimpeded, polished narrative itself. All this, we should note, was already apparent in the original charges against Robbins mounted by the Old Lights; their anxiety was expressive of the antiauthoritarian impulse reflected in Whitefield's "new style," *ex tempore* preaching itself.[4]

Thus the unfamiliar, often open-air settings and rapturous delivery of Awakening ministers were in effect revivalist gambits at social power; yet, more important, the fragmentary *style* characteristic of New Light preaching—the vertical catalogues, tonic refrains, often aggressive assault on the sensibility of the auditors (the mingling of apocalyptic despair with millennial hope, the impassioned summons to immediate action yet the simultaneous reminder of human helplessness, and so on)—betrays the *social marginality* of the evangelical actors/agents themselves. Their challenge to normative discourse is the linguistic sign of their outsider status; their rejection of and assault on traditional (linear) modes was an effort at religious and political displacement.

From this perspective, the fragmentary mode of Awakening preaching was the rhetorical strategy and *sign* of the New Light desire to overturn, religiously and politically, the authority of those who, in their experience, controlled the pulpits. Indeed, the antinarrative form and extremist tone of Awakening discourse were verbal weapons in a debate about social power. That is, the spoken word as event carried a charged political valence for those religious radicals in stylistic revolt against the hegemonic formalism of the standing clergy.

To a great extent, the New Lights won the battle, at least in eastern

Connecticut and in the rural pulpits of the country backwaters, where Joseph Bellamy and Samuel Hopkins presided, keeping the Edwardsean flame alive. The interconnections—filial, educational, and doctrinal—among the elder Robbins (who appears in this study as representative of the first generation of New Lights) and a trio forming the rising generation (Edwards, Jr., Hart, and West) convey how the New Divinity men kept the faith and maintained their considerable cultural weight up to and through the American Revolution. Yet by the end of the century, as virtually all historians of colonial America agree, the once-powerful cohort of ministers was displaced by the new class of lawyers, whose rhetorical eloquence and political vision enabled the emergent nation to evolve from traditional to modern society.[5] The great irony in the monumental turnings enacted by the Revolution, of course, is that the revolutionary ministers reached the height of oracular power and attained perhaps their most compelling sway over the lives of their auditors at precisely this threshold, when the world they labored to deliver into being would soon delimit their mediatorial offices as watchman and guide.

The rhetoric of the patriot clergy everywhere registers the transformed cultural landscape. As the preachers mobilized for war, appealing to the doctrine of inalienable rights and warning of the dire threat of a once affectionate and now designing and cruel mother country, they also entered into a new world of modern political systems, of secular modes of political dispute and accommodation—modern forms of social organization that displaced *their* world view (of providential history, human depravity, predestination, and so on) to the margins of emergent middle-class culture.

In this respect, we should recognize the profoundly *conservative* impulse behind the revolutionary preachers' desire to contain the whirl of secular history with a figuralist mentality shaped by the Bible. Whatever issued from the antiauthoritarian tendencies of "mobilizing" rhetoric, either imaginatively or socially considered, the ministers' pulpit orations were so many attempts to order history experienced as reeling out of control. Thus the compulsion to narrate was more than a reflexive effort to explain (to paraphrase Paul Ricoeur); instead, the impulse to plot the arc of history was the sign of their human desire to arrest a metaphysical fall into interpretive contingency, the hermeneutic void of utter disconnectedness.[6]

I have argued that the fragmentary mode—the impeded, disfluent, at times even manic narrative characteristic of revolutionary discourse—is the rhetorical site of the struggle itself. And in both the Awakening and the Revolution the fragmentary style served to rouse the populace to challenge the moral and political authority of the symbols of control. During the Awakening, the claims of the clerical status quo were subverted by an overturning rhetoric oppositional to the sermonic norm; the return (conscious or unconscious) to revivalist modes during the Revolution, however, yields two ironies.

First, while the revivalists, often reveling in a confrontational style, consciously strove (despite the admonitions of Jonathan Edwards) to disrupt, the revolutionary preachers worried over the social and moral implications of libertarian sentiments. Yet despite their fears of social discord, their own revivalist-inflected rhetoric ironically betrays (as it fueled) the antiauthoritarian spirit of the times that they nevertheless imbibed.

Second, the revivalists sought to displace politically those "unconverted" ministers in unsanctioned control of pulpits; the Awakening style of preaching was thus both the rhetorical sign of the New Lights' (temporary) social marginality—fragmentary rhetoric is historically the linguistic vehicle of an adversarial stance—and their *method* of gaining power.[7] In contrast, the evangelical ministers, at the height of their religious and social power (circa 1776), reacted to cultural crisis with rhetoric that, ironically, betrays their own looming marginality later in the century.

In this regard, the breakdown of narrative in the revolutionary pulpit uncannily foreshadows the ministerial loss of authority reflected in a discourse historically identified with those *outside* the dominant culture. In short, the revolutionary preachers fell into rhetorical outlooks characteristic of those marginalized groups in quest of social power *at the height of* their own hegemonic sway. From this perspective, we can now hear the mixed messages sounding from their pulpits: the call to retreat into the safety of Christ's chamber till the storms pass over and the clouds disperse, an exhortation to steer courageously amidst tempest-tossed seas of history, and the itch to escape history yet the desire to oppose tyranny in all temporal guises. We may now understand such psychic ambivalencies as expressions of the imagination in conflict; we may now recognize their legacy of fragmented narratives as the poignant, telling literary traces of their historical and vocational dilemma. In the end, the struggle to narrate and explain was *already* the sign of the clergy's decline in social status and oracular authority.[8] That the patriot clergy preached better than they knew is perhaps the greatest irony in this study of how religious rhetoric helped deliver the country into the modern, secularized world.

I conclude with an allusion to the rhetoric of collective deliverance, for ministerial language during the Revolution was filled with biblical tropes drawn from Exodus, Daniel, Esther, Isaiah, and especially Revelation. It may be a commonplace to observe that the patriot orators were both witnesses to and agents of the political contractions leading to the birth drama of the American republic; what I have tried to show is how a group of ministers responded to the historic convulsions in their midst and how their narrative-imposing imaginations labored to give shape to a secular "story" that was utterly new, despite the typological parallels pointed out again and again between America's "story" and "republican" Israel. My subject has been, in this respect, the various linguistic reflections of that imaginative effort, and, above all, a gauging of the psychic and rhetorical energy spent in the cultural work of interpretation itself. In the process, *Rhetoric and History* recovers that too frequently dismissed or ignored cohort of evangelicals—it is self-evident that the New Divinity men who appear in this history are not abstracted from the spiritual needs of their congregations—by restoring their own frameworks of meaning.[9] In the wake of such a rehabilitation, these figures take on a more recognizable shape, fleshed out by their need to seek connections, to draw a comforting myth out of temporal confusion.

In addition, the collective portrait adds weight to the assertions of recent scholarship about the ritual aspect of revolutionary discourse.[10] In the betwixt and between atmosphere within which patriot orators composed and preached, language itself became unmoored from traditional contexts, referents, and canons of style and form. Rhetorically speaking, that is, the revolutionary era was "an instant of pure potentiality," one of those liminal moments when the multivocal dimensions of ritual discourse incorporate both old and new meanings, a linguistically creative juncture witness to the creation of new cultural myths. New stories are required when the old no longer resonate with explanatory power.[11]

The fragmentary style manifest in the manuscript sermons served, in this respect, as an ideological challenge to the smooth flow and moral authority of the biblical myths that sustained the ministers' prophetic office. In this respect, too, the fragmentary mode highlights the famous "eclipse of biblical narrative" of eighteenth-century religious culture in general.[12] We may follow that key hermeneutic transition in Stephen

West's almost manic shorthand sermon notes applying the prophetic pouring of the vials in Revelation to Stockbridge's provincial, yet at the same time cosmic, fate.

Of course, after the Revolution there would be a "return" to narrative with a vengeance in the spate of multivolume histories (David Ramsey, Mercy Otis Warren, and others). Only after the Revolution could a new narrative incorporating both Founding and Revolutionary fathers, the typological parallels between the Old Testament and 1776, and the sacred story of biblical–republican origins be fashioned through a myth whose textual authority blurred sacred and secular history in the figure/*figura* of Washington.[13]

What, then, can we now say about the role of religious rhetoric and the coming of the American Revolution? Or of the interaction of religious and political languages? Has this survey of the mental landscape of the patriot ministry altered its contours? I have shown that the scholarly debate over religion and politics in the Revolution has itself resulted in an unfortunate scholarly deafness; historians too often have neither read nor heard the religious overtones of revolutionary discourse as expressive of a still compelling (however soon to be outmoded) world view. Literary and religious interpreters, on the other hand, have perhaps strained to hear echoes of revival brimstone in arguing for the Awakening as a necessary prelude to Revolution. My own view is that the links between Awakening and Revolution exist not in a uniquely shared theological vision or along strict doctrinal allegiances but rather on the level of rhetoric itself. Clearly, the upheavals wrought by the Revolution issued in denominational leveling; the sacred cause of liberty enabled Old and New Lights to blend their voices together despite variations in class, temperament, and beliefs about self and society. Still, if Samuel Cooper of Brattle Street can be taken as representative, there are clear rhetorical distinctions in preaching between the guardians of the Edwardsean heritage and the liberal Cooper. My argument has involved the connections among religious stance, literary form, and evangelical identity. By showing, in light of what Hans Frei calls "the great reversal"[14] in the world of eighteenth-century religious narrative, how the private jottings of a group of affiliated preachers might be read, *Rhetoric and History* offers an alternative way of construing the "mobilizing" agency of religious language during cultural crisis as it unearths, layer by psychic layer, what the oracular spokesmen may have been thinking as they mounted their pulpits. Clearly, their sermons embodied public belief. Clearly, too, the sermon's agent carved out a political space during delivery, speaking under the assumption that his words would affect his listeners.[15]

Of course, I have been concerned with only one side of that dialogue; how the laity responded to the endless cascade of words uttered at countless ritual occasions during the Revolution remains as a challenge to those historians in search of recovering the voices of the inarticulate.[16] I believe, however, that we can already encounter a version of the people's dialogic response in the worried yet hopeful, adversarial yet tempered voice to be heard in the still-evocative overtones of the fragile, dusty, hand-stitched sermon booklets. Artifacts of the Revolution in their own right, those often-crumbling remnants are in many ways the clearest reflection of the mental world of the American Revolution that we have. Ultimately they provide a profound testament to the power and presence of the spoken word in the continuing labor of people to change their spiritual and political condition.

Notes

Preface

1. Of course, more recently the work of William G. McLoughlin, Joseph A. Conforti, Mark R. Valeri, William Breitenbach, Bruce Kuklick, and other scholars cited throughout the study has effectively challenged this judgment.

2. Harry S. Stout's *The New England Soul: Preaching and Religious Culture in Colonial New England* (New York, 1986) incorporates a wealth of manuscript materials; his focus, however, remains on the thematic development of the sermon over time, rather than on a consideration of formal shifts in the genre or the shape of individual preaching careers.

3. Gary B. Nash, *Race, Class, and Politics: Essays on American Colonial and Revolutionary Society* (Urbana, 1986), xxi.

4. In this respect Charles L. Cohen's remark, that "researching manifestations of a past mentality is tricky business, especially since they are not easily quarried out of the sources, and their ambiguities pose difficult interpretive problems," is indeed relevant to the business of this study, which extracts kernels of revolutionary mentality from the core of extant manuscripts. Charles L. Cohen, *God's Caress: The Psychology of Puritan Religious Experience* (New York, 1986), 14.

5. David T. Courtwright, "Fifty Years of American History: An Interview with Edmund S. Morgan," *William and Mary Quarterly* 44 (1987), 363.

Introduction

1. Jonathan Edwards, Jr., sermon 485, June 30, 1776, Edwards Papers, Hartford Seminary Library. The literature on mobilization during the Revolution is cited throughout the introduction and Chapter 1, but see especially,

Bernard Bailyn, "The Central Themes of the American Revolution: An Interpretation," in Stephen G. Kurtz and James H. Hutson, eds., *Essays on the American Revolution* (Chapel Hill, 1973), pp. 3–31 (especially p. 11).

2. Richard Slotkin, *The Fatal Environment: The Myth of the Frontier in the Age of Industrialization, 1800–1900* (New York, 1985), pp. 24, 22. The key work for Slotkin and other cultural critics who seek to "historicize" American mythology is Roland Barthes, *Mythologies* (New York, 1972).

3. Slotkin, *The Fatal Environment*, p. 25.

4. Nathan O. Hatch, *The Sacred Cause of Liberty: Republican Thought and the Millennium in Revolutionary New England* (New Haven, 1977), pp. 181–82. On the issue of political ideology and mobilization, see Harry S. Stout, "Religion, Communications, and the Ideological Origins of the American Revolution," *William and Mary Quarterly,* 3d ser., 34 (1977), 519–41; on the influence of the sermon in shaping popular religious culture, see Harry S. Stout, *The New England Soul: Preaching and Religious Culture in Colonial New England* (New York, 1986).

5. Perry Miller, "From the Covenant to the Revival," in Miller, *Nature's Nation* (Cambridge, Mass., 1967), pp. 90, 100, 97. Perhaps the most extreme version of Miller's position is voiced by William G. McLoughlin: "I am convinced that the Revolution would never have occurred had it been left to the deists and rationalists. Their cool, judicious, scientific arguments for republicanism did not carry enough weight with the average man to lead him into rebellion." " 'Enthusiasm for Liberty': The Great Awakening as the Key to the Revolution," *American Antiquarian Society Proceedings* 87 (1977), 72. "Pamphlets could never represent the primary source for radical republicanism," summarily declares Stout ("Religion, Communications," p. 536). His assertion is too emphatic. Ministers did expound Lockean tenets to an audience sensitive to the meanings of "liberty," "property," and "sovereignty." For McLoughlin's more extended treatment of religion and the Revolution, see William G. McLoughlin, "The Role of Religion in the American Revolution: Liberty of Conscience and Cultural Cohesion in the New Nation," in Kurtz and Hutson, eds., *Essays,* pp. 197–255.

6. Bernard Bailyn, *The Ideological Origins of the American Revolution* (Cambridge, Mass., 1967); Bailyn, "Religion and Revolution: Three Biographical Studies," *Perspectives in American History* 6 (1970), 134. For a succinct account of developments in recent scholarship on religion and the Revolution, see Robert E. Shalhope, "Republicanism and Early American Historiography," *William and Mary Quarterly* 39 (1982), 334–56 (especially pp. 354–56).

7. Alan Heimert, *Religion and the American Mind from the Great Awakening to the Revolution* (Cambridge, Mass., 1966). Although dismissed when it first appeared, Heimert's still-controversial work continues to shape the debate about the evangelical legacy to the Revolution. This is not the place for re-evaluation, but we should note that most critics have missed Heimert's

major point: that the *affective* preaching modes of the Edwardsean clergy were instrumental in the coming of the Revolution.

8. Hatch, *The Sacred Cause,* pp. 88 [I have transposed Hatch's declarative statement into an interrogative], 35n, 36, 46. On the "apolitical" dimension of the New Divinity men, see James West Davidson, *The Logic of Millennial Thought* (New Haven, 1977), pp. 213–54. Note one of the most recent efforts to describe the religious and political nature of the discourse: "The thesis of this article is that the large majority of ministers who published sermons during the Revolutionary era justified the war effort by a rationale that was *more political* than religious" (emphasis added). Melvin B. Endy, Jr., "Just War, Holy War, and Millennialism in Revolutionary America," *William and Mary Quarterly,* 3d ser., 42 (1985), 3. "Religious leaders," Endy asserts, "were incorporating political developments into their salvation history." The process of "incorporation," as well as the question of published versus manuscript sermons, concerns me here.

9. J. G. A. Pocock, *Virtue, Commerce, and History: Essays on Political Thought and History, Chiefly in the Eighteenth Century* (Cambridge, 1985), p. 9. I am indebted to Pocock's Introduction to this recent collection, subtitled "The State of the Art," as well as to his important "Languages and Their Implications: The Transformation of the Study of Political Thought," in Pocock, *Politics, Language and Time* (New York, 1971), pp. 3–41.

10. Hatch's contention, that an obsession with lofty metaphysics detached some New Lights from history and politics, is a kind of standard by which he measures a figure like Bellamy. "Without mentioning a single contemporary event, either religious or political," Hatch argues, "Bellamy offered Christians *only* the timeless hope that some day Christ would prevail." *The Sacred Cause,* p. 35 (emphasis added). The manuscript evidence, however, reveals that Jonathan Edwards, Bellamy, and Samuel Hopkins were *consumed* by events. On Bellamy's revolutionary pulpit themes see Mark R. Valeri, "Joseph Bellamy: Conversion, Social Ethics, and Politics in the Thought of an Eighteenth-Century Calvinist," Ph.D. Diss., Princeton University, 1985.

11. Lyman, quoted in Charles Royster, *A Revolutionary People at War: The Continental Army and American Character, 1775–1783* (Chapel Hill, 1979), p. 19. For a discussion of Bellamy's preaching during the American Revolution see Valeri, "Joseph Bellamy."

12. Rhys Isaac, *The Transformation of Virginia, 1740–1790* (Chapel Hill, 1982), p. 263. On the semantic problems scholars have faced in trying to describe "incendiary," "explosive," "incandescent" patriot rhetoric see Chapter 1, below.

13. "A purely religious, even evangelical, conception of liberty," observes Ruth H. Bloch, "continued to overlap with the political, whig definition." Ruth H. Bloch, *Visionary Republic: Millennial Themes in American Thought, 1756–1800* (New York, 1985), p. 45. Elsewhere Bloch speaks of the "dou-

ble meanings" of the rhetoric (p. 63). The imprecision of "to overlap" suggests the descriptive fix historians encounter when they try to explain the complex dynamics of revolutionary discourse. Cf. Bailyn, "Religion and Revolution," p. 137: the "conflation of Biblical and secular historical worlds" in sermons. Cf. Stout, "Religion, Communications," p. 533: "If we are to understand the cultural significance of the Revolution, we must move beyond the rhetorical world of informed publications to the social world of popular assembly. We must *listen* as the 'inarticulate' would have listened and determine to what extent religious and political meanings had a common rhetorical denominator that reached a revolutionary *crescendo* in the movement for independence" (first emphasis in original; second, added).

14. Abner Cohen, *Two-Dimensional Man: An Essay on the Anthropology of Power and Symbolism in Complex Society* (Berkeley, 1974), p. 23. Extrapolating from Victor Turner's seminal *The Ritual Process* (1969), Cohen asks, "How are purely political interests converted to the most intimate moral and ritual obligations which are capable of impelling men to action without coercion from the outside?" The answer lies in the ritual office of dominant symbols: "At the ideological level," Cohen explains, "there is a cluster of meanings referring to moral values, principles of social organisation, rules of social behaviour. . . . At the sensory pole . . . there are gross sensations, desires and feelings. . . . The ritual symbol effects an interchange of qualities between the two poles of the symbol. Norms and values become saturated with emotion, while the gross and basic emotions become ennobled through contact with social values." Abner Cohen, "Symbolic Action and the Structure of the Self," in Ioan Lewis, ed., *Symbols and Sentiments: Cross-Cultural Studies in Symbolism* (London, 1977), pp. 120, 121.

15. I borrow these terms from Richard Bauman, *Let Your Words Be Few: Symbolism of Speaking and Silence among Seventeenth-Century Quakers* (Cambridge, 1983), pp. 14, 10. I am indebted to Bauman's study of the oral modes of Quaker rhetoric for my analysis of revolutionary language.

16. David D. Hall, "Religion and Society: Problems and Reconsiderations," in Jack P. Greene and J. R. Pole, eds., *Colonial British America: Essays in the New History of the Early Modern Era* (Baltimore, 1984), pp. 336, 337. For recent studies of Puritan mentality see Charles Hambrick-Stowe, *The Practice of Piety: Puritan Devotional Disciplines in Seventeenth-Century New England* (Chapel Hill, 1982); Charles L. Cohen, *God's Caress: The Psychology of Puritan Religious Experience* (New York, 1986); David D. Hall, "Toward a History of Popular Religion in Early New England," *William and Mary Quarterly* 41 (1984), 49–55. For a comprehensive overview of recent scholarship see David D. Hall, "On Common Ground: The Coherence of American Puritan Studies," *William and Mary Quarterly* 44 (1987), 193–229. I take the phrase "regular preaching" from Stout, *New England Soul*, 32.

17. On these issues see Lester H. Cohen's important *The Revolutionary*

Histories: Contemporary Narratives of the American Revolution (Ithaca, 1980).

18. This observation is based on scanning the Wheelock Papers, Baker Library, Dartmouth College and the Edwards Papers, Beinecke Library, Yale University. Edwards, for example, began preaching with notes by the spring of 1741. See ms sermon Zech. 12:10 (April 1741).

19. Here I draw on Hall, "Religion and Society," p. 332. Stout speaks of the stylistic differences between New Light and Old Light sermons as "constitut[ing] homilectic badges." Stout, *New England Soul,* 219.

20. Cohen, *The Revolutionary Histories,* p. 21.

21. The Robbins chapter is much longer compared to the other case studies because I use him more emblematically, as a model of Awakening discourse in general and as a figure whose rich preaching career enables me to develop *organically* the argument of subsequent chapters.

22. James A. Henretta, "Social History as Lived and Written," *American Historical Review* 84 (1979), 1309.

23. Here I draw on Victor Turner, especially the essays collected in *Dramas, Fields and Metaphors: Symbolic Action in Human Society* (Ithaca, 1974) and "Liminal to Liminoid in Play, Flow and Ritual"; An Essay in Comparative Symbology," in Turner, *From Ritual to Theatre: The Human Seriousness of Play* (New York, 1982), pp. 20–60.

24. Samuel Sherwood, *The Church's Flight into the Wilderness* (New York, 1776), p. 9.

Chapter 1

1. Philemon Robbins, "Diary, 1730–33," Robbins Family Papers, Yale University Library (hereafter cited as YUL).

2. C. K. Shipton, *Sibley's Harvard Graduates* (Boston, 1951), 7:616. On the ministry in eighteenth-century New England see Christopher M. Jedrey, *The World of John Cleaveland: Family and Community in Eighteenth-Century New England* (New York, 1979); Joseph Conforti, *Samuel Hopkins and the New Divinity Movement* (Grand Rapids, 1981); Donald M. Scott, *From Office to Profession: The New England Ministry, 1750–1850* (Philadelphia, 1978); Joseph Conforti, "Joseph Bellamy and the New Divinity Movement," *New England Historic and Genealogical Register* 137 (1983), 126–38; and Mark R. Valeri, "Joseph Bellamy: Conversion, Social Ethics, and Politics in the Thought of an Eighteenth-Century Calvinist," Ph.D. Diss., Princeton University, 1985. Of course the groundbreaking study of the patriot clergy is that by Alice M. Baldwin, *The New England Clergy and the American Revolution* (Durham, 1928).

3. Robbins, "Diary," YUL.

4. Robbins usually appears in colonial religious history as a figure in the

early stirrings of Baptist revolt against the standing Congregational clergy in Connecticut. See C. C. Goen, *Revivalism and Separatism in New England, 1740–1800* (New Haven, 1962), passim; Richard L. Bushman, *From Puritan to Yankee: Character and the Social Order in Connecticut, 1690–1765* (New York, 1967), pp. 211, 235, 237; and William B. McLoughlin, *New England Dissent, 1630–1833: The Baptists and the Separation of Church and State*, 2 vols. (Cambridge, Mass., 1971), 1:444–46. On pulpit longevity see Scott, *From Office to Profession*.

5. I refer to Jon Butler, "Enthusiasm Described and Decried: The Great Awakening as Interpretive Fiction," *Journal of American History* 69 (1982), 305–25. See, in this respect, Ammi Robbins's assessment of his father's preaching career in a letter to Benjamin Trumbull, a few days after Philemon Robbins died (August 13, 1781): "As to his success in his ministry perhaps it may be well to mention the great harvest he had in Anno 42 & 43 & as well as some other seasons now & then." Ammi R. Robbins to Benjamin Trumbull, Aug. 17, 1781, Trumbull Papers, Beinecke Library, Yale University. A portion of the son's letter later appeared in a local obituary notice. "He preached the gospel," the younger Robbins continued to Trumbull, "with great plainess of speech, yet with uncommon zeal, affection, & solemnity." See the sketch of Robbins in *Sibley's Harvard Graduates*, 7:626.

6. Merton M. Sealts, Jr., ed., *The Journals and Miscellaneous Notebooks of Ralph Waldo Emerson* (Cambridge, Mass., 1973), 10:177. I am indebted to Robert A. Gross for this reference.

7. I refer to the work of a host of scholars whose work I cite throughout this study: Patricia U. Bonomi, Ruth Bloch, Rhys Isaac, Harry S. Stout, Nathan O. Hatch, Alan Heimert, Lester H. Cohen, Charles Royster, Catharine Albanese, Stephen Lucas, Philip Greven, and others.

8. Philemon Robbins, sermon on Gal. 5:1, Dec. 24, 1732, Robbins Family Papers, Connecticut Historical Society (hereafter cited as CHS).

9. Cf. Rhys Isaac, *The Transformation of Virginia, 1740–1790* (Chapel Hill, 1982), p. 263. On the multivocality of political discourse see the references to Ruth Bloch and J. G. A. Pocock cited in the Introduction, above.

10. Robbins, sermon on Gal. 5:1, pp. 4, 6, CHS.

11. Ten years later Robbins himself would become embroiled in just such a controversy. See below for a discussion of his role in the charged preaching atmosphere of the 1740s.

12. Robbins, sermon on Gal. 5:1, p. 9, CHS.

13. Ibid., p. 10.

14. Cf. Charles Chauncy, *Enthusiasm Described and Caution'd Against* (Boston, 1742) and Chauncy, *Seasonable Thoughts on the State of Religion* (Boston, 1743). For Chauncy's response to the revivalists see Edward M. Griffin, *Old Brick: Charles Chauncy of Boston, 1705–1787* (Minneapolis, 1980) and Charles H. Lippy, *Seasonable Revolutionary: The Mind of Charles Chauncy* (Chicago, 1981). For a provocative rereading of the famous Ed-

wards–Chauncy debate, see Amy Schrager Lang, "'A Flood of Errors': Chauncy and Edwards in the Great Awakening," in N. O. Hatch and H. S. Stout eds., *Jonathan Edwards and the American Experience* (New York, 1986).

15. Robbins, sermon on Gal. 5:1, p. 11, CHS.

16. Bushman, *From Puritan to Yankee,* pp. 194, 195. "The revivalists undermined the social order," writes Bushman, "not by repudiating law and authority, but by denying them sanctifying power" (p. 193).

17. Robbins, sermon on Gal. 5:1, p. 11, CHS.

18. Philemon Robbins, "Diary, 1737–45," Houghton Library, Harvard University.

19. Ibid. According to the Branford Church Records, 1738 represented the highest yield in new members (11; 4 men, 7 women counting one "Thankful Burgess"); in 1739: 6 (2 men, 4 women); in 1740: 4 (2 men, 2 women); in 1741: 10 (3 men, 7 women); throughout the 1740s women constitute the new members of the Branford Church. And as for those "who have owned the covenant," Robbins's Church recorded only women from 1738 to 1742—with each year seeing only *one* person owning the covenant. Branford Church Records, Connecticut State Library, Hartford. In light of Robbins's own accounting the son's testimony to Trumbull (cited in note 5) suggests more family myth than historical accuracy.

20. Philemon Robbins, ms sermon Matt. 13:18–23, April 6, 1740, Robbins Family Papers, YUL.

21. Philemon Robbins, ms sermon Amos 3:6, March 4, 1741, pp. 8–9, Robbins Family Papers, YUL. Robbins will return to the shipwreck metaphor as perhaps the key sermonic trope of his revolutionary imagination.

22. Ibid., p. 2.

23. Philemon Robbins, ms sermon Rev. 3:21, Oct. 30, 1740, p. 2, Robbins Family Papers, YUL.

24. *Sibley's Harvard Graduates,* 8:619. "In spite of the known opposition of Parson Whittelsey [the settled minister of Wallingford], in spite of the formal protests of some members of Whittelsey's congregation and of neighboring ministers," Robbins preached to the separated Baptists. In the wake of the controversy, he "drew up a series of confessions, all of which the Association rejected as arrogant and stiffnecked" (8:621).

25. Philemon Robbins, *A Plain Narrative* (Boston, 1747), quoted in Benjamin Trumbull, *A Complete History of Connecticut* (orig. 1818; New London, 1898), pp. 11, 172.

26. Trumbull, *A Complete History,* pp. 11, 172; Philemon Robbins, *A Plain Narrative* (Boston, 1747), p. 19.

27. Robbins, *A Plain Narrative,* pp. 5, 3.

28. Branford Church Records, Jan. 22, 1747, Connecticut State Library. The records also confirm that Robbins had invited Davenport to preach in his pulpit and had welcomed David Brainerd "to hold a meeting at his

house," which, the scribe admits, "we could not some of us so well approve of, under circumstances."

29. Robbins, *A Plain Narrative*, p. 10; Philemon Robbins to Nathaniel Chauncy, June 11, 1747, YUL. That rhetoric was sounded a year later in a letter to Bellamy which further chronicled Robbins's pastoral ills: "And as to a full answer to what they say upon the Remarks [the work which rebutted Robbins's *A Plain Narrative*] I believe that may be expected, if I should print anything further—but O tis perplexing fatiguing & killing—my people wont contribute for they think 'twill do no good—my purse is low—not having cleared for the Narrative yet—and some friends advise to let it alone . . . do write & tell me what I had best do . . . you have heard the Assembly advised us to call a Council [including] Adams of New London Williams of Pomfret (a great friend to Liberty—he abhors Tyranny)" Philemon Robbins to Joseph Bellamy, July 1, 1748, Gratz Collection. Historical Society of Pennsylvania. Even George Whitefield was concerned for Robbins's pastoral welfare: "he enquired," one of Robbins's sympathetic correspondents related, "(he knew where I belong'd) about Mess. Mills, Robbins, & Wheelock, and having heard of your difficulties, wanted a particular account. I gave him a narrative which he was extremely glad of—he charged me over & over to give his love to you . . . says next summer he designs to visit you." Isaac Foot to Philemon Robbins, Aug. 25, 1747, Robbins Family Papers, CHS. In the end, however, Robbins seems to have survived his pastoral controversy, unlike his fellow evangelical Jonathan Edwards, who advised Robbins in 1746 (at the beginning of the Wallingford affair) about what course of action he might take: "From all that I can learn of the affair," Edwards wrote, in response to Robbins's call for advice, "it appears to me by no means advisable for you to lay down your ministry at Branford if the major part of the people will stand by you." Jonathan Edwards to Philemon Robbins, Nov. 3, 1746, CHS.

30. From surviving manuscripts it is possible to narrow the compositional moment when Robbins shifted from linear narrative to abbreviated sermon notes. Robbins continued to write out his sermons at least through early May 1741 (the last extant linear–narrative sermon is dated May 3, 1741, Robbins Family Papers, YUL); by mid-June Robbins had transformed his mode of composition (the threshold sermon seems to be that of June 14, 1741, "Sabbath before the raising the new meeting House Here," Robbins Family Papers, CHS). The "Wallingford" sermon (analyzed below) dates from July 12, 1741, and the surviving sermons from the Awakening years all bear the stamp of the new style. While Jonathan Edwards altered his compositional mode at the height of the Awakening, his more liberal protagonist upriver, Jonathan Ashley of Deerfield, continued to compose his sermons in traditional linear form. The manuscript evidence thus adds weight to Stout's assertion that sermon format amounted to a "homiletic badge" (Harry S. Stout, *The New England Soul: Preaching and Religious Culture in Colonial New*

England [New York, 1986], p. 219), at least during the Great Awakening. See Jonathan Ashley, ms sermon April 8, 1742, New York Public Library. Ashley, of course, earlier opposed Edwards politically in the Robert Breck affair.

31. Nathan Cole, *The Spiritual Travels of Nathan Cole,* in David Levin and Theodore L. Gross, eds., *America in Literature* (New York, 1978), p. 359; Harry S. Stout and Peter Onuf, "James Davenport and the Great Awakening in New London," *Journal of American History* 70 (1983), 558.

32. Cole, *Spiritual Travels,* pp. 360, 366. The following contemporaneous report enhances Cole's dramatic portrait: "Last Sunday I had the greatest satisfaction (I sometimes wish our Language would admit of a Degree of comparison . . . above the Superlative) of hearing the Dear, meek, humble, gentle, compassionate—awful, powerful awakening Preacher Mr. Whitefield. I think he had more than ordinary freedom when he made application to Secure Sinners . . . I never heard the Thunders of Sinai so powerfully Delivered." Isaac Foot to Philemon Robbins, Aug. 25, 1747, CHS. The admixture of thunder and meekness provides an index to the complexities of the evangelical temperament. "Through his preaching," writes Stephen A. Marini, "Whitefield became the principal architect of a new oral culture for Radical Evangelicalism." *Radical Sects of Revolutionary New England* (Cambridge, Mass., 1982), p. 15.

33. Walter J. Ong, *The Presence of the Word: Some Prolegomena for Cultural and Religious History* (New Haven, 1967), p. 285.

34. Stout and Onuf, "James Davenport and the Great Awakening," p. 572; Chauncy, *Seasonable Thoughts,* p. 51 (quoted in Stout and Onuf, p. 567); Stout and Onuf, "James Davenport and the Great Awakening," p. 569.

35. Richard Bauman, *Let Your Words Be Few: Symbolism of Speaking and Silence among Seventeenth-Century Quakers* (New York, 1983), p. 35. I am indebted to Bauman for my discussion of oral-religious rhetoric.

36. Philemon Robbins, ms sermon Gen. 6:3, July 12, 1741, Robbins Family Papers, YUL. On each margin of the first page, above the doctrinal heading, Robbins lists (without date of delivery) the various pulpits/places where he preached the sermon: after "Brandford July 12, 1741" on the top left, he adds "New Haven/Waterbury/Newtown/Guilford"; on the top right, "Bapt/Wallingford" followed by Cambridge/Ripton/Grafton/Natoring?) /Rowley/E. Point." In light of the dozen or more occasions upon which Robbins spoke from these particular sermon notes it would be interesting to know whether the preacher himself felt in any way constrained by the potential *routinization* in the re-voicings of the Genesis text, the repetitions of its points of doctrine. That is, was there a qualitative difference in the audience experience of extemporaneous preaching as compared to that of the revivalist who, in preaching the same sermon, had perhaps come to expect, or anticipate, certain responses. Of course we imagine that the Wallingford Baptists (along with Robbins's other Connecticut audiences) felt the *immediate* impact of

the new style, even if for Robbins the faintings and cryings out said to be induced by revivalist rhetoric had become pro forma. In this respect students (or admirers) of the charismatic Whitefield should perhaps wonder if the son of thunder was ever *unengaged* by the routine of itinerant preaching.

37. Ibid., p. 1.

38. Bauman, *Let Your Words Be Few*, p. 149.

39. Robbins, ms sermon Gen. 6:3, p. 1, YUL. On the dialogic aspect of biblical rhetoric see Amos N. Wilder, *Early Christian Rhetoric: The Language of the Gospel* (Cambridge, Mass., 1964; 1971), pp. 14–15: "The very nature of the Gospel imposes upon [Paul in his letters to the Galatians] ways of expression that suggest dramatic immediacy: devices and rhythms of the speaker rather than the writer; imagined dialogue; the situation of a court hearing or church trial with its accusations and defences; the use of direct discourse; challenges not so much to understand the written words but to listen and behold; queries, exclamations and oaths." The revivalists' appropriation of Paul's social and rhetorical stance issued in denunciations from the pulpits and pens of ministers like Charles Chauncy and Isaac Stiles, who felt that the prophetic moment announced in the New Testament could never be reassumed or recovered, at least not by the likes of James Davenport. In Chauncy's view, Davenport put all ministers on trial by storming into their studies to question the authenticity of their piety. For a discussion of Whitefield's dialogic rhetoric and Davenport's "unorthodox tactics" see Marini, *Radical Sects*, pp. 16–19 (quote from p. 18).

40. Kenneth Burke, *A Rhetoric of Motives* (1950; 1969); quoted in Bauman, *Let Your Words Be Few*, p. 78). On the subject of incantorial rhetoric see Jackson I. Cope, "Seventeenth-Century Quaker Style," *PMLA* 76 (1956), 725–54.

41. I refer to Bushman, *From Puritan to Yankee*. On the question of women converts during revivals see Cedric B. Cowing, "Sex and Preaching in the Great Awakening," *American Quarterly* 20 (1968), 624–44.

42. On the question of age of conversion during the Awakening, see Stout and Onuf, "James Davenport and the Great Awakening," p. 562; on the links between the evolution of colonial society and age of religious conversion see John M. Murrin, "Review Essay," *History and Theory* 11 (1972), 226–75 (esp. pp. 241–42); Philip J. Greven, Jr., "Youth, Maturity, and Religious Conversion: A Note on the Ages of Converts in Andover, Massachusetts, 1711–1749," *Essex Society Historical Collections* 108 (1972), 119–34; and Ross W. Beales, Jr., "Cases for the Rising Generation: Youth and Religion in Colonial New England," Ph.D. Diss., University of California at Davis, 1971.

43. Robbins, ms sermon Gen 6:3, pp. 2, 4, YUL.

44. Robbins, "Diary, 1737–45" Houghton Library; Philemon Robbins, ms sermon Neh. 9:33, April 11, 1744, Robbins Family Papers, CHS.

45. Robbins, ms sermon Gen 6:3, p. 1, YUL.

46. Michael Walzer, "On the Role of Symbolism in Political Thought,"

Political Science Quarterly 82 (1967), 195n, 194; Charles E. Hambrick-Stowe, *The Practice of Piety: Puritan Devotional Disciplines in Seventeenth-Century New England* (Chapel Hill, 1982), p. 135. See p. 118: "The printed sermon must become a means of recovering at least something of the originally preached sermon, opening for us the realm of religious experience." As this chapter (I hope) makes clear, manuscript sermons are perhaps a more suggestive index of what was heard—*and felt*—in New England religious culture. For an important study of how manuscript sermons refract colonial reality, see Stout, *The New England Soul*. For discussions of ritual symbols, see Victor Turner, *The Ritual Process* (New York, 1969) and Abner Cohen, *Two-Dimensional Man: An Essay on the Anthropology of Power and Symbolism in Complex Society* (Berkeley, 1974). See p. 23: "Symbols are objects, acts, relationships or linguistic formations that stand *ambiguously* for a multiplicity of meanings, evoke emotions, and impel men to action" (emphasis in original).

47. Solomon Stoddard, *The Defects of Preachers Reproved* . . . (New London, 1724), in Richard L. Bushman, ed., *The Great Awakening: Documents on the Revival of Religion, 1740–1745* (New York, 1970), p. 15.

48. Philemon Robbins, ms sermon Psalms 85:6, Dec. 25, 1757, pp. 2, 3, Robbins Family Papers, YUL. The sermon concludes, "O the happy fruits of a *revival*" (Robbins's emphasis); *Funk & Wagnalls Standard College Dictionary* (New York, 1963).

49. Eugene E. White, *Puritan Rhetoric: The Issue of Emotion in Religion* (Carbondale, 1972), p. 20. White adds: "In the Puritan schema, the arousing of emotions was a legitimate function of the *Application,* theoretically the one place in the entire sermon in which the preacher could directly address the Affections" (p. 20).

50. Clifford Geertz, "Ideology as a Cultural System," in Geertz, *The Interpretation of Cultures* (New York, 1973), p. 219.

51. Philemon Robbins, ms sermon, Nov. 16, 1757, Robbins Family Papers, YUL. After the Stamp Act was repealed Robbins continued to remind his congregation to praise God for "our civil liberties & privilidges as belonging to British Nation—& as belonging to this Collony" and thank Him for "the preservation of the Life of our gracious King." Philemon Robbins, "A Thanksgiving Sermon," Nov. 19, 1767, Robbins Family Papers, YUL.

52. Richard D. Brown, "Spreading the Word: Rural Clergymen and the Communication Network of 18th-Century New England," *Massachusetts Historical Society Proceedings* 94 (1984), 6; Scott, *From Office to Profession,* p. 13.

53. Peter Shaw, *American Patriots and the Rituals of Revolution* (Cambridge, Mass., 1981), p. 7.

54. Philemon Robbins, "A Stamp Act Fast Sermon," Dec. 18, 1765, pp. 1, 2–3, Robbins Family Papers, CHS.

55. Ibid., pp. 4–5.

56. Ibid., pp. 7, 8–9. William DeLoss Love, after quoting the last two

lines from Robbins's manuscript, concluded: "There was but one inference from these sentences, and the hearers understood it." *The Fast and Thanksgiving Days of New England* (Boston, 1895), p. 331.

57. Robbins, "Stamp Act Sermon," p. 10, CHS.

58. Shaw, *American Patriots*, p. 23; Robbins, "Stamp Act Sermon," pp. 11–12, CHS. The blending of the rhetoric of retreat with millennial expectancy is continued in Robbins's revolutionary discourses. This key trope of an ark/country besieged suggests how great indeed was the conflict to which the patriot clergy were subject about the call to human action. The itch to escape history was always a compelling tendency.

59. Philemon Robbins, "A Thanksgiving Sermon preached . . . on Occasion of the Repeal of the Stamp Act," [1766] pp. 1, 2, Robbins Family Papers, CHS.

60. Ibid., pp. 4, 6, 7.

61. Charles Chauncy, *A Discourse on "the good news from a far Country"* (Boston, 1766), in John W. Thornton, ed. *The Pulpit of the American Revolution* (orig. 1860; rept. New York, 1970), pp. 139, 137; Robbins, "A Thanksgiving Sermon . . . ," p. 6. Cf. Lippy, *Seasonable Revolutionary*, p. 72: Chauncy's "opposition to the Stamp Act represented an effort to maintain intact the structures of political authority which he believed had been operative prior to its passage." For Chauncy's reaction to the Stamp Act, see Griffin, *Old Brick*, pp. 138–43.

62. Robbins, "A Thanksgiving Sermon," p. 10, CHS. "What a Patriot wt. a friend, what a lover of his country is here," Robbins's oration goes on to pronounce. For Chauncy on Pitt see *A Discourse*, p. 135n.

63. Robbins, "A Thanksgiving Sermon," p. 11, CHS.

64. "Now our soul is escaped as a bird out of the snare of the fowler—the forementioned author expresses himself in these words—," ibid., p. 12.

65. Ibid.

66. Bernard Bailyn, "Religion and Revolution: Three Biographical Studies," *Perspectives in American History* 6 (1970), 124. See pp. 121–24 for a discussion of Mayhew's "incendiary" rhetoric.

67. Gordon S. Wood, *The Creation of the American Republic, 1776–1787* (Chapel Hill, 1969), pp. 118, 7. For another allusion to the ministry in these terms, see p. 40.

68. Brown, "Spreading the Word," p. 13; Wood, *Creation of the American Republic*, p. 37.

69. Cf. Philip Davidson, *Propaganda and the American Revolution, 1763–1783* (Chapel Hill, 1941); Harry S. Stout, "Religion, Communications, and the Ideological Origins of the American Revolution," *William and Mary Quarterly*, 3d. ser., 34 (1977), 519–41; Isaac, *The Transformation of Virginia*, pp. 263, 264.

70. Stephen E. Lucas, *Portents of Rebellion: Rhetoric and Revolution in Philadelphia, 1765–76* (Philadelphia, 1976), pp. x, xvii; Isaac, *The Transformation of Virginia*, p. 263; Bailyn, "Religion and Revolution," p. 139.

Alice Baldwin speaks of the revolutionary clergy as "among the most zeal-ous," and the "chief agitators." *The New England Clergy,* p. xi. Most re-cently Patricia U. Bonomi speaks of how "preachers . . . used their pulpits as drums for politics." *Under the Cope of Heaven: Religion, Society, and Politics in Colonial America* (New York, 1986), p. 209. See pp. 209–16 for a general discussion of the clergy and the American Revolution.

71. Cf. Stout, "Religion, Communications," pp. 520, 528, and Stout, *The New England Soul,* passim.

72. See Nathan O. Hatch, *The Sacred Cause of Liberty: Republican Thought and the Millennium in Revolutionary New England* (New Haven, 1977), passim.

73. Winthrop S. Hudson, "Fast Days and Civil Religion," in Winthrop S. Hudson and L. J. Trinterud, *Theology in Sixteenth and Seventeenth-Century England* (Los Angeles, 1971), pp. 6–7. On the colony-wide fast see DeLoss Love, *Fast and Thanksgiving Days.* The Trumbull sermon is among the Trumbull Papers, YUL; the Edwards, Jr. sermon 390 in the Edwards, Jr. Papers, Hartford Seminary; the Sherwood was published as *A Sermon Con-taining Scriptural Instructions to Civil Rulers* (New Haven, 1774). From his pulpit Sherwood observed a "patriotic spirit . . . gradually kindling up in every freeman's breast, through the continent," which, "if duly regulated by Christian principles and rules [will] ensure success to American liberty and freedom" (p. vi).

74. Philemon Robbins, ms sermon Esther 4:3 ("The Day before the Con-gress at Philadelphia . . . Aug. 31, 1774"), pp. 1, 2, Robbins Family Pa-pers, CHS.

75. Bailyn, "Religion and Revolution," p. 137. On the appropriation of the Book of Esther see Bernard Bailyn, *The Ideological Origins of the Ameri-can Revolution* (Cambridge, Mass., 1967), p. 127. I borrow the phrase "conscience patriot" from Shaw, *American Patriots.*

76. Robbins, ms sermon Esther 4:3, pp. 7, 10a (insert), CHS.

77. Ibid., This passage best conveys the incantatory style; the reverbera-tions of "darkness" powerfully render the mood of the speaker, and perhaps of his auditors as well.

78. Ibid., pp. 10–11.

79. Ibid., pp. 11, 12.

80. Philemon Robbins, ms sermon Jeremiah 18:7, 8, Jan. 19, 1777, p. 2, Robbins Family Papers, CHS.

81. Lester H. Cohen, *The Revolutionary Histories: Contemporary Narra-tives of the American Revolution* (Ithaca, 1980), p. 51.

82. Robbins, ms sermon, Jan. 29, 1777, pp. 1, 3, CHS.

83. Ibid., pp. 5, 6, 9, 11.

84. Ibid., pp. 15, 16.

85. Philemon Robbins, ms sermon Joel 2:2, April 29, 1777, pp. 5, 8, 1, 9, 12, Robbins Family Papers, YUL.

86. The "design of the founding of the college," Robbins reminded his

audience in 1778, "was the education of youths for the ministry—but there is such poor Encouragement for students to turn their minds that way . . . that great numbers take to the Law & other employments & if special providence dont intervene—the grand end of its foundation will be in a great measure frustrated." Philemon Robbins, ms sermon Psalms 9:1, Nov. 26, 1778, p. 14, Robbins Family Papers, CHS.

87. Philemon Robbins, ms sermon Joel 2.2, April 29, 1777 (P.M.), pp. 1, 2, 3, Robbins Family Papers, YUL.

88. Ibid., pp. 3, 4. Note the thoroughly imbued "oral" dimension of Robbins's rhetoric: "What shall move us—Shall an Angel or glorified saint come down from heaven & speak the inviting glories of the upper world—or shall a damned soul break out of Hell and come & tell us, what unutterable torment horrors & despair there is in the regions of darkness—alas! if they hear not Moses & the prophets" (pp. 5–6).

89. Ibid., p. 11.

90. Ibid., p. 12.

91. Ibid., pp. 14, 15, 16.

92. Scott, *From Office to Profession,* Chapter 1.

93. Philemon Robbins, "A Sermon to give Courage in war . . . ," June 8, 1777 (preached again July 17) (part 1), pp. 1, 14, 12, 13, 12, Robbins Family Papers, YUL. Jonathan Edwards, Jr. will sermonize on precisely this theme, echoing the revival phrase "distinguishing marks" to identify patriot soldiers. See Jonathan Edwards, Jr., ms sermon 454, Dec. 22, 1775, Edwards, Jr. Papers, Hartford Seminary.

94. Robbins, "A Sermon to give Courage" (part 1), pp. 6–7, 7, 15, YUL. See in this context Bonomi, *Under the Cope of Heaven,* p. 216: "Ministers [during the Revolution] did the work of secular radicalism . . . they resolved doubts, overcame inertia, fired the heart, and exalted the soul."

95. Ibid. (P.M.), pp. 14, 4–5, 10, 16, 15, 16.

96. Bailyn, "Religion and Revolution," p. 134. Richard L. Bushman describes the "fluid continuum of discourse" that "revolutionary language" established in Massachusetts by 1774. Indeed, there "was a high level of political understanding dispersed throughout the Province." Richard L. Bushman, "Massachusetts Farmers and the Revolution," in Richard M. Jellison, ed., *Society, Freedom, and Conscience: The American Revolution in Virginia. Massachusetts, and New York* (New York, 1976), pp. 81, 80.

97. See Charles Royster, *A Revolutionary People at War: The Continental Army and American Character, 1775–1783* (Chapel Hill, 1979), p. 406: "recent studies suggest that religious ideas, images, and appeals were exploited by revolutionaries to dramatize analyses and goals that originated in secular political ideology." With Royster, I am trying "to suggest the ways in which one can see a fundamental influence . . . arising from a characteristically evangelical cast of mind."

98. Philemon Robbins, "A Thanksgiving Sermon," Dec. 18, 1777, p. 5, Robbins Family Papers, CHS.

99. Ibid., p. 6.

100. Ibid., p. 15; Wood, *Creation of the American Republic*, p. 37.

101. Philemon Robbins, "A Thanksgiving Sermon" Nov. 26, 1778, pp. 5–7, Robbins Family Papers, CHS.

102. On the various levels of the meaning of liberty see Ruth H. Bloch, *Visionary Republic: Millennial Themes in American Thought, 1756–1800* (New York, 1985), p. 45.

103. Robbins, "A Thanksgiving Sermon" Nov. 26, 1778, pp. 3, 11, CHS.

104. Ibid., p. 15.

105. Ibid., p. 16.

106. Philemon Robbins, ms sermon Psalms 2:11, Dec. 9, 1779, p. 19, CHS.

107. Robbins, "A Thanksgiving Sermon," Nov. 26, 1778, p. 16, CHS.

Chapter 2

1. Philemon Robbins to Joseph Bellamy, Aug. 2, 1757, Bellamy Papers, Hartford Seminary Library. It seems that Robbins's elder son, Ammi, transferred from Princeton to join his brother, Chandler, at Lebanon. See the sons' letters home, Ammi Robbins to Philemon Robbins, July 7, 1957, Robbins Family Papers, Yale University and Chandler Robbins to Philemon Robbins, Jan. 14, 1957, Robbins Family Papers, Yale University. At the end of his letter to Bellamy Robbins cannot resist inquiring about matters Edwardsean: "You have seen that Ingenious Saucy Piece against the President— the Enemies to calvinism are numerous. . . ." Throughout the eighteenth and nineteenth centuries Edwards was referred to as "President"; his son (who eventually became president of Union College) was called "Doctor."

2. Ezra Stiles, *The Literary Diary of Ezra Stiles*, ed. F. B. Dexter (New York, 1901), 3:275; Edmund S. Morgan, "The Revolution Considered as an Intellectual Movement" (1963), in Morgan, *The Challenge of the American Revolution* (New York, 1976), p. 72.

3. Jonathan Edwards, Jr., "Miscellaneous Observations on Preaching" (undated), Trask Library, Andover–Newton Theological School, quoted in Robert L. Ferm, *Jonathan Edwards the Younger, 1754–1801: A Colonial Pastor* (Grand Rapids, 1976), p. 88; Timothy Mather Cooley, quoted in William B. Sprague, *Annals of the American Pulpit* (New York, 1859), 1:659.

4. Morgan, "The Revolution Considered as an Intellectual Movement," p. 61.

5. Benjamin A. Dean, ALS to Hartford Seminary, May 31, 1897, Hartford Seminary Library.

6. Jonathan Edwards, Jr., *Observation on the Language of the Muhhekaneew Indians* (1788), in *The Works of Jonathan Edwards, D.D.*, ed. Tryon Edwards (Boston, 1850), 1:467; Gideon Hawley to J. W. Edwards (Edwards, Jr.'s son), June 10, 1802, Beinecke Library, Yale University.

7. Jonathan Edwards, Jr., "Diary," Beinecke Library, Yale University; Edwards, Jr.'s earliest extant sermon is inscribed "Sermon III Composed at Bethlem August 1766–Preached–at G. Barrington Oct 27, 1766–at Bethlem Nov. 2, 1766 at Princeton with appendix on christmas, 1766." "Sermon III" (Aug. 1766), Edwards, Jr. Papers, Hartford Seminary Library (hereafter cited as Edwards Papers).

8. The White Haven Church Council voted to invite Edwards as their pastor on September 16, 1768; at the Council meeting of December 6 the Half-way covenant was abolished: "Voted that whereas on the 6th Day of August in the year 1760 it was voted by this church that the Infants of such as own the covenant (being civil & moral Persons) shall be admitted to Baptism–Upon further consideration and Enquiry into the Qualifications required by the Gospel of Christ for Admission to Baptism this Church is of the opinion that the same Qualifications are necessary for Admitting persons to receive Baptism for themselves or children as for admission to full communion, and that none ought to be admitted but those who make a credible profession of real Christianity"; Edwards accepted the call on December 15 (noted in records on December 19) and was ordained on January 4, 1769. The story of a disaffected party's petition against Edwards's settlement and the council's efforts at placation may be followed in White Haven Church Records, Connecticut State Library (hereafter cited as CSL).

9. Philemon Robbins, "An Ordination Sermon Preached at White Haven Jan. 4th 1769 when Mr. Jonathan Edwards was ordained," Robbins Family Papers, CHS. The local Connecticut clergy assembled for the ordination, and Joseph Bellamy traveled down from Bethlehem. After delivering a sermon the young minister was evidently grilled by the council "with regard to his knowledge & orthodoxy in divinity & his religious experiences." White Haven Records, CSL.

10. Robbins, "An Ordination Sermon," CHS.

11. On the important distinctions between "regular" and "occasional" preaching see Harry S. Stout, *The New England Soul: Preaching and Religious Culture in Colonial New England* (New York, 1986), especially Chapter 2.

12. Tryon Edwards, "Memoir," in *Works of Jonathan Edwards, D.D.*, 1:xxxii; Benjamin A. Dean ALS to Hartford Seminary, May 17, 1899, Hartford Seminary Library.

13. Although I do not examine this sermon later, let me note here that it expresses virtually every trope of the patriot pulpit as described in Nathan O. Hatch, *The Sacred Cause of Liberty* (New Haven, 1977): the fear of imperial enslavement, the figure of the Whore of Babylon (applied now to England), the fear of the English church, the threat of Popery, and so on. The sermon is filled as well with recent political history, suggesting that Edwards the New Divinity man was fully attuned to the events around him and preaching in the tradition from which Hatch's logic would exclude him. See Jonathan Edwards, Jr., sermon 390, Aug. 31, 1774, Edwards Papers, Hart-

ford Seminary. The sermon is one of the fifty or so examples of Edwards's writing out the text of his address (fifty out of some 1200 extant sermons), usually for an occasion rather than as part of his regular preaching.

14. Jonathan Edwards, Jr., sermon 74, Aug. 31, 1769, Edwards Papers, Hartford Seminary. On Edwards's earliest orations see note 7 above. On the issue of evangelical sermonic styles see Stout, *The New England Soul,* pp. 219 ff.

15. Edwards, Jr., sermon 74.

16. Ibid.

17. Ibid.

18. Jonathan Edwards, Jr., sermon 454, Dec. 22, 1775, Edwards Papers, Hartford Seminary. The only discussion of Edwards, Jr.'s revolutionary sermons I am aware of is that by Wesley C. Ewert, "Jonathan Edwards the Younger: A Biographical Essay," Th.D. Diss., Hartford Theological Seminary, 1953, pp. 78–86.

19. Jonathan Edwards, Jr., sermon 400, Nov. 24, 1774, Edwards Papers, Hartford Seminary.

20. Jonathan Edwards, Jr., sermon 93, Jan. 1770, Edwards Papers, Hartford Seminary.

21. Jonathan Edwards, Jr., sermon 156, March 1771, Edwards Papers, Hartford Seminary.

22. Ibid.

23. William Gordon to Joseph Bellamy, July 14, 1769, Bellamy Papers, Hartford Seminary.

24. Edwards, Jr.'s symbol for "world," ☉, seems a hieroglyphic custom of the evangelical pulpit. Jonathan Edwards himself employs the shorthand in his sermons, and I have seen it occasionally in letters among the New Divinity men.

25. Jonathan Edwards, Jr., sermon 347, Sept. 1773, Edwards Papers, Hartford Seminary. Interestingly, this sermon combines linear narrative with the fragmentary mode of evangelical style. In general, Edwards's few fully penned orations are occasional in origin, yet at the end of this particular sermon Edwards concludes with four pages of shorthand notes, and later, when repreaching a version of the sermon in May 1777 ("Address to the officers & soldiers of the Continental army present"), he continues the fragmentary style that characterizes the bulk of his extant sermon manuscripts.

26. Jonathan Edwards, Jr., sermon 400, Nov. 24, 1774, Edwards Papers, Hartford Seminary. Unlike Philemon Robbins, Edwards did not pronounce publicly on the Stamp Act. Of course he was only twenty-one at the time, but his characterization of a "dumbstruck," fearful clergy suggests that in the case of the ministerial reaction to the Act they may have *followed* the more vocal populace in joining the resistance; the people, that is, dared to say nay. On the Stamp Act riots see Dirk Hoerder, *Crowd Action in Revolutionary Massachusetts 1765–1780* (New York, 1977), pp. 85–143.

27. Edwards, Jr., sermon 400, Hartford Seminary. For another nostalgic

invocation of the Great Awakening see the discussion of Levi Hart (Chapter 3). Although Jon Butler's recent polemic against the extent and import of the revivals of the 1740s is compelling on a number of points, his challenge that the Awakening is a scholarly "fiction" is belied by the testimony—and nostalgia—of numerous historical actors to the "great work" that visited the country between 1740 and 1742. *Something* happened in colonial American religious culture to which evangelicals looked back with glowing memories. See Jon Butler, "Enthusiasm Described and Decried: The Great Awakening as Interpretive Fiction," *Journal of American History* 69 (1982), 305–25. On the political consciousness-raising agency of the Great Awakening, see Bruce Tucker, "The Reinvention of New England, 1691–1770," *New England Quarterly* 59 (1986), 315–40, especially p. 333.

28. David Austin to Roger Sherman, Feb. 20, 1790, Yale University, quoted in Ferm, *Jonathan Edwards the Younger,* p. 141; Jonathan Edwards, Jr. to Benjamin Trumbull, July 7, 1772, Trumbull Papers, Yale University. The son's 1774 edition of *Work of Redemption* realized a longstanding desire of the evangelical clergy. "Tho I long to see Mr. Edwards' confutation of the different branches of Arminianism," John Erskine (Edwards's longstanding Scottish correspondent) confessed to Joseph Bellamy, "yet I more long to see his intended history of man's redemption. From such a pen upon such a subject, something highly valuable may be expected. May a kind providence preserve from danger a life to important!" John Erskine to Joseph Bellamy, March 24, 1755, Bellamy Papers, Hartford Seminary. The son continued his filial–textual labors after *Work of Redemption.* Joseph Bellamy mentions in a letter to his daughter that "Mr. Edwards is transcribing his Fathers sermons for the press—plain, practical, serious, solemn, full of life & spirit, Selected out of many hundreds, to be printed as soon as times will admit." Joseph Bellamy to Rebecca Hart, July 3, 1775, Bellamy Papers, Hartford Seminary. In the same letter Bellamy read the times as a moment when "the God of Zion who is Come to visit the Land."

29. Jonathan Edwards, sermon Neh. 4:14, June 1746, Beinecke Library, Yale University; Jonathan Edwards, sermon Rev. 7:11, July 10, 1746, Beinecke Library, Yale University. For discussions of Edwards's apocalyptic thought see Stephen J. Stein, Introduction, Edwards, *Apocalyptic Writings,* vol. 4 of *The Works of Jonathan Edwards* (New Haven, 1977) and Stout, *The New England Soul,* pp. 237 ff.

30. Jonathan Edwards, "History of Redemption Notebook 'A,' " p. 37; Jonathan Edwards, sermon, Dec. 5, 1745 (preached again Nov. 1757), Beinecke Library, Yale University. For a description of the "Redemption Notebooks" see John F. Wilson, "Jonathan Edwards's Notebook for 'A History of the Work of Redemption,' " in R. B. Knox, ed., *Reformation, Continuity and Dissent: Essays in Honour of Geoffrey Nuttall* (London, 1977), pp. 239–54.

31. Edwards, "History of Redemption Notebook 'A,' " pp. 34, 35.

32. Edwards, Jr., sermon 400, Hartford Seminary.

33. Edwards, Jr., sermon 454, Hartford Seminary. This sermon is one of Edwards's fully written out performances.

34. Ibid.

35. Ibid.

36. On the "multivocal" dimension of rhetoric see the work of Pocock, Turner, Bloch, and Abner Cohen cited in the Introduction.

37. Jonathan Edwards, Jr., sermon 460, Jan. 17, 1776, Edwards Papers, Hartford Seminary. This sermon was delivered later in the year (May, June, and November) at various New Haven area pulpits.

38. Jonathan Edwards, Jr., sermon 420, April 19, 1775 ("Preached at the annual Fast; Preached at East Haven April 23, 1775"), Edwards Papers, Hartford Seminary. In the preacher's shorthand the phrase appears as "w. wt. of night—/common to ask."

39. Ibid. Note how the contrapuntal rhythm of the rhetoric recalls the earlier pattern of historical challenges to liberty and the (reflexive) response of spiritual renewal.

40. Ibid. My phrase "engineering for the millennium" borrows from Emerson's famous words, "engineering for America," spoken in eulogy over Thoreau.

41. Ibid. I refer of course to Edmund S. Morgan's important "The Puritan Ethic and the American Revolution" (1967), in Morgan, *The Challenge of the American Revolution*, pp. 88–138. Edwards continued the theme of frugality later that spring; "in private and public," he advised, "in eating—drink—equipage—Let the rich set the example/Do everything for the good of our country." Jonathan Edwards, Jr., sermon 424, June 4, 1775, Edwards Papers, Hartford Seminary. Edwards repeated the sermon "At Milford Society" the following Sunday (June 11).

42. Edwards, Jr., sermon 420. The date of Edwards's sermon (April 1775) argues against his consciously adopting the language of Paine's *Common Sense* which appeared in January 1776. On the Lockean influence on revolutionary ideology see Jay Fliegelman, *Prodigals and Pilgrims: The American Revolution against Patriarchal Authority, 1760–1800* (New York, 1982).

43. Edwards, Jr., sermon 420, Hartford Seminary. The asterisked passage, which concludes the sermon, reads as follows:

> *but if not—how ill prepared for either?
> at war with G[od]
> how—to go towards fellowmen?
> How prepared for peace?—no peace for the wicked
> How for life?
> Life in sin—
> treasure up wrath

> How—for death?
> go to hell
> How for this night
> God against—who
> /for you?

44. Jonathan Edwards, Jr., sermon 459, Jan. 17, 1776, Edwards Papers, Hartford Seminary. (This sermon, the same date as sermon 460, was probably delivered in the morning.) Michael Walzer, *Exodus and Revolution* (New York, 1986). "Walzer's book is written from the perspective of victory," observes Edward W. Said, in an important critique of the political narrative implicit in Walzer's study. In Edwards's case the rhetoric of Exodus sounded from the pulpit of a historical actor uncertain about the outcome of the battle; still, the preacher was not voicing the language of captivity and deliverance from below, and we should always bear in mind (as Said reminds us) the uses, political and psychological, to which the rhetoric of Exodus has been employed. Edward W. Said, "Michael Walzer's 'Exodus and Revolution': A Canaanite Reading," *Grand Street* 5 (1986), 86–106 (quote from p. 105).

45. Edwards, Jr., sermon 459, Hartford Seminary. On the "Olive Branch" petition of 1775, to which Edwards may be alluding in the sermon, see Jack N. Rakove, "The Decision for American Independence: A Reconstruction," *Perspectives in American History* 10 (1976), 247–49, 272–75.

46. Edwards, Jr., sermon 459, Hartford Seminary. The dire phrase, quoted at the end, is from Jonathan Edwards, Jr., sermon 485, June 30, 1776, Edwards Papers, Hartford Seminary.

47. Jonathan Edwards, Jr., sermon 588, Nov. 26, 1778, Edwards Papers, Hartford Seminary. The processual aspect of the rhetoric derives from the phrases "about to," "may come out"—in each case, history is represented as passing through a juncture, a threshold.

48. Jonathan Edwards, Jr., "Submission to Rulers," in *The Works of Jonathan Edwards, D.D.* ed. Tryon Edwards, 1:245, 246.

49. Jonathan Edwards, Jr., sermon 844, April 12, 1784 ("At the Freemen's meeting"), Edwards Papers, Hartford Seminary. "This the liberty," the preacher goes on to explain, "which was in Israel" when there "was no king . . . no government/everyone with right in own eyes."

50. Ibid.

51. Ibid. The following passage from an Edwards sermon of late April 1775 suggests how the myth of the Founding Fathers was transmitted in the evangelical pulpit; it also places Edwards firmly in the tradition of the revolutionary preachers outlined in Hatch, *The Sacred Cause of Liberty*. Listen to Edwards, the so-called metaphysical preacher, in the wake of Lexington and Concord:

> We are also threatened with the loss [of] our religion. The first & chief motives which our fathers in coming into this land, & forming a settle-

ment was the free & unmolested enjoyment of religion here. They co'd not enjoy freedom in religion in their own native land; & theref[ore] they sought it in the howling wilderness of America. Here they found it, & have for a considerable time, they & their posterity enjoyed it. But now we are threatened with the total loss of it. The parliament of G.B. have lately established popery in Canada, from this & fr. other facts it is supposed that the chief men in power in G.B. are papists, & they wo'd be glad of an opportunity to establish popery thro out all these American colonies. Such an opportunity they will have, if they shall conquer us; & we have the greatest reason to think they will not let the opportunity slip, but will introduce popery or some other religious tyranny as bad in its consequences.

Jonathan Edwards, Jr., sermon 421, April 30, 1775, Edwards Papers, Hartford Seminary.

52. Richard D. Shiels, "The Second Great Awakening in Connecticut: Critique of the Traditional Interpretation," *Church History* 49 (1980), 404. "From our perspective," summarizes Edwards's modern biographer, "the tragedy of his life seems to be his incapacity to see beyond his times. He failed to offer new life to Reformed Theology." Ferm, *Jonathan Edwards the Younger,* p. 175. Even Bruce Kuklick's recent study of the New Divinity and its legacy continues this judgment. See his *Churchmen and Philosophers: From Jonathan Edwards to John Dewey* (New Haven, 1985).

53. Stiles, *Literary Diary,* 3:344, 438, quoted in Ferm, *Jonathan Edwards the Younger,* p. 138. For an account of Edwards's dismissal, see Ferm, pp. 134–47. One particular episode of alienation occurred in March 1777, when "brother Punderson" asserted, *"viva voce,"* that "the church was degenerated from what it was 30 years ago, in not insisting on long & particular relations of experience, in candidates for admission . . . He also objected to the preaching of the pastor & of the ministers in general of the present day." The dispute continued for almost a year, until mid-January 1778, when a form of reconciliation was reached: "Jan. 18. 1778–This day brother Thomas Punderson made his confession, as was proposed . . . & was restored by the church to wonted charity & communion. A confession was made before the congregation, as usual." On January 1 Punderson had charged Edwards with "designedly arrogating to himself . . . the power & office of the Holy Ghost." White Haven Church Records, CSL.

54. According to his son-in-law, "Dr. Edwards' irritability was an obvious, and evidently a constitutional, characteristic. Of this trying infirmity no person could be more sensible than himself. In his confidential interviews he used not unfrequently to speak of it." Quoted in Sprague, *Annals of the American Pulpit,* 1:658.

55. Edwards joined his New Haven area pastoral colleagues (including Stiles and James Dana) in welcoming George Washington to town on October 17, 1789, praying that the General be preserved, and announcing that

"you have been carried triumphantly & gloriously through the late War, terminating in the Establishment of American Liberty, & perhaps the Liberty of All Nations . . . And may this new rising Republic, under your auspices, the most glorious for Population, Perfection of Policy & happy Administration of Government that ever appeared on Earth." Ezra Stiles et al., "To the President of the United States," Oct. 17, 1789, Stiles Papers, Beinecke Library, Yale University. The next day Edwards, Jr. preached on the theme of fathers and sons: "Let children submit to the instructions & restraints of their pious parents." Sermon 1109, Oct. 18, 1789 ("when President Washington was in New Haven, & present at the delivery of this sermon"), Edwards Papers, Hartford Seminary.

56. Cf. Richard D. Brown, "Spreading the Word: Rural Clergymen and the Communication Network of 18th-Century New England," *Massachusetts Historical Society Proceedings* 94 (1984), 1–14.

57. Jonathan Edwards, Jr., sermon 741, Dec. 13, 1781 ("Thanksgiving after the capture of Lt. Cornwallis & his army on 19 of Oct. 1781"), Edwards Papers, Hartford Seminary.

Chapter 3

1. Levi Hart, *Liberty Described and Recommended* . . . (Hartford, 1775), in *American Political Writing during the Founding Era, 1760–1805,* vol. 1, ed. Charles S. Hyneman and Donald S. Lutz (Indianapolis, 1983), p. 312. On Hart's key sermon, see Alan Heimert, *Religion and the American Mind from the Awakening to the Revolution* (Cambridge, Mass., 1966), pp. 395, 457. On Hart's abolitionist labors, see Joseph A. Conforti, *Samuel Hopkins and the New Divinity Movement* (Grand Rapids, 1981), pp. 139, 151–53; James D. Essig, *The Bonds of Wickedness: American Evangelicals Against Slavery, 1770–1808* (Philadelphia, 1982).

2. Levi Hart, "Diary," Oct. 22, 1760, Gratz Collection, Historical Society of Pennsylvania (hereafter cited as HSP); Levi Hart, "A Diary began January 24, 1761," Gratz Collection HSP. In subsequent entries Hart comments on finishing the Life, remarking that he "was very tenderly touched with some parts of it," especially the deaths of Sara Edwards and Esther Burr, Edwards's daughter.

3. Jonathan Edwards, Jr. to Levi Hart, Jan. 6, 1786, Houghton Library, Harvard University.

4. Hart, "A Diary," HSP. "In order to discern the relationship between religious rhetoric and Revolutionary thought," asserts Bruce Tucker, "historians need to understand how New Englanders were influenced to remember the Awakening and how that memory impinged on their consciousness about political issues." In light of the manuscript evidence and the examples of Edwards, Jr. and Hart, this observation takes on even more suggestive weight for assessing the connections between revival and revolution. Bruce

Tucker, "The Reinvention of New England, 1691–1770," *New England Quarterly* 59 (1986), p. 333.

5. Hart, "A Diary," HSP; Benjamin Lord, *Christ's Embassadors* . . . (Providence, 1763), p. 36. Hart ministered in Preston, Connecticut for almost sixty years. On Bellamy's powers in the pulpit, even Samuel Hopkins admitted that the 'Pope" of Litchfield County had no peer; "Thursday August 28 [1755] This Day being attend as a publick Fast, Mr. Bellamy preach'd for me all Day—I believe there is not a better Preacher in America on all accounts." Samuel Hopkins, Diary, July 15, 1754–Nov. 13, 1756, Trask Library, Andover–Newton Theological School. Jonathan Edwards's son, however, was not as laudatory in estimating Bellamy's career. "Was greatly excelled in preaching," Jonathan Edwards, Jr. remarked in a funeral sermon for Bellamy in 1790, "had talents to have made a preacher of first character—but his education not equal to his abilities." Edwards goes on to say that Bellamy "lived in a part of the country where niceties of style & delivery not so much noticed." Jonathan Edwards, Jr., sermon 1132, March 21, 1790, Edwards Papers, Hartford Seminary. For a discussion of the social divisions in the eighteenth-century pulpit (with specific reference to Bellamy) see Heimert, *Religion and the American Mind*, pp. 208–9.

6. Levi Hart, "Sunday Diary," Connecticut Historical Society (hereafter cited as CHS). "A thin congregation," observed Hart in late December 1766, "but enough for God to be glorified in." "A Diary," HSP.

7. Hart, "A Diary," Gratz Collection, HSP.

8. Levi Hart, Thanksgiving Sermon, June 26, 1766, CHS.

9. Levi Hart, "Notebook," Aug. 28, 1759, CHS.

10. Hart, Thanksgiving Sermon, June 26, 1766, CHS.

11. Ibid.

12. In fact, Robbins's son Ammi addressed the same question on monarchy in his Notebook at virtually the same educational moment as Hart. Responding to the query "Whether Monarchical Government is most conducive to the general good of a kingdom or nation?", Ammi answered with the following reply, which anticipates the rhetoric (and the psychic conflict with sanctioned authority) of the patriot clergy fifteen years later: "Negatively. The great Favor & Blessing of Liberty is one of the invaluable Blessings of Heaven on the Possessors of it . . . Tis the prime Blessing and Chief Requisite to the imperfect Happiness (for the greatest that can be attended to, in this Life is imperfect) . . . but on the contrary, slavery and Tyranny (for I can call it the state of those under monarchical Governments at least in many instances little better) I say, tend to make those who enjoy the blessing of true Liberty to shudder & tremble"; there follows a series of cautionary examples, including Nero and Caligula. The younger Robbins concludes his meditation on the "Destructive nature and tendency of monarchical Government" with "the thot of living under such monarchs . . . is sufficient to strike silence to all those who appear in the Defence of it. Thus

I've . . . endeav'd to defend the Negative of our debate, but shall defer the decision to our tutor." Ammi R. Robbins, "Question Book begun July 4, 1758," Robbins Family Papers, CHS.

13. See, for example, the following representative passage from Hart's Diary for Nov. 1, 1770: "Wrote to Dr. Erskine & sent a pacquet from Dr. Bellamy which was to have gone last fall but was thro neglect of friends to whos case it was commited put off till this time—His disappointment I mention in his letter as also my writing in May last in answer to his of July— 1769—expresd my desire of receiving the most noted publications on divinity in Scotland . . . The revival of religion in the College at N– Jersey–the death of Mr. Whitefield–the dark state of public affairs in America." Gratz Collection, HSP. Many of Hart's unpublished writings deal with doctrinal disputes. On the theological debates among the Edwardsean guardians and their more liberal brethren, see Conrad Wright, *The Beginnings of Unitarianism* (Boston, 1955) and Conforti, *Samuel Hopkins and the New Divinity Movement.* For a contemporary account see Ezra Stiles, *The Literary Diary of Ezra Stiles,* 3 vols., ed. F. B. Dexter (New York, 1901).

14. Hart, Diary, Nov. 16, 1775, Gratz Collection, HSP. The context is "a day of public thanksgiving in this colony. my text Psal 124"; Levi Hart, sermon 31, Dec. 1775, CHS.

15. Hart, Diary, April 1, 1774; June 30, 1774; Aug. 31, 1774, Gratz Collection, HSP. That New Light Hart, Joseph Bellamy's son-in-law, would fill in the pulpit for the more liberal Stiles (whose father Isaac was an avowed anti-revivalist) suggests that doctrinal and filial allegiance was of less import in the summer of 1774 than the need for clerical bonding.

16. Hart, Diary, Aug. 21, 1774, Gratz Collection, HSP.

17. Levi Hart, sermon, Aug. 21, 1774, CHS.

18. The Jeremiah sermon (from Jeremiah 8:22) is undated but falls between the August 21 oration discussed earlier and a sermon of August 28 (from Romans 10:4) from whose "Improvement" I quote the passage on the work of redemption. Levi Hart, sermon, Aug. 28, 1774, CHS. In the Diary Hart recorded, "Weak in body, but favor'd with some degree of divine presence my text all day, Rom 10:4." Hart, Diary, Aug. 28, 1774, Gratz Collection, HSP.

19. Levi Hart, Diary, April 23, 1775, Gratz Collection, HSP.

20. In this respect John M. Murrin's admonition to those who insist on the *agency* of evangelical mentality in mobilizing for revolution is probably correct. "We might argue," he asserts, "that the evangelical style of exhortation found its truest role in winning the war, not bringing it on . . . They [in this case the Baptists] responded to what others created." The nature of the evangelicals' *response,* however, leads to more interesting, suggestive areas of inquiry than the issue of religious–political *origins* of dissent. John M. Murrin, "No Awakening, No Revolution? More Counterfactual Speculations," *Reviews in American History* 11 (1983), 168.

21. Levi Hart, Fast Sermon, April 19, 1775. CHS.

22. Ibid. The Diary entry for that same day reads: "This day was general fast in this colony, my text AM Isaiah 22: 12, 13, 14. pm Esther 3:15—was favor'd with a degree of freedom of thought & expression—may it please God to forgive the sins of our humiliations & grant salvation to the land & nation." Hart, Diary, April 19, 1775, Gratz Collection, HSP.

23. Hart, Fast Sermon, April 19, 1775; CHS; Levi Hart, sermon, May 24, 1775, CHS.

24. Hart, Fast Sermon, April 19, 1775, CHS.

25. "Was favoured with a degree of freedom of thought & expression," Hart confided on April 19, "may it please God to forgive the sins of our humiliations & grant salvation to the land & nation, & his dear church & Kingdom." Hart, Diary, Gratz Collection, HSP.

26. Levi Hart, Diary, April 23, 1775, Gratz Collection, HSP.

27. The phrase is from James W. Davidson, *The Logic of Millennial Thought* (New Haven, 1977). On the question of politics and millennialism in the revolutionary pulpit see Ruth H. Bloch, *Visionary Republic: Millennial Themes in American Thought, 1756–1800* (New York, 1985) and Harry S. Stout, *The New England Soul: Preaching and Religious Culture in Colonial New England* (New York, 1986).

28. Levi Hart, Diary, April 30, 1775, Gratz Collection, HSP. Hart repeats the phrase on July 30, 1775, Sept. 22, 1776, and April 14, 1777.

29. Levi Hart, Diary, July 2, 1775, Gratz Collection, HSP.

30. Levi Hart, sermon, Dec. 31, 1775, CHS..

31. Ibid.; Hart, Diary, Dec. 31, 1775, Gratz Collection, HSP.

32. Levi Hart, "Continental Fast" sermon, May 17, 1776, CHS.

33. Ibid.

34. Ibid. The shift in case is not sustained in Hart's oration to Preston the following week: "This controversy is not between great Britain & the colonies for according to the best accounts a great majority of the most knowing & wealthy people there are on our side." In the same sermon, however, Hart speaks of "all that hath been said by fawning sycophants in favor of the divine right of kings, & his doctrines of passive obedience & non resistance"—quite a shift from his early exercises. Levi Hart, sermon, May 24, 1776, CHS.

35. Levi Hart, Diary, Sept. 15, 1776; Sept. 8, 1776, Gratz Collection, HSP.

36. Levi Hart, Thanksgiving Sermon, Nov. 26, 1777, CHS.

37. Levi Hart, Thanksgiving Sermon, Dec. 9, 1779, CHS.

Chapter 4

1. Ruth H. Bloch, *Visionary Republic: Millennial Themes in American Thought, 1756–1800* New York, 1985), p. 63. On the "multivocal" overtones of "liberty" see p. 45.

2. Quoted in Sarah Cabot Sedgwick and Christina Sedgwick Marquand, *Stockbridge: 1739–1939, A Chronicle* (Great Barrington, Mass., 1939),

p. 112; Franklin B. Dexter, *Biographical Sketches of the Graduates of Yale College* . . . (New York, 1885–1912), 2:391. Catherine Sedgwick offered a very different portrait of West in a letter for Sprague's compendium of the Protestant ministry. See W. B. Sprague, *Annals of the American Pulpit* (New York, 1859), 1:551. On Allen's rhetoric see Theodore M. Hammett, "Revolutionary Ideology in Massachusetts: Thomas Allen's 'Vindication' of the Berkshire Constitutionalists, 1778," *William and Mary Quarterly* 33 (1976), 514–27.

3. Theodore M. Hammett, "The Revolutionary Ideology in Its Social Context: Berkshire County, Massachusetts 1725–1785," Ph.D. Diss., Brandeis University, 1976, pp. 227–28. Hammett's study nevertheless offers a rich social history of the region. On western Massachusetts see Robert J. Taylor, *Western Massachusetts in the Revolution* (Providence, 1954) and Richard D. Birdsall, *Berkshire County: A Cultural History* (New Haven, 1959), especially Chapter 3.

4. Richard D. Brown, *Revolutionary Politics in Massachusetts: The Boston Committee of Correspondence and the Towns, 1772–1774* (Cambridge, Mass., 1970), p. 212. On the question of political ferment see also Stephen E. Patterson, *Political Parties in Revolutionary Massachusetts* (Madison, 1973), pp. 108–9: "By the fall of 1774, the revolutionary movement in Massachusetts had developed three significant characteristics: first, an awakened backcountry . . . second, both the course of events and the attitudes of the people, particularly in rural areas, had contributed to an increase in the practice of democracy; and third . . . the activities of rural towns . . . tended to be more radical and daring than those of the eastern commercial towns." I have also learned much about the religious and social world of Berkshire County from John Brooke, " 'Let Virtue be Your Practice Here Till We do Meet Again': A Case Study in the Social Context of a Grammar of Gravestone Symbolism," seminar paper, University of Pennsylvania, 1978.

5. See, for example, Stephen West, sermon 594 ("To the Indians," Dec. 17, 1769), West Papers, Trask Library, Andover–Newton Theological School (hereafter cited as West Papers): "You do not seem to consider that there is a God every where present. / You do not consider what a great & glorious being he is. [There follow four more admonitory statements.] You do not consider in what a dangerous state you are in." I am indebted to my colleague at the Charles Warren Center, Christopher Miller, for the suggestion about a possible translator.

6. Stephen West, sermon 311, Dec. 1, 1764, West Papers.

7. Stephen West, sermon 417, Nov. 30, 1766, West Papers.

8. Stephen West, sermon 712, Dec. 3, 1772, West Papers.

9. Stephen West, sermon 763, March 13, 1774, West Papers.

10. Ibid.

11. Ibid. The previous July West had concluded a sermon with a recognition "that poor Stockbridge sinners" may be "awakened." "If a number have

been converted," he ecstatically explained. "O what joy—heaven." Stephen West, sermon 741, July 18, 1773, West Papers.

12. Of course the social reality of prerevolutionary Stockbridge can be abstracted only partially from the language of its minister; and of course Thomas Allen and the Constitutionalists were perhaps closer in expressing the sentiments of the majority of Berkshire colonists. Still, despite West's conservative politics and elitist perspective his rhetoric refracts the polemical atmosphere of the region; indeed, his rhetoric everywhere *confirms* his troubled, skittish response to looming revolution.

13. Stephen West, sermon 765, March 27, 1774,, West Papers.

14. Ibid.

15. Ibid.

16. For a discussion of West's sermonic output see "A Note on Manuscript Sources."

17. Stephen West, sermon 775, June 6, 1774, West Papers. This sermon, from Amos 4:12 (one of Levi Hart's favorite texts), opens with the following ominous gloss: "The Prophet wrote before the final captivity and destruction—Israel."

18. On the convening of a County congress and the designation of the Fast Day see E. F. Jones, *Stockbridge, Past and Present* (Springfield, Mass., 1854), p. 168.

19. Stephen West, sermon 781, July 14, 1774, West Papers.

20. Ibid.

21. Ibid.

22. On the multivalent aspects of "liberty" see Bloch, *Visionary Republic,* pp. 44–46.

23. Stephen West, sermon 800, Dec. 15, 1774, West Papers. "Let us remember, my hearers,—called this day to rejoyce with a holy, reverential joy in God," West penned at the beginning of one of the sermon's "Reflections." We should also remember West's consciousness of audience—"my hearers"— as we listen to the implicit continuous dialogue within the oration.

24. Ibid.

25. Stephen West, sermon 813, May 11, 1775, West Papers. This key sermon takes as its doctrine the following passage from Jeremiah 18:7, 8 concerning the prophet's voice and the movement of history: "At what instant I shall speak concerning a nation, and concerning a kingdom, to pluck up, to pull down & to destroy it." In this passage we may observe West following his own advice, not "to preach smooth things [to] people" (sermon 792, Nov. 20, 1774); "That is smooth, which appears practicable & easy to human nature." Yet the jagged, disfluent tones of West's rhetoric betray his own effort to smooth over the rough, exposed edges of history.

26. Stephen West, sermon 818, Fast sermon, July 20, 1775, West Papers.

27. On this point I follow the work of Gary Nash and Harry Stout, among others.

28. West, sermon 818.

29. Stephen West, sermon 829, Nov. 23, 1775, West Papers. Note, of course, the allusion to the Passover/Exodus. The sermon is filled with references to the Stockbridge context, including "the Canadian Indians—to be ever remembered—have among them captives taken from N. England, adopted into their principle families—now become chiefsmen." But what was remarkable in this season was how God's providence had caused "those who used to be our natural enemies to be at peace with us . . . We did not know that God sent them therefore for such a time as this."

30. For the military experience of Robbins's son Ammi see his letters home to Branford. "To give you an idea of human misery & compleat earthly wretchedness such as is exhibited in these Hospitals I will not attempt. Only reflect a minute that here are the dregs of the most sickly Army that ever was in America . . . Thus the destroying Angel passes thro our Northern Army . . . This is one of the cords with which God's scourge is composed & with which he is now chastising wicked America." Ammi Robbins to Philemon Robbins, July 22, 1776, Robbins Family Papers, CHS. On John Cleaveland's patriotic efforts during the Revolution see Christopher M. Jedrey, *The World of John Cleaveland* (New York, 1979).

31. Stephen West, sermon 834, Feb. 11, 1776, West Papers; Stephen West, sermon 858, "Thanksgiving," Dec. 12, 1776, West Papers.

32. Stephen West, sermon 841, May 17, 1776, West Papers.

33. Stephen West, sermon 847, Fast, Aug. 1, 1776, West Papers.

34. Listen, in this respect, to Samuel Hopkins on the "happy" apocalyptic news of the Indian wars of the 1750s: "I send this by the special Post, who will bring you the sad news of our Forts being Beset by the Enemy!—Worse News is doubtless yet behind—Will this wake the Country up?—I think not—I believe Albany must be taken first if not Sheffield [,] Canaan etc." Samuel Hopkins to Joseph Bellamy, Aug. 5, 1757, Bellamy Papers, Hartford Seminary Library. The following week Hopkins wrote Bellamy again that "Darkness yet attends us. We want [i.e., need] something much worse, to bring us to a feeling." Samuel Hopkins to Joseph Bellamy, Aug. 12, 1757, Bellamy Papers, Hartford Seminary Library.

35. West, sermon 847.

36. West, sermon 852.

37. Still, we might apply Stephen Marini's description of the effect of millennial preaching during the New Light Stir of the 1780s to West himself, and perhaps his audience as well: "For rural revivalists, the Dark Day, the wartime atmosphere, and the revival itself all were indications of prophetic fulfillment portending the Last Days. Understanding themselves as experiencing the narrative of the Book of Revelation, revivalists urged their hearers to join the last witnesses to the gospel and claim the powers of spiritual and physical perfection granted to the apostolic remnant." West, at least, experienced the times as his personal apocalyptic narrative. Stephen A. Marini,

Radical Sects of Revolutionary New England (Cambridge, Mass., 1982), p. 47.

38. West, sermon 852.

39. Stephen West, sermon 861, Fast, Jan. 29, 1777, West Papers.

40. Ibid. For all of West's trans-Atlantic anxiety, the Fast sermon of late January 1777 betrays a more local concern—West's conservative stance in Berkshire politics. When, in the Improvement, he declares, "Such prayers for deliverance as we are encouraged to make will be accomplished—good will—towards enemies—Such a spirit will suppress revenge—shan't think or talk of them as being worst themselves—Therefore That spirit which vents—curses—king—parliament—tories, is unfit for [?] good," West may be alluding to the community's rebuking estimate of his "mild" patriotism. Still, West would speak in 1779 of "a government founded in—hearts—people." Sermon 919, May 6, 1779, West Papers.

41. Stephen West, sermon 884, Thanksgiving, Nov. 20, 1777, West Papers.

42. See Hans W. Frei, *The Eclipse of Biblical Narrative: A Study in Eighteenth and Nineteenth Century Hermeneutics* (New Haven, 1974).

43. Stephen West, sermon 1039, Thanksgiving, Dec. 11, 1783, West Papers, Stockbridge Memorial Library; Jack P. Greene, "Search for Identity: Social Response in Eighteenth-Century America," *Journal of Social History* 3 (1970), 189–220.

44. West, sermon 1039, West Papers, Stockbridge Memorial Library.

Chapter 5

1. The familial rhetoric of the American Revolution is most provocatively explored in Edwin G. Burrows and Michael Wallace, "The American Revolution: The Ideology and Psychology of National Liberation," *Perspectives in American History,* 6 (1972), 167–306; and Jay Fliegelman, *Prodigals and Pilgrims: The American Revolution against Patriarchal Authority, 1750–1800* (New York: 1982).

2. C. K. Shipton, *Sibley's Harvard Graduates* (Boston, 1960), pp. xi, 203; Charles W. Akers, "Religion and the American Revolution: Samuel Cooper and the Brattle Street Church," *William and Mary Quarterly* 3d ser., 35 (1978), 478. The definitive biography is by Charles W. Akers, *The Divine Politician: Samuel Cooper and the American Revolution in Boston* (Boston, 1982).

3. Nathan O. Hatch, *The Sacred Cause of Liberty* (New Haven, 1977), p. 74; Richard L. Bushman, *King and People in Provincial Massachusetts* (Chapel Hill, 1985), p. 263.

4. See Alan Heimert, *Religion and the American Mind: From the Awakening to the Revolution* (Cambridge, Mass., 1966), passim.

5. Ephraim Eliot, Commonplace Book, quoted in Shipton, *Sibley's*

Harvard Graduates, p. 194; John Adams, *Works* (Boston, 1850–1856), pp. ii, 305, quoted in Shipton, p. 195.

6. Akers, *Divine Politician,* 131; Akers, "Religion and the American Revolution," pp. 478, 493; Akers, *Divine Politician,* pp. 27, 348. For Cooper's response to Jonathan Edwards, Akers follows Shipton, p. 195: "He read the writings of Jonathan Edwards, but they had no effect at all upon him." Compare, in this respect, Akers, "Religion and the American Revolution," p. 481, with Shipton, p. 194.

7. Akers, "Religion and the American Revolution," p. 493.

8. Bushman, *King and People,* p. 212. "It is astonishing," observes Charles L. Cohen in his essay review of *King and People,* "that someone who has authored a brilliant volume on the Great Awakening has absolutely nothing to say about religion's role in shaping Massachusetts' political culture and mobilizing revolutionary sentiment." "Crowning Assumptions," *Reviews in American History,* 14 (1986), 67. Cohen is perhaps a bit unfair in this estimate; nonetheless it is curious how Bushman privileges political rhetoric over religious. On this issue see Introduction (above) and the Epilogue (below).

9. "What the merchants had in mind," writes Larzer Ziff, "was a church that was distinctly predestinarian in theology but one that was responsive to an age in which sensibilities were more highly developed among the cultivated rich." *Puritanism in America: New Culture in a New World* (New York, 1973), p. 268. Ziff's discussion of the founding and influence of the Brattle Church (pp. 268–279) is illuminating.

10. For a discussion of the controversy centering around Whitefield and earlier the publication of Edwards's *Narrative of Surprising Conversions* see C. C. Goen, ed., *The Great Awakening,* Vol. 4 in *The Works of Jonathan Edwards* (New Haven, 1972); William Cooper's Diary is at the Massachusetts Historical Society.

11. Samuel Cooper, sermon 76 (Dec. 1744), Cooper Papers, Huntington Library (hereafter cited as Cooper Papers). Cooper preached the sermon at least three more times, including "At ye workhouse."

12. In this respect, Alan Heimert's claim of "a rhetorical division" separating evangelical and rational ministers after the Awakening seems valid. See *Religion and the American Mind,* p. 159.

13. Cooper, sermon 76, Cooper Papers. The probation sermon "reveals a remakable ability to appeal to all segments of his audience . . ." writes Akers; it "contained more diplomacy than divinity." *Divine Politician,* p. 15.

14. Akers, "Religion and the American Revolution," p. 487. On Cooper's pulpit rhetoric see John G. Buchanan, "The Justice of America's Cause: Revolutionary Rhetoric in the Sermons of Samuel Cooper," *New England Quarterly,* 50 (1977), 101–24. "Cooper began to use the Brattle Street pulpit to broadcast his political views," says Akers, "but through double meanings, biblical references appropriate to recent events, oral additions to very bland written sermons, and other devices that defy the historian." Charles W.

Akers, "The Lost Reputation of Samuel Cooper as a Leader of the American Revolution," *New England Historic and Genealogical Register,* 130 (1976), 32. What follows below offers a reading of Cooper's sermons that tries to penetrate to the core of Cooper's strategies.

15. Akers, "Religion and the American Revolution," p. 486.

16. Samuel Cooper, sermon 149 (July 3, 1755), Cooper Papers.

17. Samuel Cooper, sermon 170 (July 1758), Cooper Papers.

18. Akers, "Religion and the American Revolution," p. 491.

19. Samuel Cooper, sermon 140 (April 4, 1754), Cooper Papers.

20. Ibid.

21. Ibid. On the incantatory mode see Jackson I. Cope, "Seventeenth-Century Quaker Style," *PMLA,* 76 (1956), 725–754 and the discussion of revivalist preaching modes above. In his emended 1777 text Cooper added the same ritual invocation—a significant compositional return.

22. Ibid.

23. Ibid.

24. Ibid. For a different reading of this rich, palimpsest-like text see John G. Buchanan, "The Pursuit of Happiness: A Study of the Reverend Doctor Samuel Cooper, 1725–1783," Ph.D. Diss., Duke University, 1971, p. 350ff. "Rebellion is the most atrocious offense that can be perpetrated by man," observed Daniel Leonard in 1775. But "by the spring of 1775," glosses Bernard Bailyn, "such sentiments, fulminous and despairing, were being driven underground." In Cooper's erasure of "rebellion" we may observe an instance of compositional repression before the collective release of anxieties over the charge of rebellion found expression after 1776. Bernard Bailyn, *The Ideological Origins of the American Revolution* (Cambridge, Mass., 1967), p. 314.

25. Akers, "Religion and the American Revolution," p. 493.

26. Samuel Cooper, sermon 162 (Nov. 17, 1757), Cooper Papers.

27. Akers, *Divine Politician,* p. 228; Cooper, sermon 162, Cooper Papers.

28. Samuel Cooper, Diary, Massachusetts Historical Society.

29. Samuel Cooper, sermon 170 (July 1758), Cooper Papers. The passages quoted are from a separate addition to the version of April 1762, preached as a Fast sermon on the same text.

30. Samuel Cooper, sermon 141 (April 1754), Cooper Papers.

31. Cooper, sermon 170; Cooper, sermon 141, Cooper Papers.

32. Cooper, sermon 141, Cooper Papers. The observation about Cooper's otherworldliness is by Akers, "Religion and the American Revolution," p. 493.

33. Cooper, sermon 162, Cooper Papers. On the ritual rhetoric of the American Revolution see Sacvan Bercovitch, *The American Jeremiad* (Madison, 1978). For a provocative study of the behavioral variations in colonial mentality see Philip Greven, *The Protestant Temperament* (New York, 1977).

34. Akers, *Divine Politician,* p. 246. In response to the Quebec Act

"patriot clergy, both Old Light and New Light, joined the laity in publicly condemning Great Britain as an agent of the Antichrist," asserts Ruth Bloch. But Cooper's surviving sermonic corpus belies that generalization. See above for examples of how Robbins and Edwards, Jr. employ Old Testament *exempla.* See Bloch, *Visionary Republic,* p. 58. *Millennial Themes in American Thought, 1756–1800* (New York, 1985), p. 58.

35. Akers, *Divine Politician,* 198.

36. Samuel Cooper, sermon 225 (July 1777), Cooper Papers. This July 1777 sermon was delivered some eight times by 1781. "But what is the shadow of God's wings are these Chambers into which we are invited to enter," Cooper asked his audience; he replied, "The Language you at once perceive is figurative, and signifies in general, the safety, tranquility & comfort, which Religion affords to evr'y one who throly [sic] enters into it." The description of Cooper comes from Akers, *Divine Politician,* p. 198.

37. Samuel Cooper, sermon 224 (ca. 1778), Cooper Papers.

38. Ibid.

39. Samuel Cooper, sermon 226 (titled "Sabbath after Burgoyne's Surrender"), Cooper Papers.

40. Cooper, sermon 224.

41. Cf. Bushman, *King and People,* p. 212; Heimert, *Religion and the American Mind,* pp. 159, 216–217. "Quite apart from the question of the Revolution," writes Heimert, "the contrasts between Liberal and Calvinist social thought were possibly of less ultimate significance than the remarkable differences between their oratorical strategies and rhetorical practices." "The issue," Heimert contends, "was indeed, at bottom, one of style." *Religion and the American Mind,* pp. 18, 164. By "style" Heimert means (in this specific context) "class," or social behavior, but embedded in the rhetoric of *Religion* is an implicit argument about preaching styles and modes of communication. See also pp. 225, 226, 232–233. By "hieroglyphic leveling" I mean how Cooper represents the word "world" by the sign ⊙. That figure I have only seen in evangelical sermons. Samuel Cooper, sermon 162, Cooper Papers.

42. Cooper, sermon 224.

43. Ibid.

44. In this respect the figure of Cooper offers some telling contrasts with Bernard Bailyn's rich portrait of revolutionary hesitancy, Andrew Eliot. Eliot was, temperamentally, a "reluctant revolutionary," yet, despite his "psychological as well as intellectual readiness" for the logic of rebellion, Eliot could not embrace the cause of liberty. Cooper, on the other hand, was able to *act,* despite his real anxieties over the charge of rebellion. Somehow Cooper was able to work through the collective hesitancy of the Protestant clergy by literally repressing (on the page) the idea/word "rebellion." Eliot, however, remained "distressed for my country, in which I include Great Britain. I should fear a disconnection with it as one of the greatest evils." Andrew Eliot, quoted in Bernard Bailyn, "Religion and Revolution: Three Biographi-

cal Studies," *Perspectives in American History,* 4 (1970), pp. 99, 106. With this last portrait of revolutionary mentality I hope it is clear that I share with Professor Bailyn a recognition of "the difficulty of explaining by any simple formula the role of religion in the origins of the American Revolution." "Religion and Revolution," p. 88.

Chapter 6

1. Bernard Bailyn, *The Ideological Origins of the American Revolution* (Cambridge, Mass., 1967), p. 142.

2. On this point see Gary B. Nash, "The American Clergy and the French Revolution," *William and Mary Quarterly,* 3d ser., 22 (1965), 397.

3. James M. Banner, Jr., *To the Hartford Convention: The Federalists and the Origins of Party Politics in Massachusetts, 1789–1815* (New York, 1970), p. 163. "The political leaders," Banner continues, "took over the entire intellectual heritage of Calvinist religion and appropriated it to secular, profane, and partisan purposes" (pp. 162–63n).

4. Robert W. Ferguson, " 'We Hold These Truths': Strategies of Control in the Literature of the Founders," in Sacvan Bercovitch, ed., *Reconstructing American Literary History* (Harvard English Studies 13) (Cambridge, Mass., 1986), pp. 21–22; Banner, *To the Hartford Convention,* pp. 156, 157; Donald M. Scott, *From Office to Profession: The New England Ministry, 1750–1850* (Philadelphia, 1978), p. 22.

5. Jonathan Edwards, Jr.'s *Brief Observations on the Doctrine of Universal Salvation* (New Haven, 1784) answered Chauncy's *Salvation of all Men . . .* (Boston, 1782). The parallels between the careers of Edwards father and son were noted by nineteenth-century commentators.

6. In 1790 Hart published a millennial tract (as part of an ordination sermon) called *The War Between Michael and the Dragon* (Providence, 1790); in 1800 he received the honor of Doctor of Divinity from Princeton and helped create the *Connecticut Evangelical Magazine,* which had its inception the same year.

7. He "was dissatisfied with what President Edwards had written on Freedom of the Will," notes West's early nineteenth-century memoirist. Alvan Hyde, *Sketches of the Life . . . of the Rev. Stephen West* (Stockbridge, 1819), p. 7. In 1798 West wrote to Samuel Hopkins about a local gathering of ministers to discuss West's most recent theological reflections: "Dr. Edwards being there," West relates, and "made fewer objections than was expected." Stephen West to Samuel Hopkins, April 14, 1798, Simon Gratz Collection, Rare Books and Manuscripts Division, New York Public Library, Astor, Lenox and Tilden Foundations. Edwards, Jr. had preached at least once before West's Stockbridge congregation, in September 1787, from a sermon composed in December 1772. See Jonathan Edwards, Jr. Papers, Hartford Seminary.

8. On Edwards's dismissal from White Haven Church see Robert L. Ferm,

Jonathan Edwards the Younger, 1745–1801: A Colonial Pastor (Grand Rapids, 1976), pp. 134–47. Ferm quotes a letter from a vexed member of the congregation on p. 141.

9. Ronald P. Formisano, *The Transformation of Political Culture: Massachusetts Parties, 1790–1840s* (New York, 1983), p. 86. Cf. also p. 391 on "the clergy's more general retreat from political life" during the nineteenth century.

10. Ferguson, " 'We Hold These Truths,' " pp. 25, 24.

11. Ruth H. Bloch distinguishes between periods of "francophilic millennialism" and "francophobic reaction" in *Visionary Republic: Millennial Themes in American Thought, 1756–1800* (New York, 1985).

12. Jonathan Edwards, Jr., ms sermon, Nov. 29, 1792, Edwards, Jr. Papers, Hartford Seminary (hereafter cited as Edwards Papers).

13. Jonathan Edwards, Jr., ms sermon, Nov. 27, 1794, Edwards Papers.

14. Jonathan Edwards, Jr., ms sermon, Feb. 19, 1795 ("Whiskey Rebellion sermon"), Edwards Papers. Among Edwards the father's other sons, the younger Timothy became a staunch Federalist (opposing the Shaysites in the 1780s), but the youngest son, Pierpont, became a republican lawyer in Connecticut and lobbied in 1792 against the current Vice President John Adams, claiming that "a too strong tendency to aristocracy is a trait in Mr. Adams's character" and urging that his correspondent "guard against the first advances of tyranny." After the election of 1800 Pierpont redelivered Jefferson's inaugural address to a local Connecticut audience. Pierpont Edwards to [?], Oct. 4, 1792, Society Collection, Historical Society of Pennsylvania (hereafter cited as HSP). On Pierpont's oration see David Austin, *Republican Festival* (New Haven, 1803).

15. John C. Miller, *The Federalist Era, 1789–1801* (New York, 1960), p. 160; Edwards, Jr., ms sermon, Feb. 19, 1795 ("Whiskey Rebellion sermon"), Edwards Papers. On the revival of libertarian symbols during the Whiskey Rebellion see Bloch, *Visionary Republic,* p. 180. For recent studies of the Whiskey Rebellion see Steven R. Boyd, ed., *The Whiskey Rebellion: Past and Present Perspectives* (Westport, Conn., 1985), and Thomas P. Slaughter, *The Whiskey Rebellion: Frontier Epilogue to the American Revolution* (New York, 1986).

16. Edwards, Jr., "Whiskey Rebellion sermon," Edwards Papers. For an example of the antirevival rhetoric about "change" see Isaac Stiles's 1743 election sermon, *A Looking-Glass for Changelings,* excerpted in Alan Heimert and Perry Miller, eds., *The Great Awakening* (Indianapolis, 1967), pp. 305–22.

17. Edwards, Jr., "Whiskey Rebellion sermon," Edwards Papers. "Elusive malcontents" is how historian John C. Miller styles the "Whiskey Boys." *The Federalist Era,* p. 159. Edwards's "heart" language echoes the rhetoric of his father's famous treatise on *True Virtue.*

18. Levi Hart's revolutionary Diary neatly inscribes Edwards's belief:

"Lord's Day 21 May 1775—The public calamities still continue, but blessed be God He remains the same." Hart, Diary, Gratz Collection, HSP. The evangelical desire for timeless realms is discussed later.

19. Stephen West will also invoke a key revival trope—the rhetoric of "filthy rags"—to warn against the social discord in his midst. That the New Divinity men employed *antirevivalist* modes of argument in the 1790s suggests their embattled position as leaders of individual towns. On the "unqualified" authority of local ministers in the Federalist era see Banner, *To the Hartford Convention,* p. 159.

20. Before he preached in 1799 and later published his funeral oration on the death of Washington, Levi Hart spoke to his Preston audience on a Continental Thanksgiving in 1795 comparing David and Washington as monarchs. Levi Hart, ms sermon, July 19, 1795, Hart Papers, Connecticut Historical Society. On the figure of Washington in postrevolutionary American culture see Jay Fliegelman, *Prodigals and Pilgrims: The American Revolution against Patriarchal Authority, 1750–1800* (New York, 1982), pp. 197–226, and Michael T. Gilmore, "Eulogy as Symbolic Biography: The Iconography of Revolutionary Leadership, 1776–1826," in Daniel Aaron, ed., *Studies in Biography* (*Harvard English Studies* 8) (Cambridge, Mass., 1978), pp. 131–57.

21. Jonathan Edwards, Jr., ms sermon, Nov. 29, 1798, Edwards Papers, Trask Library, Andover–Newton Theological School.

22. Ibid. At the base of the passage just quoted the preacher cites, presumably as the authority for the perspective voiced in the passage, "A. Cloots's report, presented with the sanction of the Assembly." Before Melville, Edwards, Jr. alluded to the French Revolution's antinomian crowd leader—Cloots stripped himself of his original baronic title and declared that he incorporated the voice of all people before the National Assembly in June 1790—as an agent of social and religious subversion. I distill from Milton R. Stern's note about Melville's use of Cloots as "a lasting type of democracy" in his edition of *Billy Budd* (Indianapolis, 1975), p. 4n.

23. Nash, "The American Clergy and the French Revolution," pp. 404–5.

24. Banner, *To the Hartford Convention,* p. 163n.

25. Edwards, Jr., ms sermon, Nov. 29, 1798, Trask Library.

26. Stephen West was dismissed after fifty-six years in the Stockbridge pulpit on a charge of drunkenness. "His fate," writes Richard D. Birdsall, "came to symbolize . . . the fading respect due to the pastor as leader of his parish and the growing impossibility of maintaining the parish system amid the increasing number of social and political cleavages within the congregations." *Berkshire County: A Cultural History* (New Haven, 1959), pp. 91–92.

27. Stephen West, ms sermon 1563, Oct. 30, 1796, West Papers, Trask Library. Note how both Edwards, Jr. and West still compose in the syntactic shorthand of their religious affiliation, although in the case of West the style

is not as pervasive. For a discussion of the implications of that style see the Epilogue.

28. West, ms sermon 1563, Trask Library.

29. Ibid. I refer to the work of historians Richard L. Bushman, Robert A. Gross, and others mentioned earlier.

30. I borrow here from Sacvan Bercovitch, *The American Jeremiad* (Madison, 1978), p. 180, and in general from his "The Rites of Assent: Rhetoric, Ritual, and the Ideology of American Consensus," in Sam B. Girgus, ed., *The American Self: Myth, Ideology, and Popular Culture* (Albuquerque, 1981), pp. 5–42.

31. "There had to be a way," writes William Breitenbach, "to conceive of self-interest so that it would seem legitimate, limited, and orderly. New Divinity theology met all three of these demands." William Breitenbach, "Unregenerate Doings: Selflessness and Selfishness in New Divinity Theology," *American Quarterly* 34 (1982), 500.

32. Joseph Bellamy to Stephen West, Feb. 6, 1785, Bellamy Papers, Yale University Library. "26 are admitted in Mr. Smalley's church," Bellamy appended. "45 at Waterburry begin to kneel & groan & believe . . . they begin meeting there twice every week." "Doc Chauncy's late Book is come to N. Haven & makes noise there," Bellamy also related. "It makes much noise in & about Boston—I have not seen it." Thus theological controversy and numerical evidence of the spirit sustained the acknowledged leader of the New Divinity at the end of his life.

33. West to Hopkins, April 14, 1798, Gratz Collection, New York Public Library.

34. Stephen West, ms sermon 1700, Sept. 8, 1799, West Papers, Trask Library. The sermon's text derives from Matt. 25:41.

35. A letter from Stockbridge newspaper publisher Loring Andrews to fellow elite (and later Unitarian) Theodore Sedgwick speaks of Andrews's "idea that it might afford you some amusement" to describe the scene of local party politics being played out during one of West's Thanksgiving discourses; opponents of Sedgwick's federalism, "the murmurers against Government," squirmed during the preacher's sermon. "It would have occasioned a smile," Andrews went on, "had you seen the *champion of Democracy* among us change his situation at the time—he was in an erect posture; he seated himself in a moment and his fingers were employed in drumming dissatisfaction on the sides of the pew, while his eyes contemplated the floor which supported him. On the whole, all things considered, we had a tolerable discourse, and the Doctor may be said to have 'Deserved well' of the friends of order and good government." Loring Andrews to Theodore Sedgwick, Dec. 26, 1796, Sedgwick Collection, Stockbridge Memorial Library. Andrews, it would seem, was more alert to the nuances of political gesture in church than to West's Thanksgiving sermon. On the legacies of the revival in Stockbridge, Richard D. Birdsall writes of "the residue of enthusias-

tic religion which had always remained a characteristic of Berkshire religion since the days of Edwards." *Berkshire County,* p. 65. Earlier, Theodore Sedgwick had taken "an active part in suppressing the rebellion known as 'Shays' war.' " H. D. Sedgwick, "The Sedgwicks of Berkshire," *Collections of the Berkshire Historical and Scientific Society* (Pittsfield, 1899), p. 93. Birdsall mentions Andrews in *Berkshire County,* p. 51.

36. In retrospect, the revival of imprecatory rhetoric during the Second Great Awakening was a ministerial effort to recoup social power. The literature on the revivals at the turn of the century is vast, but see especially John R. Howe, Jr., "Republican Thought and the Political Violence of the 1790s," *American Quarterly* 19 (1967), 147–65; Perry Miller, *The Life of the Mind in America: From the Revolution to the Civil War* (New York, 1965); and Richard D. Shiels, "The Second Great Awakening in Connecticut: Critique of the Traditional Interpretation," *Church History* 49 (1980), 401–15.

37. Stephen West, ms sermon 1710, Nov. 28, 1799, West Papers, Trask Library.

38. Bloch, *Visionary Republic,* p. 137; Simon Hough, *The Sign of the Present Time* (Stockbridge, 1799), p. 28. Bloch is correct to call Hough "fervently anticlerical" (p. 138), for he clearly saw himself outside the boundaries of the instituted church. "I cannot find any body," he wrote in the work cited above (which he had published at his own expense), "that I think can tell me anything about the Bible, more than I know myself, and I don't want to pay any body for telling of me, what I knew before." *The Sign of the Present Time,* p. 20. Although not a member of West's own congregation—Hough was a dissenting member of David Perry's Richmond, Massachusetts, congregation (a hill town along the New York State–Massachusetts border)—Hough offers a neat instance of marginalized rhetoric, in this case directed against the New Divinity. Hough's argument takes the form of imagined dialogues between him and a would-be rebuking minister, as well as visionary poetry. On the stylistic implications between marginal rhetoric and social power see the Epilogue. I am indebted to Ruth Dagonheart of the Pittsfield Antheneum Local History department for information about the obscure Simon Hough, who died in 1819 at age 85, or about the same age as Stephen West.

39. West, ms sermon 1710, Trask Library.

40. Bloch, *Visionary Republic,* p. 131. For further important distinctions between premillennialism and postmillennialism, see Fliegelman, *Prodigals and Pilgrims,* pp. 190–91; and James H. Moorhead, "Between Progress and Apocalypse: A Reassessment of Millennialism in American Religious Thought, 1800–1880," *Journal of American History* 71 (1984), 524–42.

41. Paraphrase of Gary B. Nash, *Race, Class, and Politics: Essays on American Colonial and Revolutionary Society* (Urbana and Chicago, 1986), p. xxi.

42. Stephen West, ms sermon 2005, Oct. 19, 1805, West Papers, Trask Library.

43. On Davenport's career in the Awakening see Harry S. Stout and Peter Onuf, "James Davenport and the Great Awakening in New London," *Journal of American History* 70 (1983), 556–78. For a contemporary account of the incendiary moment see a letter in *The Boston Weekly Post-Boy* in Richard L. Bushman, ed., *The Great Awakening: Documents on the Revival of Religion, 1740–45* (New York, 1970), pp. 51–53. Of his own role in the "awful Affair of Books and Cloaths" see Davenport's *Confession and Retractions* (1744) in Bushman, *The Great Awakening,* pp. 53–55 (quote p. 55).

44. West, ms sermon 2005, Trask Library.

45. The trope of nakedness in West's rhetoric is suggestive as well of the terrible fear of apocalyptic unveiling among the evangelical clergy. If the book of Revelation offered a vision of redemption happily revealed or unveiled in God's providential plan, West's language conveys the dialectical anxiety attendant with the darker side of the clerical imagination: the "unveiling" West preaches here threatens and exposes rather than assures and confirms.

46. Ibid. For a brilliant discussion of the literary and intellectual reflections of this dialectic see Fliegelman, *Prodigals and Pilgrims,* Chapter 8, passim.

47. Levi Hart, Diary, May 21, 1775, Gratz Collection, HSP. That same week Hart "preached a sermon to Coll Tyler & his company, who are going from us in defense of our country." Diary, May 24, 1775, Gratz Collection, HSP.

48. Hart, Diary, April 24, 1777, Gratz Collection, HSP; William B. Sprague, *Annals of the American Pulpit* (New York, 1859), p. 592.

49. Cf. Hart's entries for March 13, 1790 and December 1, 1799, Gratz Collection, HSP. Two years before Bellamy died, Hart's old Bethlehem friend and classmate Ammi Robbins wrote of his own desire "to call & see the good old Doctor, while he is yet confined to the bonds of corruption." Ammi Robbins to Levi Hart, Sept. 8, 1788, Gratz Collection, New York Public Library. It was Ammi, Hart recorded in 1761, who urged that he begin keeping a diary: "After long Deliberation I have at last Determined, by the Advice of my good Friend Ammi Robbins to keep a Diary." Hart, Diary, Jan. 24, 1761, Gratz Collection, HSP.

50. Hart, Diary, entries from Oct. 23 to Nov 13, 1785, Gratz Collection, HSP. "Mr. Benedict" is Joel Benedict, who, along with Joseph Strong, later was to preach a funeral oration over Levi Hart. Intriguingly in each eulogy there is no mention of Hart's efforts in the American Revolution or even that the Revolution ever occurred. It is as if that ultimate moment, as Hart's own Diary offers eloquent proof, had been erased, repressed out of the memory of the next generation of the New Divinity. After reading these two versions of Hart's life the Revolution appears not to have taken place. See Joel Bene-

dict, *A Short Inquiry* . . . (Norwich, 1809) and Joseph Strong, *A Sermon* . . . (Norwich, 1809).

51. The final entry reads: "Lord's Day March 1 1807 preached my forty fifth anniversary from 2 Kings 2:9. May all the wisdom for mercy be blessed to me."

52. Hart, Diary, July 27, 1802, Gratz Collection, HSP.

53. Levi Hart, "Dissertation on the literal & Figural . . ." Gratz Collection, HSP. For a description of Hart's various manuscript writings on theological subjects see "A Note on Manuscript Sources."

54. Levi Hart, ms sermon, Jan. 1, 1799 ("Meeting for prayer"), Hart Papers, Connecticut Historical Society. Hart's eulogy for Hopkins appears in Stephen West, ed., *Sketches of the Life of Samuel Hopkins* (Stockbridge, 1805). Hopkins, recalled William Ellery Channing, who grew up under the New Divinity man's ministry in Newport, "took refuge from the present state of things in the Millennium. The Millennium was his chosen ground . . . He was at home in it." W. E. Channing, "Christian Worship," in *The Works of William E. Channing, D.D.* (Boston, 1849), 4:353.

55. Hart, Diary, March 22, 1799, Gratz Collection, HSP.

56. Hart, Diary entries July 2, 1800; Dec. 9, 1804; Gratz Collection, HSP. According to Dexter, Hart's older son was graduated from Dartmouth, class of 1786 (Hart's ms sermon of Sept. 29, 1786, dated at Dartmouth, was preached on the occasion; Gratz Collection, HSP); the younger son, again according to Dexter, was graduated from Brown, class of 1802. It seems clear that this is the son to whom Hart refers in the Diary. F. B. Dexter, *Biographical Sketches of the Graduates of Yale College* (New York, 1896), 2:657.

57. Indeed, the father's worry indirectly voices a judgment about the inability of the law to address the emotional health of his son. At some level the son's ailment is spiritual *and* vocational; his legal calling, that is, ignores the deeper springs where the self seeks nourishment. I am grateful to Jay Fliegelman for this insight.

Epilogue

1. Harry S. Stout, *The New England Soul: Preaching and Religious Culture in Colonial New England* (New York, 1986), p. 3; Donald M. Scott, *From Office to Profession: The New England Ministry, 1750–1850* (Philadephia, 1978) p. 16. According to Stout, the sermon was *the* most public index to what was felt and believed by colonists during the first 150 years of national development. See his calculations comparing college students' exposure to lecturing with that of the average New Englander's lifetime of sitting through sermons. *The New England Soul*, p. 317. For a critique of Stout which mentions the question of lay piety see Philip F. Gura, "Baring the New England Soul," *American Quarterly* 38 (1986), pp. 653–60.

2. David A. Hollinger, "American Intellectual History: Issues for the 1980s," *Reviews in American History* 10 (1982), 315.

3. Stout, *The New England Soul,* p. 219. For a discussion of the contrasting styles during the Awakening see Stout's sections on revivalist preaching, esp. pp. 218–21. I mean "anti-structural" in Victor Turner's sense of social stances (and styles) creatively oppositional to the forms, beliefs, and ideologies of existing social—and for my purposes sermonic—ideals. See Turner's variations on the ritual process in *Dramas, Fields, and Metaphors: Symbolic Action in Human Society* (Ithaca, 1974), especially "Metaphors of Anti-structure in Religious Culture," pp. 272–99.

4. On the influence of Whitefield's sermonic example see Stout, *The New England Soul,* pp. 192–94.

5. I draw this consensual observation from the work of Edmund S. Morgan, Richard D. Brown, and Stout himself, as voiced in the Epilogue to *The New England Soul:* "Only gradually, and with great discomfort, did New England's ministers realize that they had helped create an engine for change and reformation that they ultimately could not control. Unwittingly, their libertarian rhetoric laid the basis for their own demise as the single voice of authority in their local communities" (p. 313). See also Richard D. Brown, "Modernization and the Modern Personality in Early America, 1600–1865: A Sketch of a Synthesis," *Journal of Interdisciplinary History* 2 (1971–72), 201–28, especially p. 217. Morgan's succinct evaluation in "The Revolution Considered as an Intellectual Movement" is perhaps the most famous: "In 1740 America's leading intellectuals were clergymen and thought about theology; in 1790 they were statesmen and thought about politics." Edmund S. Morgan, The *Challenge of the American Revolution* (New York, 1976), p. 61.

6. Paul Ricoeur, *Time and Narrative* (Chicago, 1984), 1:178: "To narrate is already to explain." I would like to thank Jay Fliegelman for helping me clarify the ideas contained in this paragraph.

7. On the subject of social marginality and literary form see Nigel Smith's Introduction, in Nigel Smith, ed., *A Collection of Ranter Writings from the 17th Century* (London, 1983), pp. 7–38; and Clement C. Hawes, "Mania, Magnification, and Literary Form: A Study of Smart's *Jubilate Agno* in Its Literary and Social Context," Ph.D. Diss., Yale University, 1986.

8. See in this respect Hayden White's key observation: "The breakdown in narrativity in a culture, group, or social class is a symptom of its having entered into a state of crisis." Hayden White, "Getting Out of History," *diacritics* 12 (Fall 1982), 6.

9. The portrait continues, most recently in Bruce Kuklick's version of the New Divinity men in *Churchmen and Philosophers: From Jonathan Edwards to John Dewey* (New Haven, 1985), pp. 45ff. I borrow "frameworks of meaning" from Hollinger, "American Intellectual History," p. 314.

10. I refer to the work by David Hall, Harry Stout, Ruth Bloch, Charles Hambrick-Stowe, Rhys Isaac, and others cited earlier.

11. Victor Turner, "Liminal to Liminoid in Play, Flow, Ritual: An Essay in Comparative Symbology," in *From Ritual to Theatre: The Human Seriousness of Play* (New York, 1982), p. 44: For the discussion at the end of this paragraph and the beginning of the next I am indebted to Richard Slotkin, *The Fatal Environment: The Myth of the Frontier in the Age of Industrialization, 1800–1900* (New York, 1985), Chapter 2.

12. The reference, of course, is to Hans W. Frei's important *The Eclipse of Biblical Narrative: A Study in Eighteenth and Nineteenth Century Hermeneutics* (New Haven, 1974).

13. On the mythology of Washington see Catherine Albanese, *Sons of the Fathers: The Civil Religion of the American Revolution* (Philadelphia, 1976); and Jay Fliegelman, *Prodigals and Pilgrims: The American Revolution against Patriarchal Authority, 1750–1800* (New York, 1982).

14. Frei, *The Eclipse of Biblical Narrative*, p. 130.

15. "Language itself," observes J. G. A. Pocock, "may be thought of as constituting . . . a 'space' and as displaying the characteristics which we call 'public' and even 'political.' " J. G. A. Pocock, "The Reconstitution of Discourse: Towards the Historiography of Political Thought," *MLN* 96 (1981), 960. In this respect the affective world of eighteenth-century New England may be *more* available in manuscript than in printed documents. That is, the printed word, mediated through the colonial printing industry, the demands of the market, and so on, may be more reflective of legal, hierarchical, elitist culture, while unmediated manuscripts may register, in more authentic ways, the affects wrought by revolutionary history.

16. "The clearest indication that congregations understood sermons in terms that were similar to the ministers'," writes Harry Stout, "appears in the surviving lay sermon notes that correspond point for point with the manuscript notes of the ministers." *The New England Soul*, 317. For recent discussions of lay piety see Stephen J. Stein, " 'For Their Spiritual Good': The Northampton, Massachusetts, Prayer Bids of the 1730s and 1740s," *William and Mary Quarterly* 37 (1980), 261–85; George Selement, *Keepers of the Vineyard: The Puritan Ministry and Collective Culture in Colonial New England* (Lanham, Md., 1984); and Charles Lloyd Cohen, *God's Caress: The Psychology of Puritan Religious Experience* (New York, 1986).

A Note on Manuscript Sources

Philemon Robbins (1709–1781)

Materials by and relating to Philemon Robbins are collected in the Robbins Family Papers at the Connecticut Historical Society and Yale University Library. The CHS has family letters, Robbins's early workbooks (in math [1727] and a 1724 transcription of *Flynt's Geography*), along with 146 sermons dating from 1732 until 1781. The Robbins Family Papers at Yale include his Diary from September 19, 1730 to 1733, as well as 190 sermons from 1731 to 1781. Another Diary fragment (1737–45) is located at Houghton Library, Harvard University. The records from Branford Church are housed at the Connecticut State Library, Hartford. Except for brief sketches of Robbins cited in the notes from Sprague (1:367–69) and Sibley (7:616–27), and his occasional appearance in accounts of New Light–Baptist histories, there is no study of Robbins's career. He is mentioned most recently in Patricia U. Bonomi, *Under the Cope of Heaven: Religion, Society, and Politics in Colonial America* (New York, 1986), p. 165.

Jonathan Edwards, Jr. (1745–1801)

The vast majority of sermons by Jonathan Edwards, Jr. are collected in the Hartford Seminary Library, Hartford. Approximately 1200 sermons, dating from 1766 until 1800 (of which only about 50 are written out in full) are catalogued. Another 60 sermons by Edwards, Jr. are in the Edwards Family Papers at the Trask Library, Andover–Newton Theological School. Edwards's early Diary (May 1764–Jan. 1765) is at the Beinecke Rare Book and Manuscript Library, Yale University, along with numerous letters to and from fellow evangelicals and politicians. For a detailed listing of all available Edwards, Jr. manuscript materials see Robert L. Ferm, *Jonathan Edwards the Younger, 1745–1801: A Colonial Pastor* (Grand Rapids, 1976), pp. 184–90. The White Haven Church records are located at the Connecticut State Library.

Levi Hart (1738–1808)

Manuscripts relating to Levi Hart may be found in two large collections: Hart's early notebooks (Aug. 18, 1759–Dec. 4, 1759; Dec. 15, 1759–March 25, 1760); volume 1 of "Miscellanies" (ca. 1763); various undated writings on religion and commentaries on other theologians' work (for example, responses "taken from the writings of Mr. Edwards"); Hart's "Sunday Diary" from the 1760s; and approximately 115 sermons from 1760 to 1807—all these items are as yet uncatalogued at the CHS. Hart's huge Diary kept between 1759 and 1807 is recently catalogued in the Gratz Collection of the Historical Society of Pennsylvania. In addition, the HSP has several sermons as well as drafts of various treatises, including the "Dissertation on the Literal & Figurative Senses of Scripture Prophecy" (1797) and the manuscript of Hart's funeral oration for Samuel Hopkins, later published in Stephen West's edition of Hopkins's *Diary* (Sketches of the Life . . . [Stockbridge, 1805]). Except for sketches in Sprague (1:590–94) and Dexter (2:656–61), only scattered references to Hart exist, notably in Heimert, Conforti, and Essig, cited above. The Preston (Griswold) Church records are at the CSL.

Stephen West (1735–1819)

The Stephen West Papers at the Trask Library, Andover–Newton Theological School contain approximately 1060 sermons, dating from January 1759, the onset of West's pastoral career, to the summer of 1818, the year before his death. The last numbered sermon is 2440. This rich collection (often listing West's sermons week by week) is supplemented by a few West items at Williams College Library and letters scattered in various collections, including the HSP and the Gratz Collection, New York Public Library. Stockbridge Memorial Library has papers relating to the history of the Stockbridge Church. The only sustained portraits of West are in Sprague (1:548–56) and Dexter (2:388–94).

Samuel Cooper (1725–1783)

The sermons of Samuel Cooper are located in two collections: the Cooper Papers at the Huntington Library, San Marino, California, houses the bulk of Cooper's 146 extant sermons, while the New York Public Library has 32, including a number of sermon fragments. Portions of Cooper's diaries have been published, although the diary quoted in this study is in manuscript at the Massachusetts Historical Society. For a description of the Cooper manuscripts see Charles W. Akers, *The Divine Politician: Samuel Cooper and the American Revolution in Boston* (Boston, 1982), pp. 427–28.

Other Collections

All students of eighteenth-century New England religious and intellectual culture are indebted to the Joseph Bellamy Papers at the Hartford Seminary Library and the Gratz Collection at the HSP. Other letters, sermons, and diaries which supplement this portrait of evangelical mentality are drawn from the archives at the CHS, Beinecke Library, Yale University Library, Connecticut State Library, Houghton Library, and the New York Public Library.

Index